CHINA BUSINESS LAW

LIBRARY

A Guide for
Lawyers and Entrepreneurs

Recommended Stockists

Australia
Lawbook Co.
Sydney, Melbourne,
Brisbane, Perth

Canada/USA
Carswell
Ontario
Canada

Hong Kong
Bloomsbury Books Ltd

Hong Kong Book Centre Ltd

Swindon Book Co. Ltd

Japan
Yushodo Fantas
Tokyo

Kokusai Shobo Ltd
Tokyo

Maruzen Co. Ltd
Tokyo, Osaka

Tokyo Publications
Tokyo

Malaysia
Sweet & Maxwell Asia
Petaling Jaya

New Zealand
Brooker's Ltd
Wellington, Auckland

Hong Kong
Sweet & Maxwell Asia
Hong Kong

Thailand
Source One Ltd
Bangkok

UK & Europe
Sweet & Maxwell Ltd
London

USA
Professional Publications
Services
New Jersey

West Group
Minnesota

Rest of the World
Sweet & Maxwell Asia
Singapore

CHINA BUSINESS LAW:
A Guide for
Lawyers and Entrepreneurs

The Law Society of Singapore

Editor-in-chief

Associate Professor Tan Lay Hong

Singapore

Sweet & Maxwell Asia

2003

Published in 2003 by

THOMSON
—————★————— ™
SWEET & MAXWELL ASIA
6 Battery Road #29-03
Singapore 049909

Affiliated Companies

AUSTRALIA
Lawbook Co.
100 Harris Street,
Pyrmont NSW 2009

CANADA
Carswell
Corporate Plaza,
2075 Kennedy Road
Scarborough, Ontario M1T 3V4

MALAYSIA
Sweet & Maxwell Asia
No 17 Jalan PJS 7/19
Bandar Sunway
46150 Petaling Jaya
Selangor, Malaysia

NEW ZEALAND
Brooker's
PO Box 6343, Auckland

HONG KONG
Sweet & Maxwell Asia
20/F Sunning Plaza
10 Hysan Avenue
Causeway Bay
Hong Kong

UNITED KINGDOM/EUROPE
Sweet & Maxwell Ltd
100 Avenue Road, London NW3 3PF

UNITED STATES OF AMERICA
West Group
PO Box 64526
St Paul, Minnesota 55164-0526

Printed in Singapore by Seng Lee Press Pte Ltd

Published 2003
First Reprint 2003

ISBN 981-04-8461-5

EDITOR-IN-CHIEF

Tan Lay Hong, LLB (Hons) (Singapore), LLM (London), Advocate and Solicitor of the Supreme Court of Singapore

Tan Lay Hong is an Associate Professor with the Division of Business Law at the Nanyang Business School (NBS). She has had considerable experience in civil litigation and commercial practice in a leading local law firm prior to joining academia in 1992. Since then, she has done extensive research on Chinese business law, particularly in foreign direct investment laws and Chinese corporate law. She has published her reseach in reputable journals such as *The Company Lawyer* (UK), *The Australian Journal of Corporate Law* (Australia) and *The Journal of World Investments* (Switzerland). She teaches a course on Chinese foreign direct investment laws to post-graduate MBA students at NBS.

CONTRIBUTORS

Samtani Anil, LLB (Hons) (Singapore), LLM (Singapore), Advocate and Solicitor of the Supreme Court of Singapore, Solicitor of the Supreme Court of England and Wales

Samtani Anil is an Assistant Professor of Law with the Nanyang Business School, Nanyang Technological University. He was formerly a State Counsel in the Attorney-General's Chambers and a partner in a Singapore law firm. His research and teaching interests include information technology law, intellectual property law and international business law. He is an advisor to the World Intellectual Property Organization (WIPO) and Chair of the Internet Corporation for Assigned Names and Numbers (ICANN)'s Membership Implementation Task Force for East Asia. He has also been consulted by and continues to advise the governments of Singapore, Thailand, Japan, India and the Philippines and several research institutes and international organizations on issues pertaining to the law and regulation of electronic commerce and intellectual property rights. He is a recipient of several awards and scholarships, including the US Fulbright Scholarship, the National University of Singapore/Hokkien Huay Kuan Foundation Scholarship and a Visiting Scholarship at the Boalt Hall School of Law at the University of California, Berkeley.

Chew Boon Kheng, LLB (Hons) (London), LLM (Singapore), Advocate and Solicitor of the High Court of Malaya

Chew Boon Kheng's main area of practice is corporate law, with a focus on capital markets, mergers and acquisitions and corporate finance.

He is also an active member of Stamford LLC's China Practice Group. His recent experience includes advising a public listed company in its joint venture with one of China's largest privately owned companies specializing in commercial and military aircraft repairs; advising a multinational media corporation on their PRC operations; acting for a major PRC bank in a multi-million facility to a Singapore government-linked company; advising in a number of initial public offerings of both local and foreign corporations seeking to list on Singapore and foreign exchanges and advising a local group of chemical companies in its acquisition by a German conglomerate.

Boon Kheng has recently published an article "Doing Business in China" in the *Law Gazette*, an official publication of the Law Society of Singapore. He has also contributed a chapter on "The PRC Revised Foreign Investment Catalogue" for the 2nd Edition of the *PRC Corporate Secretarial Manual* by Sweet & Maxwell.

Fu Rong, Law School of Beijing University, MBA, Business School of Nanyang Technological University

Fu Rong's practice focuses on various corporate matters, including the drafting, reviewing and negotiating of various contracts, dealing with foreign direct investment in the PRC, taxation, banking and finance, and shipping and admiralty.

Fu Rong has experience dealing with import and export matters in relation to state-owned trading groups in Beijing. She has worked in a well-known investment bank where she acquired in-depth knowledge in all aspects of financing. She is also familiar with the legal and practical commercial aspects of Foreign Investment Entities in the PRC such as approval processes, land ownership and transfers and foreign exchange issues. In addition, she has been actively involved in various types of direct investment in China, including foreign investment structuring, advising on the setting up of foreign investment entities in the PRC, and the acquisition of Chinese companies. In the field of capital markets, she has been involved in debt-restructuring exercises, venture capital financing and other financing activities in connection with China-related enterprises. She has advised several MNCs on the legal changes related to the accession of the PRC to the WTO, and lectured on PRC law and various legal issues at numerous conferences and seminars in the PRC and Singapore.

Terence Lin, LLB (Hons) (Singapore), Advocate and Solicitor of the Supreme Court of Singapore

Terence Lin's main area of practice is corporate law, with a particular emphasis on PRC-related matters. Terence is a member of Stamford LLC's China Practice Group and his practice includes matters relating to the securitization of assets and public offerings, including the listing of PRC companies in Singapore, the establishment of foreign investment vehicles, representative offices and non-profit organizations in the PRC and various issues relating thereto, employment law in Singapore and the PRC, licensing arrangements between a Singapore statutory board and PRC government authorities, lease agreements and franchise arrangements in the PRC, mergers and acquisitions, sales of shares and assets and transfers of businesses.

Terence has co-authored "The PRC Revised Foreign Investment Catalogue" chapter for the 2nd Edition of the *PRC Corporate Secretarial Manual* by Sweet & Maxwell

Tan Chong Huat, LLB (Hons) (Singapore), Advocate and Solicitor of the Supreme Court of Singapore, Solicitor of the Supreme Court of England & Wales, Commissioner for Oaths, Accredited Arbitrator with China International Trade and Economic Arbitration Commission, Member, Economic Committee, Singapore Chinese Chamber of Commerce & Industry, Editor and Co-author, *PRC Corporate Secretarial Manual* by Sweet & Maxwell.

Tan Chong Huat has a wide-ranging practice that focuses on corporate and commercial matters, corporate finance and banking, but also includes arbitration, litigation and property law.

Chong Huat has been actively involved in numerous equities and debt securities listings on the Singapore Stock Exchange and other major stock exchanges and has acted for listed companies in takeovers, private placements, securities and debt issues.

He has considerable experience in advising clients on investment matters in Southeast Asia, particularly in the PRC. He regularly advises on issues arising in the context of foreign investment in the PRC, including structuring of joint ventures, due diligence investigations for the establishment of companies or corporate acquisitions, asset valuation, intellectual property protection, assignment, enforcement and dispute resolutions.

Chong Huat currently acts for numerous key PRC institutions, including the State Administration of Foreign Exchange, and was involved in a number of floating rate note/bond issues by major PRC financial institutions in Singapore with listings on the Singapore

Stock Exchange. He has also acted for both borrowers and lenders on domestic and cross-border transactions and has advised on secured and unsecured lending transactions. He has worked on a wide range of financing matters, including the financing of leisure infrastructure, toll roads, water treatment plants, power stations, gas pipelines, port facilities, industrial parks, golf resorts, hotel, residential and commercial property developments, and chemicals and manufacturing facilities.

He was nominated in the 1998 edition of AsiaLaw Leading Lawyers for his China-related work and in the 1999, 2000 and 2001 editions for his PRC and Project Finance experience.

Yang Ing Loong, MA (Cantab), Barrister of the Middle Temple, Advocate and Solicitor of the Supreme Court of Singapore, Accredited Mediator of CEDR, FCIArb., FSIArb.

Before joining legal practice, Yang Ing Loong was a State Counsel and Deputy Public Prosecutor in the Attorney-General's Chambers. In his tenure there, he was Singapore's representative to the Working Group of the United Nations Conference on International Trade Law (UNCITRAL) in Vienna, Austria, and had acted as legal advisor to the Singapore government in Air Services Agreement negotiations in Norway. Upon joining legal practice, he specialized in commercial and corporate litigation and advice, handled shareholders' and directors' disputes and commercial arbitration. He is presently a partner of Allen & Gledhill, a leading local law firm, and heads its China Practice Group. He travels regularly to the PRC and has advised a number of large Singaporean corporations in their transactions in China, especially in the areas of mergers and acquisitions and banking.

Ing Loong is actively involved in international arbitration, both as counsel and arbitrator, and has delivered several papers on arbitration at conferences such as the International Pacific Bar Association Conference and the Arbitration Association of the Republic of China. He is a panel member of both the Singapore International Arbitration Centre and the Arbitration Association of the Republic of China. In April 2000, he was invited by the Taiwanese Judicial Yuan to run an advocacy workshop for the local judges on Singapore's criminal procedure. Ing Loong also sits as a Committee Member of the Disciplinary Committee of the Stock Exchange of Singapore Ltd and the Law Society of Singapore. He is a Community Mediator at the Marine Parade Community Development Council appointed by the Minister of Law. In January 2002, he was co-opted as a Council Member of the Law Society of Singapore and successfully organized a legal mission to China in August 2002.

Foreword

China is a major partner in Singapore's internationalisation efforts. It was Singapore's fifth largest trading partner in 2002 and remains one of our hottest investment destinations. Foreign trade figures in 2002 reached S$28.1 billion, a striking increase of 25.3% over 2001, while contractual Foreign Direct Investments in 2002 hit US$2.8 billion, an increase of 40% over 2001.

Despite being such an important market, Singapore-based entrepreneurs and companies are often daunted by the lack of accurate interpretation and advice on the Chinese legal system when they venture into China. I am glad that our top legal minds have come together to publish this comprehensive legal guide, and to provide answers to commonly asked questions relating to doing business in China.

For lawyers who use this book, the continuing challenges are two-fold: to provide innovative, high-value services, and to stay current on China's legislation.

I am sure this book will be an invaluable source of information to both legal practitioners and entrepreneurs.

Lee Yi Shyan
Chief Executive Officer
International Enterprise Singapore

Preface

I began research on Chinese law about 10 years ago as a post-graduate student in the King's College, University of London. In the past 10 years, I have seen countless literature and voluminous books written on Chinese law, but no one has produced an abridged version, what I would loosely call a 'nutshell' book on Chinese business law. I decided to fill that gap.

The opportunity came when the Law Society of Singapore and IE Singapore (formerly the Trade Development Board) decided that a book should be written to familiarize local lawyers with Chinese law so that they can better advise their clients in their China business dealings.

As such, this book is intended to be a *primer* for lawyers venturing into the Chinese legal market with their clients for the first time and need guidance on the position of Chinese law in relevant areas. At the same time, I have written this book with the entrepreneur in mind, so that they may also find the book useful in helping them better understand, and hopefully better structure, their China investments. In this book, I have attempted to combine breadth with depth wherever relevant to expose the reader to some of the underlying difficulties in contemporary Chinese law. Some of these in-depth discussions will certainly enthrall those who are keen on gaining a deeper and sharper understanding of Chinese law.

While the book was undergoing the editorial process, new legislation that impacted on some of the areas discussed in this book were introduced. As such, I feel that I should do a quick run of these legislation lest readers perceive that the book's value has been compromised. Firstly, in relation to Chapter 2, readers should note that the Ministry of Information Industry in China has issued a new classification of what is regarded as basic telecommunication services as opposed to value-added services. This new classification serves to clarify former grey areas and highlight business opportunities for both foreign and domestic telecommunications investors. Readers are invited to avail themselves of the details in a short article published in *China Law and Practice* May 2003, pp 23–26. Foreign investors who are in the resource exploration sector should also familiarize themselves with the recently issued draft *Administrative Regulations on the Granting of Exploration and Mining Rights by Tender, Auction and Quotation*. Again, a short commentary of the draft rules can be found in *China Law and Practice* May 2003, pp 20–22.

Secondly, in relation to Chapter 3 of the book, it should be noted that the Ministry of Foreign Trade and Economic Co-operation, now known as the Ministry of Commerce (after having merged with the State Trade and Economic Commission), has issued a regulation called the *Decision Concerning Revision of the Interim Provisions on Foreign-invested Holding Companies and their Supplementary Regulations* on

7 April 2003. The expanded rights of holding companies registered in China are as follows:

1. holding companies are now allowed to invest in all sectors that China has opened to foreign investment, including 'restricted' projects and in the services industries;

2. holding companies are authorized to lease machinery and office equipment to their subsidiaries;

3. holding companies are now allowed to provide after-sales service for the products of the holding companies' parent company;

4. holding companies are allowed to participate with other authorized Chinese enterprises in contracts for overseas construction projects;

5. foreign investors in a holding company are now allowed to make all capital contributions in *Rmb*, whereas they had to pay all capital contributions in hard currency previously;

6. holding companies are permitted to be promoters of joint stock companies, and may hold unlisted legal person shares in both foreign-invested and domestic joint stock companies (though they are still not allowed to hold listed shares or list the shares they hold); and

7. holding companies' importation rights have been increased from 20% to 35% of the holding companies' registered capital that has been paid in cash.

In essence, the new regulations on holding companies are intended to help foreign investors who have registered PRC holding companies to better streamline their group activities and perform the central treasury function.

In summary, the body of law surrounding foreign direct investment is very stable and will not be subject to much change except for the opening up of more sectors to foreign investment in compliance with China's commitments under the World Trade Organization (WTO). China's intellectual property law has also matured in the last decade and is generally aligned with international standards and protocols. The area that should be closely observed is the development of Chinese Corporate and Securities Law and Mergers and Acquisitions. These areas are in the state of flux, and due to the frequent legislative changes taking place, the law is chaotic and represents a significant challenge to foreign investors.

Last but not least, I take this opportunity to thank the Law Society and IE Singapore for making this book possible. I would also like to express my gratitude to the other contributors of this book, who despite their hectic schedules, have delivered their respective chapters on time.

Associate Professor Tan Lay Hong
July 2003

Contents

CHAPTER 3
Mergers and Acquisitions in China

CHAPTER 4
Chinese Company Law

Chapter 5
Chinese Contract Law

CHAPTER 8
Arbitration

Table of Cases

Table of Statutes

CHAPTER 1

The Chinese Legal System

Tan Lay Hong

INTRODUCTION

1-101　Chinese law can be complicated, but it need not be so. In many things, if we get the big picture then everything else falls into place and the details will begin to make sense. In addition, knowing the historical development of the law as well as its social, political and economic context may help one to understand it better than if one were merely attune to the nuts and bolts of the law. In approaching Chinese law, it is recommended that one does not attempt to understand it with eyes coloured with Western experience and practice, but instead to approach it afresh without any prior prejudices and preconceived notions. Having said that, however, appropriate comparisons with Western systems of law will still be made whenever it will enable the reader to understand the Chinese law better.

1-102　This chapter will attempt to construct a coherent under-standing of the Chinese legal system. It will look at some common attributes of a legal system such as Chinese legal theory and culture, Chinese legal concepts, the Constitution, the law making machinery, namely the National People's Congress, the State Council and their provincial counterparts and the Chinese judiciary.

CHINESE LEGAL THEORY AND CULTURE

Historical notions of law

1-201　After the overthrow of the Qing dynasty in 1911, the ruling Nationalists abrogated traditional imperial Chinese law and enacted a new body of law based largely on the European-style civil law. The main models were the French, German and Japanese civil codes. Today's Chinese Company Law, for instance, is based on the German civil code. The Nationalist civil codes were severely attacked and abrogated when the communist took power in 1949, and all bourgeois ideas, including Western law and legal theory, were severely criticized. The newly constituted communist government abolished the old Nationalists laws and began building a socialist legal system based on the Soviet model.

1-202   Despite the adoption of a Soviet-style legal theory, traditional notions of ancient Chinese law remain influential today. The ancient Chinese valued social harmony and believed that in an ideal society there is neither need for extensive legislation or litigation. The ruler had the responsibility for maintaining harmony, and he ruled based on social norms that governed relationships between people. Law was an instrument of last resort. It was used by emperors solely for maintaining the hierarchal order by punishing criminals and deterring commoners from crime. In fact, ancient China only had criminal law. Law was not directed at good people, instead people believed that its only purpose was to deter the potentially evil. Hence, the famous idiom: 'Law is meant for the base person but not for a gentleman *(fa bei xiaoren bu fang junzi)*'.

1-203   In short, the Chinese saw the law as a tool used by the ruling class for dominance, not for the protection of civil and individual rights.

Marxist legal theory

1-204   The works of AY Vyshinsky, a Soviet legal scholar of the 1930s, formed the heart of socialist legalism in China. Vyshinsky emphasized the coercive aspects of law and regarded law as an instrument used by the ruling class to suppress antagonistic forces. This theory neatly fitted the exigencies of China in the 1950s when China was in the throes of a class struggle.

1-205   Based on Vyshinsky's theory, Chinese legal scholars developed what is called the Marxist theory of law. Under this theory, the existence of law rests on class and class struggle alone.

1-206   The Marxist legal theory remains part of a compulsory legal education and training in China today. Obviously, however, it is at odds with the realities and needs of China in this present era. China's current legalization campaign, ie the building of legal institutions; the legislation of a comprehensive body of law, particularly in the economic field; and the instilling of a legal consciousness, stands in sharp contrast to this Marxist theory. The contradictions are ironed out by the Chinese leaders' use of a pragmatic approach to law.

Legal pragmatism in China

What is legal pragmatism?

1-207   The pragmatic approach to law has never been properly explained by Chinese leaders and scholars even though it plays a critical role in the legalization campaign in contemporary China. The Chinese pragmatic approach bears the following characteristics:

(a)   It overemphasizes the instrumental facets of law.

(b)   It regards law as an outcome of 'actuality'.

(c)   It treats law as a servant of policy.

(d)   It does not treat individual rights seriously.

1-208   According to this approach, the law is an instrument of the Chinese Communist Party (CCP). What this means is that after establishing 'actuality', the CCP uses the law as an instrument to legislate appropriate policy.

1-209   It was rationalized that the 'actuality' in China in the 1950s was class struggle; thus law was regarded as an instrument for class domination, an instrument that allowed the proletariat to dominate and eventually eliminate the bourgeois class and all other reactionaries. As the political imperative has moved from class struggle to economic development, the primary role of law has now changed from serving class struggle to serving economic development. But who decides what the 'actuality' is? Current practice shows that it is the CCP that decides what the 'actuality' is at any given time.

Deng's ideology

1-210   Deng Xiaoping saw the law as a necessary tool to advance socialist modernization in China. He sought a 'Chinese' path to the development of a socialist legal theory. Hence his famous adage of developing a 'socialist market economy with Chinese characteristics'. He insisted on 'four cardinal principles' – the socialist road, the dictatorship of the proletariat, the leadership of the Party, and Marxism-Leninism and Mao Zedong Thought.

1-211   Despite his 'four cardinal principles', Deng had no doubt that 'law was the highest authority'. By this, he meant that the 'rule of persons' had to be replaced by the 'rule of law', ie there must be laws to guide people's behaviour, laws must be observed, law-breakers must be punished, and lastly, law enforcement must be strict. In Deng's view, the law and legal system were seen as instruments to improve

people's material wealth, and to end the legal nihilism found in Mao's legal thought. The essence of Deng's socialist legal theory is to safeguard the people's political rights against arbitrariness and bureaucratism.

1-212   Though expedient, the danger in Chinese legal pragmatism is that it lacks a firm foundation. In the United States, legal pragmatism exists within the context of an established, sophisticated legal system, built on constant and inviolable principles, that is the rule of law. In contrast, in China, the emphasis on instrumentalism lacks a similar foundation. Thus, Deng's random views could be bent in the direction of expediency as was seen in the Tiananmen debacle. Despite Deng's conception of 'law as the highest authority', he reaffirmed the supreme position of the CCP.

Deng's socialist legal theory 'with Chinese characteristics'

1-213   What is the meaning of Deng's 'four cardinal principles'? Firstly, the 'socialist road' means maintaining a dominantly planned economy supplemented by a market economy. Secondly, the 'dictatorship of the proletariat' is synonymous with the 'people's democratic dictatorship', which means allowing a limited degree of democracy within a socialist legal system. Thirdly, 'Party leadership' must be made accountable through public supervision to curb excesses. And lastly, 'Mao Zedong Thought' must be reformulated to tackle China's realities. In practice, the 'four cardinal principles' are interpreted as 'living' (*huo*) anti-dogmatic principles, and thus open the door to emancipation.

The road ahead

Optimism in legal reforms

1-214   In China, law is still in a confused state and full of conceptual uncertainties. The study of law is in turmoil. This turmoil is, however, to be viewed positively as it throws open important questions such as: What sort of legal order does the Party intend to create? What purposes are served by creating a legal system? What is the status of the legal system in a socialist society? What is the relationship between law and politics? To what extent should law protect people's democratic rights? And so on.

1-215   But there is optimism. Firstly, people in China now view the law positively rather than negatively. Secondly, legal reforms are underway. Since 1978, China has embarked on an ambitious programme of legal reform and institution building. Much has gone into developing and improving the professionalism of the legislature, judiciary, legal profession, procuracy and public security. China has passed numerous laws such as the Organic Law of the People's Court, Judges' Law, Lawyers' Law, Procuracy Law, Police Law, Legislation Law and so on to strengthen these institutions.

Curbing abuses and excesses in state power

1-216   Thirdly, there is considerable support for the view that there must be meaningful constraints on the government. The Administrative Litigation Law was passed in 1989 to afford Chinese citizens (and even foreign investors) an important legal channel to curb abuses of state power by government agencies and officials. The Administrative Litigation Law appears to have had considerable impact since its implementation. From 9,742 tried cases in 1989, it rose to 79,527 in 1996.[1]

Jiang's ideology – continuity with Deng's 'open door' policy

1-217 Fourthly, Jiang Zemin, since taking the helm of leadership, continued with Deng's insistence on market reform within a context of social and political stability. He reaffirmed the regulative functions of law in a market economy and promoted new economic legislation. He renewed the emphasis on establishing legal infrastructure, re-enforcing judicial independence, improving the quality of legal personnel, training lawyers and promoting popular legal awareness. But Jiang made it clear that cultural and ideological purity may not be sacrificed for temporary economic growth, and reaffirmed the authority and validity of Marxism.

1-218 Concerned with leaving behind his own ideological legacy, Jiang actively promoted his 'Three Represents' theory. In Jiang's view, this theory meant that the CCP must always represent China's 'advanced productive forces', 'advanced culture' and 'the fundamental interests of the overwhelming majority of people in China'. In essence, Jiang's theory was intended to embrace capitalists and entrepreneurs into the fold of the CCP.

1-219 Although Jiang's 'Three Represents' theory is difficult to justify theoretically,[2] it enjoys broad support from many sectors of Chinese society. Its importance lies in the fact that the ruling communist party had on its own volition given up the idea of class warfare, and has embraced capitalism into China's political process. The 16th CCP Congress held on 14 November 2002 enshrined Jiang's 'Three Represents' theory into its charter. At the same time, there was a peaceful transition of power to Vice-President Hu JinTao. Although not much is known about Hu's personal views and ideology, it is widely believed that he will continue with Jiang's reforms.

China's accession to the WTO

1-220 Finally, China's accession to the World Trade Organization (WTO) will put international pressure upon her to abide by the WTO

---

1   Similar lawsuits against government agencies and officials have been filed and tried prior to the passage of the Administrative Litigation Law, but the number was relatively small in the late 1980s.

2   For instance, economists have yet to agree on who or what constitutes 'advanced productive forces'. Secondly, the term 'advanced culture' is a misnomer as culture is supposed to be multi-faceted and should not be categorized as 'advanced' or 'backward'. Thirdly, it is practically impossible for the CCP to represent 'the overwhelming majority of people' due to the diversity of Chinese society, see 'Jiang's Three Represents Theory To Meet Demands of Changing China' *The Straits Times* 15 November 2002 p A4.

obligations. The ruling regime's desire for legitimacy, both at home and abroad, will slowly but surely prod them to adopt laws and practices that accord with international standards of democracy, human rights and the rule of law.

LAW-MAKING IN CHINA

National People's Congress and its Standing Committee

Constitution and structure of the NPC

1-301   The National People's Congress (NPC) is the highest institution of state power and together with its Standing Committee exercises the legislative power of the state. The NPC comprises deputies elected from the provinces, autonomous regions and municipalities directly under the central government (ie localities) and the army. With 3,000 members, the NPC convenes a meeting every year which lasts for one to two weeks. Meetings are convened by the Standing Committee at any time the Standing Committee deems necessary or at the proposal of one-fifth of the deputies. NPC membership is an honorary position and most of the NPC deputies have little, if any, knowledge of law-making. Technically, the NPC has power to amend the Constitution and enact basic laws governing criminal offences, civil rights and other matters.

Standing Committee of the NPC

1-302   In practice, the NPC has neither the resources nor ability and time to consider draft bills for enactment. It is the Standing Committee that is the active organ in legislation. It is smaller in size and meets every two months. Its members serve on a full-time basis. Its meetings may be attended by non-voting representatives from the State Council, the Central Military Commission and other state bodies and the local governments. Minorities are proportionately represented in the NPC and its Standing Committee.

1-303   The Standing Committee has detailed rules on law-making which can be found in the Legislation Law cited below. It follows a similar procedure to the procedure adopted by the NPC for law-making (described below).

1-304   The Standing Committee has wide ranging powers despite being unable to amend the Constitution. It is charged with, *inter alia*, interpreting the Constitution and supervising its enforcement, enacting, amending and supplementing laws passed by the NPC, interpreting laws, annulling administrative rules, regulations and decisions of the State Council or other organs of state power of the localities that contravene the Constitution or the law.

Law-making process in China

How bills originate - from the State Council

1-305 In practice, a bill is first drafted by a commission or ministry under the State Council before it reaches the NPC and its Standing Committee. The State Council has detailed rules on law-making. These rules are found in the Law on the Organization of the State Council of the People's Republic of China.

1-306 In the drafting stage, expert opinion is sought from the relevant departments, scholars, practising lawyers and other professionals. Consultations take place between government officials and experts. The final draft bill is then submitted to the State Council for consideration.

1-307 Upon receiving a draft bill, the Office Legislative Affairs (OLA) of the State Council makes further revision and invites scholars and experts to give advice. Meetings are convened by the OLA to solicit views from the relevant ministries and commissions. Such meetings are in truth springboards for power brokering amongst the different factions with each vying for a larger share of the pie.

1-308 After the consultation process carried out by the State Council, the new draft is then submitted to the Legislative Affairs Commission (LAC) of the Standing Committee of the NPC. The LAC conducts a similar consultative process. At this stage, foreign laws and regulations are considered and may serve as precedents in the drafting process. The LAC may also initiate bills at the behest of the Standing Committee.

NPC procedures for law-making - a mere formality

1-309 The NPC holds an annual meeting with two-thirds of its members forming a quorum. Its members are grouped into delegations based on the localities or special state bodies such as the military. These delegations may submit bills or proposals to the NPC that fall within the scope of their functions and powers. In addition, the Presidium of the NPC, the Standing Committee, the State Council, the Central Military Commission, the Supreme People's Court, the Supreme People's Procuratorate and the special committees of the NPC may introduce bills to the NPC. In the law-making process, China does not adopt the various stages of reading bills that are commonly seen in Western legislatures.

1-310 Once a bill is placed on the agenda of a session, the sponsor (the relevant special committee or relevant office of the Standing Committee) would furnish information to enable the bill to be debated by the delegations, the Law Committee and special committees. The Law Committee gathers the views of the delegates and revises the drafts for further consideration by the NPC. If necessary, the Presidium may delegate the matter to the Standing Committee for further deliberation or action.

1-311   The final stage of law-making is when the NPC and its Standing Committee promulgate the law. The law becomes effective upon promulgation by the President. The President may not modify the law.

1-312   The NPC recently promulgated detailed rules and procedures on the law-making process of the NPC. This important piece of legislation is called the Law of the People's Republic of China on Legislation (Legislation Law). It was promulgated on 1 July 2000 and became effective on the same day.

1-313   The Legislation Law clearly states that all laws, administrative regulations and local regulations shall be published in the gazette of the respective law-making bodies and the gazetted version shall be the official version.

STRUCTURE OF CHINESE LAW

Complex interwoven web of rules and regulations

Chinese law in chaos

1-401   Anyone who thinks that the NPC and the State Council are the only sources of law in China is very much mistaken. In fact, no one can live in China for long without immediately becoming aware of the complex, interwoven web of rules that govern the economy. At the present moment, Chinese law can be described as chaotic. For instance, in the field of securities law, we have local regulations enacted by the Shanghai and Shenzhen local government in the 1980s (regional laws) that were subsequently overladden with two pieces of very significant legislation from the State Council. The establishment of the China Securities Regulatory Commission (CSRC) in 1992 added more layers of legislative and administrative rules and regulations. And finally, the National Securities Law was promulgated by the NPC on 29 December 1998. To complicate matters, most of these regulations were couched in vague language, had overlapping provisions, and until recently the Chinese legislative authorities never had the habit of clarifying whether subsequent legislation supersedes earlier regulations or whether the local rules have been repealed. As a result, officials and lawyers in China engage in a daily struggle to make sense out of the complex interwoven web of rules and regulations. The immediate question raised by any observer or businessman is how to navigate through these laws and regulations. Perhaps the answer lies in finding out what caused it in the first place.

Reasons for the complexity of Chinese law

1-402 The following paragraphs outline the reasons why Chinese law is in the state of chaos that it is in.

Post-1949 Communist 'Normative Document' System

1-403 When the Communists took power in 1949, the Party leaders adopted the Soviet principle that all state power should rest exclusively in the hands of a supreme legislature. The 1954 Constitution radically centralized the exercise of law-making powers. Only the NPC and its Standing Committee had the authority to enact national laws (*falü*) or decrees (*faling*). Regional and local governments, with the exception of the minority areas, were stripped of all legislative power. This model could not, however, sustain a workable system of law. China was just too large, and could not be governed by some scanty primary laws that were produced by a national legislature that meets every year for only two weeks.

1-404 The result was the development of the normative document system. It resembles the Qing system of sub-statutory rules, commentaries and case precedents. After finding that its documentary communication system could not meet the demands of the national government, the CCP developed a complex method of written and verbal bureaucratic communication. Officials began to use the Soviet derived term 'normative documents' (*guifangxing wenjian*) to refer to all such administrative directives. Such documents were issued at all levels of the administrative bureaucracy ranging from the State Council to village and township authorities. China's current legal order was in many respects developed out of this normative document system. In Chinese parlance, these normative documents were variously termed as '*tiaoli*', '*zhangcheng*' and '*banfa*'. These normative documents were often issued by localities and state organs to suit the needs of the local situations and exigencies.

1-405 The normative document system survived the Cultural Revolution and is now perpetuated by state bureaucratic organs and local governments alike.

Decentralization of legislative power after 1979

1-406 By 1979, the central government saw the need to decentralize administrative power and to that end, the NPC enacted legislation that extended subordinate law-making powers to the provincial level people's congresses and selected local and regional people's governments and congresses. Some have, however, argued that these administrative rule-making powers cannot properly be described as 'legislative powers'. Be that as it may, many practitioners of Chinese law would certainly agree that these rules and regulations are not to be ignored and have the force of law.

Chinese legislative practice of using interim experimental measures

1-407   The third reason for the chaotic state of Chinese law lies in the prevalent view that legislation ought to be a response to and not an instigator of change. Thus, national laws should not be enacted until the relevant circumstances are 'ripe' (*chengshu*). This practice resulted in the wide use of interim regulatory measures which are often issued on an *ad hoc* and experimental basis. Whilst the attraction of such an incremental approach to change is fairly obvious in that it allowed officials to tinker and experiment endlessly before committing themselves to legislation, such interim and experimental measures often cloud matters. Together with the normative document system, they are the cause of the complex web of inconsistent rules and regulations that plague the Chinese legal system today.

Chinese legal drafting

1-408   The final but not unimportant reason for the chaotic state of Chinese law lies in Chinese legal drafting. The fundamental principle of Chinese legislative drafting is that primary legislation should be both 'general' (*yuanzexing*) and 'flexible' (*linghuoxing*). The justification for this principle of generality and flexibility is to facilitate the implementation of the legislation throughout the country and also adaptation to local conditions. In China, national legislation must not only be unitary in nature, it must also allow for regional diversity. In addition, it must also allow for legislative stability (*wendingxing*) in that the law can be effectively amended through changes in interpretation rather than through alterations in the actual text.

1-409   It would be ideal if subordinate regulations[3] were drafted in more precise language to flesh out the primary legislation, but this is not so. Subordinate regulations are, unfortunately, often drafted in the same broad and indeterminate language as the primary legislation. Thus, they often lack the very detail which they are supposed to provide. One dire consequence of such vague drafting in national legislation is that it loses its capacity to constrain subordinate regulations.

1-410   Another point to note is that Chinese legislative language is highly contextual. In many instances, the law cannot be understood without a grasp of related Party policy documents. This poses an obstacle to those who do not have access to such materials. The result is that too much is left to administrative discretion in the hands of those who implement the law.

---

3   Subordinate regulations refer to regulations promulgated by the State Council and other state administrative organs.

Present system – 'unitary, two level, multi-layered'

Legislative hierarchy of laws, administrative regulations and rules, etc

1-411   There is now a general consensus that the present system can be described as a 'unitary, two level, multi-layered' (*yiyuan, erji, duoceng*) legislative structure. This maxim encapsulates the entire essence of legislative practice in the Chinese legal system. Firstly, it is a unified system; and secondly, legislative authority is divided between central and regional levels of authority.

Fragmented legislative powers

1-412   In China, the legislative power of the state is shared amongst many organs of the state as well as those of the local governments. The people's congresses of the localities and even the special economic zones may formulate local rules and regulations that are not contrary to the Constitution. But such rules must be adopted in 'light of the specific conditions and actual needs' of the localities.

1-413   China's legislative structure combines two different forms of legislative hierarchy. Firstly, there is the unified hierarchy of institutional bodies possessing law-making powers. At the apex stands the NPC and its Standing Committee. The next level is the State Council. Below these central government apparatus, law-making powers are divided between the territorial bureaucracies of regional and local government on the one hand, and the functional bureaucracies of the central government administration such as the State Planning Commission, the State Economic Restructuring Commission, the CSRC and so on on the other. Figure 1 shows the legislative structure of the PRC.[4] One can observe that it mirrors the government bureaucratic structure of the PRC closely. This is shown in Figure 2.

1-414   Secondly, there is the hierarchy of legislative categories of law, which can be simplified at three levels. Primary legislation stands at the top of the pyramid, just below the Constitution in legal authority. An example is the PRC Company Law 1993. This type of legislation is referred to as '*falü*' – the English translation of which is law. Only the NPC and its Standing Committee have the power to promulgate such laws. It is to be noted that the Standing Committee shall have the power to interpret such laws and the interpretations shall have the same status as the laws.

1-415   At the middle level are what is called '*fagui*' which are issued in different forms by the State Council and the regional people's congresses. This term is commonly translated in English as 'regulations'. In this

---

4   Table 1 is adapted from an article by Perry Keller, 'Sources of Order in Chinese Law' (1994) 42 *The American Journal of Comparative Law* 712 at p 728.

regard, the term 'regulation' has been generally used to refer to Chinese legislation for want of a better word. The Legislation Law has now made it clear that the regulations promulgated by the State Council are to be called 'administrative regulations',[5] whilst the regulations promulgated by the people's congresses and their standing committees of the localities are to be called 'local regulations', 'autonomous regulations' or 'separate regulations'.

Figure 1: Legislative structure of the People's Republic of China

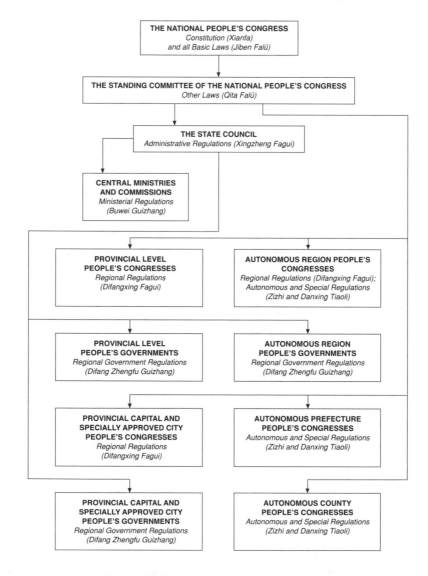

---

5   The Regulations on the Procedures for the Formulation of Administrative Regulations provide that such 'administrative regulations' may also be known as 'Rules' or 'Measures'. This Regulation was promulgated by the State Council on 16 November 2001 and became effective on 1 January 2002. It contains detailed rules and procedures on how administrative regulations are to be enacted by the State Council.

1-416 Finally, at the tertiary level, there are '*guizhang*' which are issued by the central government ministries and regional and local government. This term had also been commonly translated as 'regulations'. However, the Legislation Law has now made it clear that regulations enacted by the people's governments of the localities are to be called 'rules', whilst those enacted by the departments of state organs shall be called 'departmental rules'. They are not to be called 'regulations'.

Rules for resolving inconsistent laws and administrative regulations and rules

1-417 The Legislation Law has developed a set of rules for determining which provisions of law shall apply in the event of inconsistencies and contradictions. It provides that the authority of laws (ie primary laws passed by the NPC and its Standing Committee) is higher than administrative regulations, local regulations and rules. Next, administrative regulations are higher in authority than local regulations and rules. In turn, local regulations (ie those enacted by the people's congresses) are higher in authority than rules enacted by the people's governments. Lastly, departmental rules enacted by different departments have the same authority. And departmental rules have the same authority as rules enacted by the people's governments. Presumably, the legislation that has higher authority will prevail over those with lower authority in the event of any inconsistency or contradiction, although this is not made clear in the Legislation Law.

1-418 In addition, the Legislation Law provides that subsequent special legislation which is inconsistent with earlier general provisions shall prevail over the general provisions. In the same vein, new provisions which are inconsistent with previous provisions shall prevail over the previous provisions. Article 85 of the Legislation Law further provides that where the new general provisions of law conflict with previous special provisions, and it cannot be determined which provisions shall be applied, the Standing Committee of the NPC shall have the power to decide the question. In the case of conflicting general and special administrative regulations, the State Council shall have the power to decide the question.

1-419 In case of conflicting local regulations and departmental rules, the State Council shall have the power to decide which legislation should prevail. If the State Council decides that the departmental rules shall apply, the matter has to be submitted to the Standing Committee of the NPC for a decision. In the event that an administrative regulation that is enacted with delegated powers conflicts with the laws enacted by the NPC or its Standing Committee, and it cannot be determined which provisions should apply, the matter shall be decided by the Standing Committee of the NPC.

Issues and challenges in the present system

Imperceptible boundaries of legislative competence

1-420   The complexity of China's legislative hierarchy presents an obstacle to those who wish to develop a more rational and internally consistent and coherent body of law. The spread of legislative powers over a network of state administrative and regional organs has in effect brought the rivalries and disorder of the Chinese bureaucracy directly into the legislative structure. Administrative bodies and local governments often enhanced their status and power through the issue of regulations. In China, this works even though it is tantamount to pulling oneself up by one's own bootstrap. Such bootstrap tactics could be perpetuated because there was no law that defined the legislative competence of these bodies. It was therefore difficult for the central authorities to rein in or control aggressive uses of legislative power by the local authorities.

1-421   The Legislation Law was thus enacted to create a framework to delineate the legislative activities of the various legislative bodies. For the first time, the Legislation Law spells out the legislative competence of the NPC and its Standing Committee. Article 7 of the Legislation Law states that 'all national legislative powers' shall be vested in the NPC and its Standing Committee. It further states that the NPC shall enact and amend the criminal laws, civil laws, the fundamental laws of the national authorities and other basic laws. Article 8 sets out a list of matters which are within the legislative competence of the NPC *and* its Standing Committee. The list runs as follows:

(a)   matters concerning national sovereignty;

(b)   the creation, organization and responsibilities of the people's congresses at all levels, the people's governments, people's courts and the people's procuratorates;

(c)   the system of local national autonomies, special administrative regions, and system of grass-root mass autonomies;

(d)   crime and punishment;

(e)   the mandatory measures and punishment regarding deprivation of the political rights of citizens and restriction of personal liberty;

(f)   the expropriation of non-state-owned properties;

(g)   the basic civil law system;

(h)   the basic economic system and the basic system of revenue, taxation, customs, finance and foreign trade;

(i)   the litigation and arbitration system; and

(j)   all other matters which require the NPC and its Standing Committee to enact laws.

1-422 However, the unfortunate result of article 8 is that the legislative competence of the NPC and its Standing Committee remains undifferentiated.

Unclear boundaries of the legislative competence between the NPC and its Standing Committee

1-423 As stated above, the Legislation Law has missed the opportunity to clarify the respective boundaries of the legislative competence of the NPC and its Standing Committee. In other words, where does the legislative competence of the NPC end and where does that of the Standing Committee begin? The Legislation Law provides that the Standing Committee shall enact and amend laws 'other than those that shall be enacted by the NPC'. But what laws are to be enacted by the NPC? It is unclear. There is no law that lays down the purview of the NPC's legislative competence. The Constitution merely provides that the NPC shall 'enact and amend basic laws governing criminal offences, civil affairs, the state organs and *other matters*'. The phrase 'other matters' is a catchall word that can literally mean 'any other matters'. This mires the boundary of the NPC's legislative competence.

1-424 The problem is exacerbated by the fact that in reality, the NPC and its Standing Committee have enacted substantially similar legislation such that it is not possible to distinguish between the basic laws promulgated by the NPC and the 'other laws' enacted by its Standing Committee. Interpretations issued by the Standing Committee on those primary laws have the same status as the laws. There is thus no way of challenging the constitutionality of any laws enacted by the Standing Committee. The Legislation Law has done nothing to resolve this issue.

Overlapping legislative competence between the NPC and State Council

1-425 The same difficulty used to arise over the unclear boundaries of the respective legislative competence of the NPC and the State Council. The Legislation Law has, however, obliquely resolved this difficulty by providing that the laws enacted by the NPC and its Standing Committee are higher in authority than 'administrative regulations', a term which presumably refers to regulations enacted by the State Council.

Relationship between national laws and local regulations

1-426 The problem is magnified when the same practice is mirrored on a smaller scale at the regional level (see Figure 1). One particularly thorny question that has plagued many observers is how far the provisions of national laws could be strained to accommodate local circumstances. Indeed, can regional authorities go so far as to 'modify' (*biantong*) national law to suit local conditions by purporting to act within the spirit of the national law? The Legislation Law has left this question unanswered.

Unclear source(s) of legislative competence

1-427   The messy state of affairs is further exacerbated by the legislative practice of issuing administrative regulations and rules or measures that are not linked to any particular primary law but that are issued as part of a state organ's or local government's administrative responsibilities.

Administrative dominance in law-making

1-428   Another contributing factor lies in what is called administrative dominance in law-making. In China, the state organs are also empowered to interpret legislation and regulations. In the past, the NPC Standing Committee Resolution that empowered state administrative organs to interpret laws did not specify who should interpret the State Council administrative regulations, rules and local regulations. As a result, administrative lawmakers had been left to enjoy exclusive authority over the interpretation of their own regulations. In other words, state administrative organs and regional governments enjoyed nearly unfettered powers to issue and interpret their own regulations. The result is the plethora of legislation and administrative regulations that is found in China today.

1-429   The Legislation Law and two other administrative regulations, namely, the Regulations on the Procedures for Formulation of Administrative Regulations and Regulations for the Formulation of Rules, appear to have perpetuated this system of administrative dominance in law-making. They provide that the power to interpret any particular legislation lies in the hands of the agency that formulated the legislation.

Lack of political will to impose order

1-430   The final challenge is that there does not appear to be any single institution in China that has the authority or desire to impose order on the legal system. The Chinese courts are ill-suited to undertake the task as their powers of interpretation are restricted and they are not permitted to declare any law or regulation invalid. The administrative bureaucracies are even more unlikely candidates for the task as the rivalry amongst these bodies is in fact a contributing factor to the problem. The CCP is also not in a position to rationalize the legislative process as it is too closely enmeshed in state administration to stand above the struggles of the state organs.

CONSTITUTION

Chinese Government

Political structure

1-501 Under the 1982 Constitution, power is said to belong to the people, but it is exercised by an indirectly elected Parliament, the NPC. The NPC enacts or formally approves legislation. It also elects the President, who is the Head of State; the Premier who is the Head of the Government or Bureaucracy; and the top officials in the courts, the procuracy and a number of other state organs. Congresses in the provinces and counties exercise similar powers at their levels. In other words, they choose the governors, mayors, countyheads, presidents of the courts, chief procurators etc. In theory, Chinese citizens are guaranteed their individual rights such as the freedom of speech, assembly and religion. In addition, their social and economic rights, such as the right to employment, retirement benefits and to form labour unions, are also safeguarded by the Constitution. Figure 2 shows the political structure of the Chinese government.

1-502 The NPC is, unusual in that it is both too large (3,000 members) and meets too infrequently (once a year) to initiate any legislation on its own. When the NPC is not in session, its Standing Committee acts in its place. The actual control of the government lies in the hands of the Premier and top officials of the ministries. The Premier, government officials and the Standing Committee are not accountable to the NPC as would the Executive to Parliament in a Western democracy. However, the NPC has the power to select and remove them from office, although this has never been done before. There is no Parliamentary responsibility in the sense that a government that fails to get a majority in Parliament on a vote of confidence falls.

1-503 There is no direct election of members to the NPC. Direct elections take place only at the village and county levels. Citizens elect their representatives to the local people's congresses directly. These congresses then elect delegates to the congress at the next superior level and so on up to the NPC. At present, there are three levels in the process: the local congresses, the provincial congresses and the NPC.

1-504 Several problems arise from such a division of power. For instance, how will the Chinese solve the problem of divided control between the local congresses and the top level officials in Beijing? In particular, in the case of the courts, who is in control? The local courts are appointed by local congresses and are responsible to them. Appeals from their decisions lie to the higher courts and in some cases to the Supreme People's Court in Beijing. Are the courts accountable to the Supreme People's Court or to the local congresses that elect them? The same problem traverses the entire bureaucracy where all ministries exercise control over the local levels, but these local levels are said to be responsible to the local congresses that appoint them.

1-505   In theory, the NPC is supposed to be the supreme organ exercising state power. But in practice, the NPC is nothing more than a rubber stamp that does as it is told by whoever is in power at their level. The real political power is held by the CCP. The Central Military Commission that controls the army also holds great power although it is not directly involved in the NPC or the government.

Constitution

1-506   In China, the written Constitution is not the place to start if one wants to know what the government of China is really like. The written Constitution has actually very little to do with the real structure of the Chinese government. But that is not to say that the Constitution is to be dismissed altogether. In China, the written Constitution has one function: the adoption or amendment of the Constitution is a signal that a significant change has taken place in the government, and that it is conceived to be long-lasting.

Figure 2: Contemporary Structure of Chinese Government

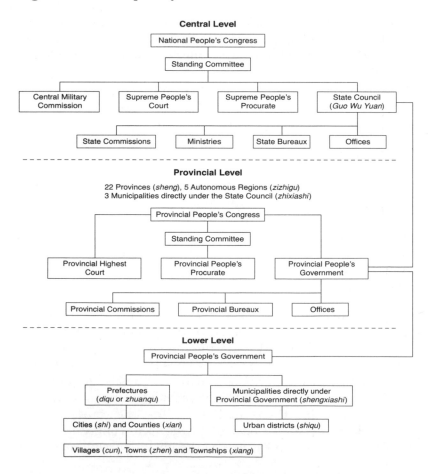

Constitutional supervision and interpretation

Who has powers of supervision and enforcement?

1-507   Do Chinese courts practise the system of judicial review that is commonly carried out in Western democracies? The short answer is no. One writer has chosen to use the term 'constitutional supervision' rather than 'constitutional review' or 'judicial review' because the word 'supervision' in China historically expressed a vertical power relationship whereby a master exerts power over its underlings. 'Review', on the other hand, has a more egalitarian connotation as between reviewer and reviewed there exists a relatively equal and independent relationship. In addition to examining cases brought before it for review, a supervisory body can also take the initiative to review and investigate cases on its own. The Chinese system fits the 'supervision' model of constitutional review more than the judicial review system found in Western democracies.

1-508   In China, there is no separation of power concept. The Constitution confers power over the state on the NPC. One major reform in recent years was an increase in the constitutional authority of the Standing Committee to supervise and interpret the Constitution. Article 5 of the 1982 Constitution provides that:

> No laws or administrative or local rules and regulations may contravene the Constitution. All state organs and military forces, all political parties and social organizations must abide by the Constitution and the law. All acts in violation of the Constitution or the law must be investigated.

1-509   Thus, the NPC has delegated the powers of constitutional supervision to its Standing Committee. In practice, however, constitutional supervision and interpretation have not been effectively carried out in China.

What is the scope of constitutional supervision?

1-510   In China, constitutional supervision is carried out in three different areas:

(a)   there is the constitutional review of legal documents, which includes the review of all legal and regulatory documents that may violate the Constitution, and in the event of a violation, the alteration or voiding of such documents;

(b)   the review of unconstitutional acts by state leaders, which includes the investigation and determination of responsibility of leaders who overstep their constitutional authority, who are derelict in duty, or who engage in any other acts that might damage the Constitution such as corruption; and

(c)   to decide jurisdictional disputes.

Types of constitutional supervision guaranteed under the Constitution

1-511   Ex Ante Review: Article 116 of the Constitution states that the NPC's Standing Committee has the power to review any local laws and regulations before they go into effect. The standing committees of the people's congresses of the localities have similar powers of approval of local rules and regulations.

1-512   Ex Post Review: Review of the constitutionality of laws that have already gone into effect can take place in two ways: active and passive review. In the former, all higher governmental organs to whom laws are reported for their record[6] are expected to actively consider the constitutionality of the legislation in question. This type of review is inadequately developed in practice. As regards the latter (passive review), it is carried out through opinions or reviews sought from higher authorities as to the constitutionality of any legal document by a relevant department who discovers that certain laws or regulations may be violating the Constitution.

1-513   Review of unconstitutional acts by officials: Article 41 of the Constitution provides Chinese citizens with 'a right to make to relevant state organs complaints and accusations against, or exposures of, any state organ or functionary for violation of the law or dereliction of duty ...'. This includes complaints of unconstitutional acts of officials that prejudice or cause hardship to the citizens. It must be noted that this is different from the actions taken under the Administrative Litigation Law 1989. The Administrative Litigation Law does not cover unconstitutional acts of officials.[7]

1-514   Modification or annulment of unconstitutional laws, regulations and normative documents: Article 62 of the Constitution states that the NPC has the power to alter or annul inappropriate decisions of its Standing Committee. In addition, article 67 provides that the NPC's Standing Committee has the power to annul any administrative rules, regulations, decisions or orders of the State Council, or local level state bureaucracies that contravene the Constitution.

---

6   Under the Legislation Law, all administrative regulations must be reported to the Standing Committee of the NPC for record. Local regulations enacted by the local people's congresses of the localities shall be reported to the NPC's Standing Committee and State Council for record. Departmental rules shall be reported to the State Council. Local rules enacted by the local people's government shall be reported to the State Council and the Standing Committee of the people's congresses of the same level.

7   The Administrative Litigation Law 1989 provides ordinary Chinese citizens, legal persons and even foreigners the right to legally challenge administrative decisions (various penalties or other measures) that adversely affect their freedom or economic interests.

1-515 Despite the existence of a legal framework for constitutional supervision, the NPC and its Standing Committee have yet to explicitly exercise its power of constitutional supervision.

Lack of a constitutional supervisory organ

1-516 Perhaps the singular factor that stymies constitutional development in China is the lack of an effective organ that has the power and legitimacy to exercise constitutional supervision and interpretation. The Chinese courts are not equal to the task as they are but mere state organs in the line of bureaucracy that is subject to the authority of the higher courts and the Supreme People's Court as well as the people's congresses at many levels that appoint them and support their budgets. The solution may be to set up *de novo* a constitutional supervisory organ. But this raises questions as to the constitutionality and political legitimacy of such an organ. It may necessitate a drastic amendment to the Constitution that at the present stage is vigorously opposed by some factions of the bureaucracy and policy-makers.

CHINESE JUDICIARY

Historical background

From 1949 to the present

1-601 For most of its history, the Chinese judiciary has been regarded as an instrument of the people's democratic dictatorship (ie the CCP), and was an instrument of oppression of the enemy class. For the first 30 years of the founding of the Republic, the focus of the courts was on criminal policy. This was in line with the Chinese view that law was meant to sanction criminals, the base and lowly, not to be an instrument for the protection of ordinary citizens' legal rights.

1-602 The highest judicial organ is the Supreme People's Court (SPC). It began operations in November 1950 with 17 members. At least four had no legal background. Most were military officers. The courts relied heavily on Party policy for criminal jurisdiction. Between 1959 and 1979, most court staff suffered at the hands of the anti-rightists, and some were sent to the countryside to be peasants. When the 'open door' policy was instituted in 1979, the courts reopened their doors, so to speak, and the NPC passed seven laws to reinstitute the court system. The most important law is the 1979 Organization Law of the People's Court. With the explosion of economic reforms, the courts began handling civil and commercial cases on a larger scale than before.

1-603   The 1982 Constitution (amended in 1988 and 1993) and the 1979 Organization Law of the People's Court (amended in 1983) provided the basic framework of the court system. Both laws state that the SPC is the highest judicial organ of the state, not the highest court of the state. Describing the SPC as an organ means that it is a specialized organ of the bureaucracy. It is responsible for exercising the adjudicatory aspect or judicial power of the state's unified power. Unlike Western systems of government, the Chinese judiciary is not one of three co-equal branches of government. There is no doctrine of separation of powers in China. The Chinese judiciary is not independent of the other state organs and its status and personnel are similar to that of other central government organs and cadres. There is, however, recent lobbying by interest groups to introduce the concept of judicial independence in China.

Court system and the CCP

1-604   Although Chinese law provides that the 'people's courts shall exercise judicial power independently, in accordance with the provisions of the law, and are not subject to any interference by any administrative organ, public organization or individual', the preamble of the Constitution emphasizes that the CCP leads the country in improving the socialist legal system. Like all state organs, the SPC has a Party organization. The SPC is subordinated to the Central Committee of the CCP, in particular the Central Political-Legal Committee (CPLC). In effect, the CPLC supervises the court system and sets nationwide legal policy.

1-605   The principle of 'dual leadership' (*shuang chong lingdao*) operates in the courts. By this it is meant that both the relevant Communist Party Committee and state organ work together in matters of organization (ie personnel), ideology and policy. All nominations of judges are vetted by the CCP before being placed before the Standing Committee of the NPC. Virtually, all judges selected to the SPC are Party members. With respect to ideology, the CPLC guides the political consciousness of the personnel in the legal institutions through regular political study and party meetings. Most importantly, the CPLC sets the direction of legal policy.

1-606   Although in the past, the court system served the CCP and enforced Party policy as part of its mandate, the CCP has now become less involved in the area of technical issues of law that the courts face in their daily work. Thus, much of the courts' work these days is performed without the direct interference of Party organs except in politically sensitive cases. In recent years, the CPLC has also issued fewer normative documents to guide the courts. Party organs are not involved in most quasi-legislation issued by the SPC and generally not involved in the review of cases considered by the SPC.

Court system and the NPC

1-607   The court system is also not independent of the NPC and its Standing Committee either. The relevant laws provide that the SPC is responsible to and reports its work to the NPC and its Standing Committee. In other words, the NPC 'supervises' the SPC, and the President of the SPC has to report on the court system to the NPC annual session. In practice, the people's congresses at all levels regularly 'inquire into' court adjudication.

1-608   The NPC supervises the court system in two ways: firstly, the NPC's Standing Committee has a permanent letters-and-visits office which receives hundreds of letters and handles petitioners' visits every day. Any letter or petition that raises a matter relating to the courts is referred to the SPC's General Office, which then directs them to the appropriate division. Secondly, the NPC supervises the SPC when the NPC representatives submit a proposal to the SPC concerning a case, which is normally controversial. Twenty to thirty such proposals are submitted annually. The SPC has a set of procedures for dealing with such proposals.

1-609   Finally, the NPC and the SPC co-operate in that the SPC frequently participates in the drafting of legislation prepared by the LAC of the Standing Committee, and in turn may solicit the opinion of the Commission's staff regarding judicial interpretations.

Structure of the court system

Court hierarchy

1-610   At the top of the structure is the SPC. Below it are 30 Higher Level People's Courts (*gaojiu renmin fayuan*) for each province, autonomous region (eg Tibet and Xinjiang) and centrally-administered city (ie Beijing, Tianjing and Shanghai). These are termed provincial courts. At the next level are 389 Intermediate Level People's Courts (*zhongji renmin fayuan*). These are established just below the provincial level in prefectures (*diqu*), provincially-administered cities and centrally-administered cities. At the bottom level are the 3,000-odd Basic Level People's Courts (*jiceng renmin fayuan*) which exist at the county level. A Basic Level People's Court may establish branch courts known as People's Tribunals (*renmin fating*) outside the town to facilitate parties staying in outlying areas to attend court. There are over 18,000 People's Tribunals in China (see Figure 3).[8]

---

8   Table 3 is taken from an article by Donald C Clarke, 'Power and Politics in the Chinese Court System: The Enforcement of Civil Judgments' (1996) 10 *Columbia Journal of Asian Law* 1 at p 9.

Figure 3: Power and Politics in the Chinese Court System

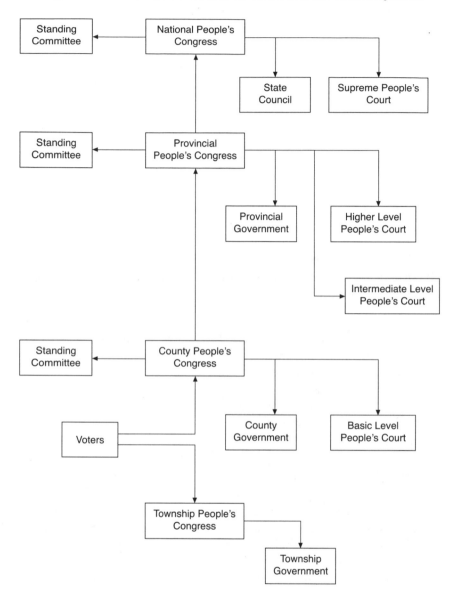

Courts as state organs

1-611   Under the present system, each court functions like a state administrative organ. The SPC and its judges, as well as the lower courts and their judges, are each assigned a bureaucratic rank.[9]

---

9   The ranking system, derived from the traditional Chinese political and legal system, is divided into 30 levels, enabling state and party entities and their personnel to appraise their status in relation to other units. Rank structures the way a unit and its officials are viewed, its relation to other units, and reflects its prestige.

1-612 Unlike their counterparts in Western democracies, Chinese judges on the SPC have no greater security of tenure than any other government official. The Constitution stipulates a limit of two continuous five-year terms for the President of the SPC, just like any senior government servant. Furthermore, the President may be removed from office at any time. No term is fixed for the other judges of the SPC. As with other central organs, administrative practice refers to judges and other court administrative personnel as *fayuan ganbu* (court cadres). Judges are called *shenpanyaun* (adjudication personnel).

Internal organization of the court system

1-613 The organization of the court system is just like any other government bureaucracy. The SPC is at the head of the court hierarchy or 'system' (*xitong*). The court system includes the hierarchy of People's Courts, funded by local governments of various levels, and courts from other hierarchies such as the Military, Railroad and Maritime Courts.

1-614 The SPC is tasked to set up its internal structure. There is the Criminal Division, Economic Division and even the Intellectual Property Division. In addition, the SPC has a Research Office that is involved in substantive legal work. Pursuant to the Organizational Law of the People's Court, the SPC has a Judicial Committee, whose members shall be nominated by the President of the Court and confirmed by the NPC's Standing Committee. The SPC's Vice-Presidents and chief judges of adjudicatory divisions sit on the Judicial Committee. Under the law, the judicial committee(s) of the courts at various levels are responsible for summarizing judicial experience and discussing large, important and difficult cases.

Functions of the SPC

Interpretation of the law

1-615 The 1982 Constitution states that the function of the SPC is to 'supervise the administration of justice (adjudication work) of the People's Courts at various levels and by the special People's Courts'. The phrase 'supervision' (*jiandu*) is a term in Chinese politics and law to mean guiding, monitoring, criticizing and making charges against, or exposing a state organ, and may be top down or bottom up. Under the rubric of 'supervision', the SPC is empowered to interpret law, hear cases in the first instance and on appeal, engage in adjudication supervision, and review and approve death sentences. In the area of civil and commercial law, the most important function of the SPC is to interpret the law.

1-616   The Chinese judiciary does not have the monopoly power to interpret the law. It shares this power with the NPC and its Standing Committee. In a Resolution of the Standing Committee of the NPC Providing an Improved Interpretation of the Law dated 10 June 1981 (1981 Resolution), the Standing Committee shared this power with the State Council and its department and the Supreme People's Procuratorate. The 1981 Resolution also authorized the SPC to interpret 'questions involving the specific application of laws and decrees in court trials'. Interpretations by the SPC and the Supreme People's Procuratorate are known as 'judicial interpretation'.

1-617   Since the 1980s, the SPC has increasingly exercised its powers to interpret law. This is largely caused by legislation lagging behind the huge economic and social change taking place in China. Oftentimes, the lower courts have found themselves in situations where the relevant rules are either missing, not promulgated yet, or vague and obsolete. The SPC has no choice but to issue interpretations to fill in the gaps to enable the lower courts to carry out their work. Thus there arises a practice where the SPC issues interpretations as administrative documents (*wenjian*). These may take the form of 'official opinions' (*yijian*), 'explanations' (*jieda* or *jieshi*), 'official answers' (*pifu* or *dafu*), 'letters' (*fuhan*), 'notices' (*tongzhi* or *tonggao*) and 'conference summaries' (*jiyao*). Such documents are also routinely issued by other administrative organs, ministries and departments.

Types of interpretation issued by the SPC

1-618   Official opinions and explanations: These are the most important documents issued by the SPC. 'Official opinions' are general statements of normative rules. They are not made in connection with any pending litigation. They may be authoritative opinion concerning the whole of a new major law, or issued in the absence of the relevant law, while others may merely interpret a section of an existing law. Some of them are even longer and more detailed than the original legislation. For example, the 'official opinion' interpreting the 1986 General Principles of Civil Law contains 200 articles, which is longer than the primary law which had 156 articles.

1-619   Problems arise when the 'official opinion' establishes new rules or contradicts the primary law. For instance, a 1988 'official opinion' called Opinion (for trial use) of the Supreme People's Court on Questions Concerning the Implementation of the General Principles of Civil Law of the PRC interpreting the General Principles of Civil Law contradicted the law itself and recognized oral partnership agreements when the primary law states that partners must draw up a written agreement. Without doubt, the SPC makes law through issuing these 'official opinions and explanations'. These interpretations have been termed 'quasi-legislation'. Drafting of such interpretations is carried out in much the same way as drafting of national legislation. There is consultation between the relevant departments and the lower courts and government ministries, with views of experts from research institutes and law schools solicited. Views from the public are, however, not solicited. Once a consensus on a draft opinion is reached, it is submitted to the SPC's Judicial Committee for approval. The whole process may take six months to two years.

1-620 Most 'official opinions and explanations' are published in the SPC's official gazette, the Gazette of the Supreme People's Court (*Zuigao Renmin Fayuan Gongbao*). Sensitive 'official opinions' are, however, kept from the general public and are circulated within the court system as internal documents.

1-621 Judges rely heavily on 'official opinions' to provide the relevant legal rules in making their judgments. 'Official opinions' may be cited in rulings and judgments, and are often used by lawyers in making their arguments in court.

1-622 Official replies and letters: These take the form of an official reply or letter in response to a lower court's request for advice on a specific legal question. Such requests probably sound scandalous to a legal practitioner from a Western democracy who is accustomed to judicial independence, even from the lowest court in the court hierarchy. Official replies (*pifu*) issued by the SPC are binding on the requesting lower court. They are akin to directions or instructions issued by a superior state or Party organ to its subordinate units.

1-623 Other responses from the SPC may take the form of a 'letter' (*fuhan*) or an advisory reply to a letter requesting for advice on how to interpret a particular provision of law. In contrast to a *pifu,* the requesting body is not obliged to obey the advice in a *fuhan.* Although there is no clear basis for asking higher level courts for instructions on deciding cases that they consider difficult, for the most part of their history, courts in China have engaged in this practice and will likely continue to do so.

1-624 Official responses from the SPC generally have legal binding force. The SPC will not accept requests submitted directly by the intermediate or basic level courts. It only accepts requests which have been considered by a provincial Higher People's Court and discussed by its Judicial Committee. Generally, neither the lawyer nor his clients would know whether the court hearing their case has requested for official replies or letters unless they have a good relationship with the presiding judge.

1-625   More than one division may issue official replies on the same law. Problems arise when conflicting replies are given by different divisions. For instance, in 1985 the Economic Division of the SPC interpreted the Civil Procedure Law to mean that a party who has withdrawn his original complaint could not file suit again on the same issue. In 1990, however, the Civil Division of the SPC decided that such a party could file suit again. The issue was finally resolved in the revised Civil Procedure Law.

1-626   Not all 'official replies' are published. It is often issued only to the requesting court. Sometimes, however, 'official replies' are distributed in the court system, or even published in the Gazette of the SPC.

1-627   Notices (circular) and conference summaries: In bureaucratic practice, a 'notice' (*tongzhi*) is a document in which a higher level organ transmits regulations or other measures to its lower level organs requiring them to implement or enforce such measures. A *tonggao* is a notice transmitting regulations or measures, but its distribution is limited. A conference summary is a document that transmits important conference decisions for implementation or enforcement.

1-628   Such notices and summaries are technically speaking not judicial interpretations, but in practice they function as such. Not all of such notices interpret law, many are mere administrative circulars. The SPC has frequently issued notices to amend the Criminal Law. The SPC has, in practice, issued notices with other state organs such as the Supreme People's Procuratorate, Ministry of Public Security and so on. Such notices are called joint notices. Lower courts such as the basic and intermediate level courts have no authority to issue notices. Only the Higher People's Courts, the SPC and specialized courts such as the Military Court have authority to issue notices.

1-629   Conference summaries are issued by the SPC when its leadership feels insufficiently informed about the practice to draft an opinion yet, but the vagueness of the relevant law requires some clarification. Although the authority of a conference summary is lower than an 'official opinion' or 'official reply', the lower courts generally follow its provisions, unless they run contrary to local interests. 'Official opinions' have been issued based on conference summaries augmented by subsequent judicial practice.

Problems with judicial interpretations

1-630   There are four problems arising from the Chinese courts' practice of issuing judicial interpretations:

(a)   What documents constitute judicial interpretations? And which bodies have the authority to issue them?

(b)   Many judicial interpretations exceed the scope of the court's legal authority.

(c)   No fixed rule exists on the distribution or circulation of judicial interpretations within the court system or to the general public.

(d)   The lack of consistency in issuance and authority makes it difficult for the lower courts to know when an interpretation is no longer valid.

1-631   Lastly, the whole problem is compounded by the fact that the NPC's Standing Committee does not monitor the courts' exercise of their authority to interpret the law, even when the interpretations contradict the original legislation.

Adjudication supervision

Theoretical basis

1-632   A unique system of adjudication supervision exists in China that is not found in Western legal systems. Adjudication supervision (*shenpan jiandu*) or supervisory review is a procedure for additional, but discretionary reviews of final judgments. It is available in both civil and criminal cases. In a civil case, a party to the lawsuit may petition the court which originally tried the case, or a higher court for a review of the judgment. In a criminal case, the party to the criminal case, a victim or his family or any citizen may petition to reopen the case. As such, it has been said that there is no finality to a judgment in China.

1-633   There are several theoretical underpinnings to the practice of adjudication supervision. Firstly, the power of adjudication supervision derives from an individual's constitutional right to petition for redress of grievances. This is called *shensu* which may take many forms. In filing a *shensu*, the petitioner may be complaining about an unlawful judgment made by a court, or that the presiding judge had violated trial procedures, or that the general validity of the judgment is challenged. Secondly, the ability of citizens to file for adjudication supervision reinforces Mao's theory of mass line supervision of law and justice. This mass line approach means that the authority of law comes from the masses, and thus the masses, both prior to enacting the law and after the law is enacted, are enlisted in the investigation of cases, or their opinions are considered. The practice of adjudication supervision epitomizes this approach by providing that a People's Court in administering justice is still subject to the supervision of the people. The right of any citizen, whether or not a party to the action, to seek an adjudication supervision in criminal cases is thus symptomatic of this approach.

1-634   Thirdly, adjudication supervision can be traced back to Soviet law in the 1920s where the supreme courts could set aside a decision if there was error or if major policy required a change. In part, this process of reopening judgments also reflects the Communist Party's distrust of its judges in the lower courts, and the desire to preserve a method of reviewing their decisions. In China, adjudication supervision reflects the Chinese preference for the mass line approach to the administration of justice, and specifically, the principle of 'seeking truth from facts and correcting mistakes whenever discovered'. In China, 'correcting errors' is the cornerstone of socialist legal work, and correcting mistakes is perceived to be more important than the finality of judgments.

Ambits of adjudication supervision

1-635　Under the Criminal Procedure Law, there is no restriction on the time or the grounds for the reopening of a legally effective judgment under adjudication supervision. The sole criterion is that the judgment must have contained some error. In civil cases, the 1991 Civil Procedure Law provides that the reopening of cases is limited to circumstances of new evidence, insufficient evidence, erroneous application of law, prejudicial violations of law and judicial misconduct. Although adjudication supervision should not be used to seek a change in the judgment following a change in the law or policy, or for complaints that the punishment was too lenient, in practice adjudication supervision has been used to reverse judgments after a policy change as well as to increase punishment.

1-636　Adjudication supervision is different from an appeal in the sense that in an appeal, only parties to the lawsuit may lodge an appeal, whilst in adjudication supervision, a Court President, a Party or government official may invoke the process. Adjudication supervision involves the legal system's sense of correctness. In the process of adjudication supervision, the court is not obliged to seek the parties' views or representations.

1-637　Adjudication supervision may be initiated by the SPC, the Supreme People's Procuratorate, or petitioned by a party to the lawsuit, a victim and his family, or in criminal cases by any citizen. Oftentimes the SPC or government official may initiate adjudication supervision of a case after the case has gained notoriety in the media, in its efforts to protect the court system's reputation.

Chinese judges

1-638　The first Judges' Law of the PRC was promulgated on 28 February, 1995. It was amended on 30 June 2001 and the amended law took effect on 1 January 2002. The Judges' Law reaffirmed the status of judges as government officials of state administrative organs.

The lack of security of tenure of Chinese judges is shown by article 40 of the Judges' Law, which provides that any judge shall be dismissed or have his post removed in the following circumstances:

(a)   where he is confirmed by annual appraisal to be incompetent for two successive years;

(b)   where he becomes unqualified for the present post and declines to accept other assignments;

(c)   where he refuses to accept a transfer of posts due to the restructuring of the court system;

(d)   where there is no need to maintain his original post after a change of post;

(e)   where he is transferred out of the court;

(f)   where he stayed away from work without leave or exceeded his leave without good reasons for 15 days or more in succession, or for 30 days or more in a year;

(g)   where he fails to perform a judge's duty and makes no rectification after criticism;

(h)   where he is unable to perform a judge's duty for a long period of time due to poor health;

(i)   where he is disqualified from the post because of violation of discipline, law or a commission of a crime.

1-639   In order to raise the professional standing and etiquette of judges, the SPC issued a Notice called the 'Basic Code of Professional Ethics for Judges of the PRC' on 18 October 2001 to instill good work style, probity and a high standard of professional ethics for judges across China.

CONCLUSION

1-701   The foregoing chapter hopes to give the reader a glimpse into the workings of the Chinese legal system so that the reader may understand the ensuing chapters better. In essence, the Chinese legal system is totally different from that of a Western democracy, and has traditionally developed along Marxist legal theory. The procedural laws of the Chinese legal system are clearly developed from Marxist-Leninism and Mao Zedong Thought. However, many of the substantive laws of modern China, particularly in the economic and commercial fields are increasingly adapted from Western democracies. For example, China's Company Law is based on the German civil code whilst its Securities Law is adapted from the American model.

REFERENCES AND FURTHER READING

Books

Perry Keller, *Chinese Law and Legal Theory* (Ashgate Publishing Company, 2001).

Pitman B Potter, *The Chinese Legal System: Globalization and Local Legal Culture* (Routledge, 2001).

Wang Guiguo and John Mo, *Chinese Law* (Kluwer Law International, 1999).

Articles

Cai Dingjian, 'Constitutional Supervision and Interpretation in the People's Republic of China' (1995) 9 *Journal of Chinese Law* 217.

Donald C Clarke, 'Power and Politics in the Chinese Court System: The Enforcement of Civil Judgments' (1996) 10 *Columbia Journal of Asian Law* 1.

Susan Finder, 'The Supreme People's Court of the People's Republic of China' (1993) 7 *Journal of Chinese Law* 145.

William C Jones, 'The Constitution of the People's Republic of China' (1985) 63 *Washington University Law Quarterly* 707.

Perry Keller, 'Sources of Order in Chinese Law' (1994) 42 *The American Journal of Comparative Law* 711.

Carlos Wing-Hung Lo, 'Socialist Legal Theory in Deng XiaoPing's China' (1997) 11 *Columbia Journal of Asian Law* 469.

Minxin Pei, 'Citizens v Mandarins: Administrative Litigation in China' 152 *The China Quarterly* 832–862.

Margaret Y K Woo, 'Adjudication Supervision and Judicial Independence in the PRC' (1991) 39 *The American Journal of Comparative Law* 95.

Yu Xingzhong, 'Legal Pragmatism in the People's Republic of China' (1989) 3 *Journal of Chinese Law* 29.

CHAPTER 2

Law on Foreign Investment in China
Tan Lay Hong

INTRODUCTION

Background to Deng's 'open door' policy

2-101 Deng's 'open door' policy undoubtedly heralded an era of momentous political and economic change in China. One of the prominent features of the 'open door' policy was the aim to attract inward foreign direct investment (FDI) to China to achieve Deng's four modernizations. In 1975, when Deng re-emerged from political obscurity, he identified three areas where China was sorely lagging behind. They are: (a) the need for China to adopt advanced technology from foreign countries and expand international trade; (b) the need to introduce and improve modern industrial management methods; and (c) that China should import technology and equipment for natural resource exploitation by paying with coal and petroleum.

2-102 The major economic movements of the 1950s and 1960s such as the 'Great Leap Forward' together with the 'Cultural Revolution' bankrupted the entire nation. But with two decades of the 'open door' policy, China today boasts a Gross Domestic Product (GDP) of Rmb 7,168.2 billion (2002), total imports and exports of US$590.8 billion (2002) and foreign exchange reserves of US$286.4 billion (2002).

Breakdown of FDI between 1980-2001

2-103 Table 1 shows the flow of inward FDI into China from 1980 to 2002. The total FDI stock in China stands roughly at US$826.137 billion (2002).

Table 1: Foreign Direct Investment from 1980 to 2002

Year	No of Projects	(US$ billion)	
		Amount by Contract Value	Amount Actually Invested
1980–82	921	6.010	1.166
1983	471	1.732	0.636
1984	1,851	2.649	1.258
1985	3,073	5.932	1.658
1986	1,662	2.834	1.875
1987	2,233	3.709	2.314
1988	5,786	5.297	3.190
1989	5,784	5.595	3.392
1990	7,237	6.596	3.487
1991	12,978	11.977	4.366
1992	48,764	58.123	11.007
1993	83,473	110.852	25.759
1994	47,490	81.406	33.800
1995	37,126	90.300	37.700
1996	24,529	73.210	42.350
1997	–	51.780	45.300
1998	23,022	51.945	45.421
1999	21,406	41.540	40.390
2000	22,532	62.660	40.770
2001	26,139	69.190	46.840
2002	34,171	82.800	52.700
Total	410,648	826.137	445.377

REGIONAL OPEN POLICIES FOR FDI

The Special Economic Zones (SEZs)

2-201   Following the promulgation of the Sino-Foreign Equity Joint Venture Law (EJV Law) in July 1979, China established the four special economic zones (SEZs). They are Shenzhen, Zhuhai, Xiamen and Shantou, located in Guangdong and Fujian provinces. These SEZs were considered crucial to China's policy of attracting inward FDI.

2-202   Firstly, the SEZs were chosen because of their geographical proximity to the homes of the overseas Chinese. It was hoped that the overseas Chinese network could be tapped to accumulate capital, technology and management knowhow and to gain access to international markets. This strategy has largely paid off as, in the early years of China's 'open door' policy, the great majority of inward FDI came from Hong Kong and Taiwan.

2-203 Secondly, the SEZs served as 'laboratory' experiments for China's 'open door' policy to gauge whether the preferential policies and incentives given to foreign investors in the SEZs would attract more inward FDI. The result was an astounding success for the SEZs which could not be contained within their boundaries for long. Soon other provinces were clamouring for the same special treatment that was given to the SEZs. In 1984 the Chinese authorities extended the concept of SEZs to 14 coastal cities and Hainan Island.

Preferential policies in the SEZs and ETDZs

2-204 Among the preferential policies for FDI firms operating in the SEZs were a 15% reduction in income tax, a tax exemption in the first two profit-making years and a 50% reduction in the third profit-making year (*mianer jiansan*). The FDI firms were also granted an exemption from income tax on their remitted share of profits, exemption from import duties for equipment and machinery imported for use in the production activities of the firm, and the easing of entry and exit formalities. The coastal open cities were permitted to offer tax incentives to FDI firms that were similar to, but less generous than those offered in the SEZs. In particular, they were encouraged to establish 'economic and technological development zones' (ETDZ) that could offer terms as generous as those offered in the SEZs. Again, the 14 coastal cities proved to be a great draw for foreign investors due to their proximity to the ports and other infrastructure. The 14 coastal open cities together with the SEZs virtually formed a coastal belt which, from a geographical viewpoint, is important not only for linkage with foreign markets but also for its wide connection with the massive domestic inland areas.

The 'three development triangles'

2-205 In order to attract more FDI to speed up China's ambitious plans for modernization, in May 1985, three 'development triangles', namely, the Yangtze River Delta Region (around Shanghai), the Pearl River Delta Region (around Guangzhou) and the Minnan Delta Region (around Xiamen), were designated as coastal open economic areas. These 'development triangles' were granted most of the FDI preferential policies implemented in the 14 open coastal cities. Again ethnic ties played an important role in the development of these areas as seen in the gravitation of Taiwanese investors to the Minnan Delta region and Hong Kong and Macao investors to the Pearl Delta Region. In 1988, the 'coastal development strategy' was implemented to extend the 'open door' policy to the entire coastal area. It was felt that despite the risks of the growing gap between the coastal and inland areas, the coastal areas should be allowed to move ahead and develop faster by using its better labour, communications and infrastructure. It was stressed that labour-intensive industries should be encouraged to locate in the coastal areas and to export so that they can help China develop its international trade links.

Uneven regional open policy

2-206   The implementation of the uneven regional open strategy enabled the coastal region to gain more benefits than the other regions. This resulted in a growing gap in economic development and income level between the coastal regions and the inland areas. As a result, in the 1990s the Chinese government moved to close the gap by extending the preferential policies to other parts of China. In 1990, the concepts of SEZs and ETDZs were extended to Shanghai when the Shanghau Pudong New Area development project was announced.

Areas for growth in the new millennium: High-tech industries and Western region development

2-207   In the mid to late 1990s, two prominent areas were earmarked for growth by the Chinese government. They were the promotion and development of high-technology industries and the Western region development plans. The former involves the push for the establishment of high-tech industrial zones in the sectors of information and communication technology, new materials, bio-engineering, bio-technology, photo-electromechanical integration and others. There are currently 53 high-tech zones in China reaping a revenue of Rmb 656 billion. These zones earned US$10.6 billion in exports in 1999. Recently, it was reported that US electronics giants such as Microsoft Corp, IBM Corp, Lucent Technologies and Intel Corp have also located their research and development facilities in China.[1]

2-208   The Western region development plans were implemented, in part, to close the economic development and income gap between the coastal areas and inland provinces. The plans called for the accelerated development of infrastructure in the area of utilities, communication, transportation, telecommunications, TV and radio facilities in the central and western provinces. In addition, it also hopes to tap into China's vast natural resources in those regions. Beginning in September 1996, local authorities in the central and western regions are empowered to approve FDI with total investments up to US$30 million.[2] Several documents and regulations have been actively promulgated to grant tax and other preferential incentives to foreign investors who invest in these regions. A separate catalogue

---

1   Catherine Gelb, 'Software Research In-and For-China' *The China Business Review* July–August 2000 pp 40–44.
2   Previously, the approval limit of local authorities in these regions was US$10 million.

called The Guiding Foreign Investment in the Dominant Industries of the Central and Western Regions Catalogue (the Investment Catalogue) was issued by the State Council on 16 June 2000 to guide FDI in these regions.

EVOLUTION OF CHINA'S FDI LAWS

First phase 1979–86

The Sino-foreign Equity Joint Venture Law 1979

2-301 At the Second Session of the 5th NPC Plenary Meeting on 1 July 1979, China's first FDI law, the Equity Joint Venture Law (EJV Law) was promulgated. It was a short piece of legislation with only 15 articles. The EJV Law was amended in 1990 and 2002. Its Implementing Regulations were promulgated by the State Council in 1983 and contained 118 articles. The first phase of FDI laws from 1979 to 1986 comprised these two pieces of legislation and the Regulations of the People's Republic of China on Special Economic Zones in Guangdong Province.

2-302 The EJV Law was China's first law permitting the establishment and operation of foreign economic entities in its territory since 1949. It resembles more a series of political declarations allowing the legal entry of FDI into China than a set of statutory rules for governing joint ventures. The EJV Law explicitly states that the establishment of a joint venture in China must be 'on the principle of equality and mutual benefit'. This reflected the fear and distrust of the Chinese people of foreigners mercilessly exploiting them as happened in the ending years of the Qing dynasty as well as during the turbulent period of the warlords between 1911 and 1949.

2-303 To rectify the shortcomings of the EJV Law and accommodate the needs of foreign investors, the State Council issued a set of Implementing Regulations in 1983 which provided greater details on all aspects of equity joint venture operations in China.

Regulations on SEZs: SEZ and WFOE

2-304 The issue of the regulations relating to SEZ not only created the SEZs but also permitted the establishment of wholly foreign-owned enterprises (WFOE) within them. Unlike joint ventures, which the Chinese government seemed to have greater confidence in dealing with and was willing to launch on a national scale, the WFOE was a lot more problematic ideologically and politically. Thus, WFOEs were initially permitted only in SEZs, and they had to use advanced technology and equipment or export more than 50% of their output. To allow WFOEs to go beyond the SEZs required an ideological and policy shift which was finally attained in 1984 when the Chinese government formally announced that the private sector was a supplementary part of the socialist economy, and granted the private economy legal status. The first WFOE that was established outside the SEZs was the 3M Company of the US (1984).

Second phase 1986–90

The WFOE Law 1986

2-305   Two important pieces of legislation marked the second phase of FDI laws in China. The first was the Law of the People's Republic of China on Enterprises Operated Exclusively with Foreign Capital (WFOE Law) and the second was the Provisions of the State Council of the People's Republic of China for the Encouragement of Foreign Investment, popularly known as the '22 articles'.

2-306   The WFOE Law formally recognised WFOEs and protects their lawful rights and interests. The WFOE Law was needed when foreign investors increasingly preferred to operate alone rather than with Chinese partners. Two reasons exist as to why foreign investors preferred WFOEs: (a) to maintain maximum operating independence from Chinese participation and to have a high degree of control over financing, marketing, pricing and even external relations of its various subsidiaries; and (b) the need to protect its technology.

The '22 articles' 1986

2-307   The '22 articles' were promulgated to meet the challenge from China's South-East Asian neighbours for FDI. The provisions offered a slew of incentives to FDI such as: (a) granting special preferences to 'export-oriented' and 'technologically-advanced' foreign-funded enterprises through a reduction in land use fees, preferential tax treatment, and priority in obtaining utilities and other infrastructure services; (b) establishing a limited foreign exchange market for foreign-funded enterprises; and (c) guaranteeing the autonomy of foreign-funded enterprises in management and production decision-making.

The Co-operative Joint Venture Law 1988

2-308   In order to implement the '22 articles' more effectively, both the central and local governments issued various implementing regulations. In 1988, the Co-operative Joint Venture Law (CJV Law) was promulgated. The second phase witnessed both a rapidly growing body of FDI laws and regulations and a great improvement of the FDI regulatory framework. Basically, the FDI legal regime became more liberalized, systematic and consistent.

Third phase 1990–present

Major amendments to JV Laws

2-309   In the 1990s, the Chinese government further liberalized its FDI policies to attract a more rapid and healthy development of FDI inflows into China. In 1990, the EJV Law underwent two major amendments. The first was to allay the fears of foreign investors against expropriation, and the second was to provide for equal opportunities for foreign investors to appoint the Chairman to the joint venture. Previously, only the Chinese side could appoint the Chairman.

2-310   In line with its WTO commitments, China amended its JV laws to remove the following restrictions and requirements:

(a)   Foreign exchange balancing requirement.

(b)   Local content requirement.

(c)   Domestic sales ratio restrictions.

(d)   Requirement to be 'export-oriented' and 'technologically-advanced'.

(e)   Mandatory filing of production and operation plans.

Strengthening the legal regime to protect foreign investors

2-311   In 1990, the Implementing Regulations for WFOEs were also promulgated. The legal and regulatory framework for FDI continued to be fleshed out by the Chinese government, and in the 1990s a series of laws relating to FDI were adopted. They include the Foreign Investment Enterprise and Foreign Enterprise Income Tax Law, the Copyright Law, the Software Protection Regulations, the Patent Law Amendments, the Trademark Law, the Company Law, the Securities Law, the Banking Law and Foreign Exchange Regulations, and the long-awaited Co-operative Joint Venture Law (CJV Law), Implementing Regulations. In this phase, the Chinese government also introduced measures to address the problem of over-valuation of equipment and technology contributed as capital to the joint ventures, and round-tripping.[3]

Investment Catalogue to guide FDI, 1995 (amended in 2002)

2-312   In June 1995, the Chinese government introduced even more transparency into its FDI legal framework. It enacted the Provisional Regulations on Guiding Foreign Investment (Guiding Provisions) and a Catalogue (Investment Catalogue) to guide the absorption of FDI

---

3   Round-tripping refers to FDI that actually came from domestic Chinese capital but re-entered China solely for the purpose of taking advantage of the special preferential and fiscal incentives.

towards sectors which suit China's national economic and social development plans, and state industrial policy. The Guiding Provisions and Catalogue were amended in 1998 and 2002.

'Encouraged', 'Permitted', 'Restricted' and 'Prohibited'

2-313 The Guiding Provisions classified FDI into four categories, namely 'encouraged', 'permitted', 'restricted' and 'prohibited' (see Box below for details). Originally, the 'restricted' category was further sub-divided into 'A' and 'B' groups. Under the former group, the joint venture had to export at least 70% of their output unless they were located in the central and western regions of China. The 'B' group initially comprised the sensitive sectors such as the services sector as well as pillar industries like automobiles, electronics, telecommunications and transportation. In the 2002 amendment, the telecommunications and automobiles sectors were shifted from the 'restricted' category to the 'encouraged' category. The 2002 amendments also eliminated the distinction between group 'A' and 'B' industries.[4]

Sectoral Restrictions in China's FDI Policy

Encouraged

(1) Agricultural projects using new technology or integrated development agricultural projects and energy industry projects, transport industry projects and major raw material industry projects;

(2) high-tech projects or advanced-application technology projects that can improve product performance, improve the technological and economic results of enterprises or produce new equipment and new materials for which domestic production capability is inadequate;

(3) projects that can meet market demand and that can improve product grades, open new markets or improve the international competitiveness of products;

(4) projects using new technology or new equipment that can conserve energy, that involve raw materials, integrated utilization of resources or recycling of resources, or that can prevent and treat environmental pollution;

---

4   For details of the revised 2002 amendments to the Catalogue, please see 'The New Foreign Investment Guidelines and Market Reform in China' *China Law & Practice* April 2002, pp 19–22 and 'The Revised Foreign Investment Catalogue: Grounds for Optimism?' *China Law & Practice* April 2002, pp 23–25.

(5)   projects that can make use of the special manpower and resource advantages of the central and western regions and that comply with state industrial policies; and

(6)   other kinds of projects stipulated by laws and administrative regulations.

Permitted

Any FDI that does not come under any of the other categories, including projects that export at least 70% of its total sales which were previously in the 'restricted' category.

Restricted

(1)   Projects where the level of technology is outdated;

(2)   projects that are detrimental to energy conservation and environmental improvement;

(3)   projects for the exploration and mining of specially designated minerals for which protective mining is required by the state;

(4)   projects in industries to be liberalized gradually by the state; and

(5)   other kinds of projects stipulated as restricted by laws and administrative regulations.

Prohibited

(1)   Projects that endanger national security or harm the public interests;

(2)   investments that cause pollution and damage to the environment as well as destroy natural resources or damage people's health;

(3)   projects that occupy large tracts of agricultural land and jeopardize the development of land resources or the use of military facilities;

(4)   projects that apply production techniques that are unique to China; and

(5)   other projects that are prohibited by state laws and administrative regulations.

The 'encouraged' category

2-314 The number of sectors in the 'encouraged' category has increased from 186 to 263, the number of sectors in the 'restricted' category has been reduced from 112 to 75 and there are 33 sectors in the 'prohibited' category. The 'encouraged' category covers agricultural and mining activities, manufacturing activities ranging from simple food processing, textile and other raw materials processing, petroleum and coking industries, to high tech industries like bio-engineering, chemical fibre and plastic engineering, equipment and transport equipment manufacturing as well as electronic and communications equipment manufacturing.

2-315 In the 2002 amendments, previously 'restricted' sectors such as telecommunications, automobile, coal, water and nuclear power equipment and power transmission equipment, railway network construction and operation, planting and nurturing of Chinese medicinal plants, paper, natural incense, higher education, accounting and auditing have all been moved to the 'encouraged' category.

The 'permitted' category

2-316 This category comprises any investments that do not come within any of the other categories. In the 2002 amendments, 'restricted' sectors such as taxis, financial, insurance and foreign exchange consultancies, and the production, processing and trading of gold and silver and jewellery ornaments are now in the 'permitted' category. The production of consumer products such as washing machines, refrigerators, televisions and video cassette recorders for which there is now an overcapacity have also been moved to the 'permitted' category.

The 'restricted' category

2-317 Sectors previously in the 'prohibited' category such as the construction and management of large municipal gas, heat, water supply and drainage networks and cinemas have now been moved into the 'restricted' category.

The 'prohibited' category

2-318 Sectors of industries that are closed to foreign investors, ie the 'prohibited' category, include broadcasting and television, construction and operation of power grids and aviation transport control companies. New sectors added to this category include the production of genetically modified seeds and aquatic fishing in offshore territory.

CHINA'S ACCESSION TO WTO

Opening up and liberalization

Slashing tariffs

2-401 On 11 November 2002, China formally acceded to the World Trade Organization (WTO). Generally, WTO membership will open the door even wider for foreign investors to the Chinese economy. Firstly, tariffs will be slashed significantly. Table 2 below sets out the tariff barriers on imports and the impact of WTO membership on imports.

Table 2: Tariff Barriers and WTO Commitments

Existing Tariff Barriers	WTO Commitments
(1) Average import tariffs for industrial goods at 14.8%.	(1) Average tariffs for industrial goods will be slashed to 8.9%. The tariff rate ranges from 0 to 47% of which the highest rates will be applied to photographic films and automobiles.
(2) Average import tariffs for agricultural goods at 18.9%.	
(3) Average import tariffs for all other goods at 15.3%.	(2) Average tariffs for agricultural goods will be slashed to 15%.
(4) Import Tariff Rate Quota applicable to 16 products.	(3) A new Tariff Rate Quota will be introduced for some sensitive agricultural products such as sugar and cotton. Quotas will be eliminated for barley, soybeans, rape seed, peanut oil, sunflower seed oil, corn oil and cottonseed oil.
	(4) Tariffs on information technology products will be eliminated by 2005.

Opening up of key industries[5]

2-402 Under the WTO commitments, China has promised to open up various key sectors to foreign participation, notably the services sector. The following discusses the impact of WTO membership on several of China's key industries.

Wholesale and retail sector

2-403 The sector that will be greatly impacted by WTO membership is services. One prominent sector is the wholesale and retail trading sector. Upon accession to the WTO, China undertook to eliminate the state-trading enterprises so that parties may import and export on their own without these middlemen.

---

5 Detailed reports on the impact of WTO membership on China trade and investment can be found at http://www.info.gov.hk/tid/wto_accession/content.htm and http://www.tdctrade.com/main/china.htm.

Trading rights of FIEs expanded

2-404   Previously, manufacturing foreign-invested enterprises[6] (FIEs) were only allowed to export the products they made in China with a restricted ratio on domestic sales. Upon accession to the WTO, the trading and distribution rights of manufacturing FIEs have been expanded. They are immediately allowed to distribute domestically and internationally all the products that they make in China, purchase goods (non-quota goods) from third parties for export, and bid for export quotas for their own products.[7] All foreign service providers in the wholesale and retail trade can establish joint ventures in China. Within one year of WTO membership, all manufacturing FIEs can distribute imported products domestically and internationally. Foreign service providers may have a majority share in joint ventures with local partners. Within three years, all restrictions on foreign ownership in services joint ventures will be abolished.

Foreign participation in wholesale sector

2-405   In terms of wholesale trade, up to 50% foreign ownership in joint ventures will be allowed within the first year of WTO accession. These wholesale joint ventures are allowed to trade in *all* products excluding salt and tobacco. Within the second year, these wholesale joint ventures will be allowed majority foreign ownership with no geographical restrictions or quantitative restrictions. In the third year, WFOEs will be allowed in the wholesale sector. In the fourth year, all market restrictions will be removed, and in the fifth year, wholesale traders will be permitted to engage in the distribution of chemical fertilizers, processed oil and crude oil.

Foreign participation in retail sector

2-406   In the retail sector, foreign investors are allowed to establish retail businesses in the five SEZs and in Beijing, Shanghai, Tianjin, Guangzhou, Dalian, Qingdao, Zhengzhou and Wuhan. They must, however, operate as joint ventures with local partners. In the second year following accession, foreign majority ownership of retail joint ventures will be allowed. WFOEs will be allowed from the fifth year onwards. These retail businesses will be permitted to retail in all products except tobacco, books, newspapers, magazines, pharmaceutical products, pesticide, mulching films and processed oil and chemical fertilizers. The categories of products prohibited will be

---

6   In this book, the term FIEs refer to equity joint ventures, co-operative joint ventures and wholly foreign-owned enterprises.

7   Previously, manufacturing FIEs were often subjected to domestic sales ratio which stipulates that only one-third of their output can be distributed domestically.

gradually lifted from the third to fifth year, so that by the fifth year only tobacco and those products subjected to state trading will be prohibited from being retailed by joint ventures.

Telecommunications sector

Opening up to foreign participation

2-407   Immediately upon accession to the WTO, China promised to allow foreign ownership in value-added services and paging services of up to 30%. These joint ventures are, however, restricted to Beijing, Guangzhou, Guangdong province and Shanghai. Within two years, the proportion of foreign ownership in value-added services will be increased to 50%. All geographical restrictions will be removed. From the fifth year onwards, 49% foreign ownership will be allowed in mobile voice and data services. In the sixth year, foreign majority ownership and WFOEs will be permitted in all domestic and international services, with all geographical restrictions removed.

Legal framework

2-408   On 11 December 2001, the State Council promulgated the Administration of Foreign-funded Telecommunications Enterprises Provisions[8] (Telecom Regulations) effective 1 January 2002, to set out the minimum requirements for opening the sector to foreign investors. Presently, all telecommunications FIEs must be joint ventures of which the maximum capital contribution ratio of the foreign investor in basic telecommunications services shall not exceed 49%, while that of value-added services shall not exceed 50%. The minimum registered capital of such FIEs that provide basic services nationwide shall not be less than Rmb 2 billion, whereas those providing value-added services shall not have registered capital of less than Rmb 10 million. FIEs that operate in the provinces and municipalities in basic services shall have registered capital of not less than Rmb 200 million, whereas those providing value-added services shall not have registered capital of less than Rmb 1 million. The Telecom Regulations spell out the detailed procedures on how to establish a telecommunication FIE. It is expected that the Provisions will be further amended to bring China in line with its subsequent WTO commitments.

2-409   The 81-article Telecommunications Regulations were issued by the State Council on 20 September 2000 to govern the telecommunications industry in China. The Regulations basically contain China's agreement to abide by the WTO's Basic Tele-

---

8   An English translation of the Telecom Regulations can be found in *China Law & Practice* February 2002, pp 48–55. A commentary on the Provisions can be found in *China Law & Practice* February 2002, pp 30–34.

communications Agreement. Pursuant to these commitments, China will have to implement pro-competitive measures in the area of regulatory independence, competitive safeguards, transparent licensing procedures, interconnection rights, universal service and allocation of scarce telecom resources.[9]

2-410   Vendors of telecommunications equipment (including foreign manufacturers) are required to obtain a licence from the Ministry of Information Industry before they can commence selling their products and services in China. The relevant law is the Measures for the Administration of the Network Connection of Telecommunications Equipment, effective on 10 May 2001. The licence, called a network connection permit, is valid for three years. Annual inspections are carried out on these vendors to ensure that their equipment satisfies the technical standards set out by the Ministry.

Banking and securities sector

Post-WTO liberalization

2-411   Presently, there are 170 foreign bank branches operating in China. Most can only conduct businesses in foreign currencies with foreign firms and individuals. Only 32 foreign branches have obtained licences to operate Rmb business with foreign firms and individuals. And these are in restricted geographical areas such as Beijing, Shanghai and the open coastal cities. Within two years after accession to the WTO, foreign banks will be permitted to conduct Rmb business with corporate clients, and within five years, foreign banks will be allowed to conduct Rmb business in retail banking with Chinese individuals.[10]

2-412   In the securities sector, WTO membership commits China to permit foreign securities companies to establish joint ventures to underwrite and trade in 'A', 'B' and 'H' shares[11] within three years of accession. Next, China committed to allow 33% foreign ownership in fund management companies immediately upon accession, which can be increased to 49% after three years.

---

9   An excellent article commenting on the Telecommunications Regulations can be found in 'China's New Telecommunications Regulations and the WTO' *The China Business Review* July–August 2001, pp 34–37, 41.

10   A comprehensive discussion on post-WTO banking in China can be found at http://www.aial.com/prcccMay02.html#4.

11   'A' shares are shares that are issued domestically in China and can only be traded by Chinese nationals. 'B' shares are shares issued domestically in China but may only be traded by foreigners whilst 'H' shares are shares issued by Chinese companies and listed/traded on the Hong Kong stock exchange.

Legal framework for banks and finance companies

2-413   The relevant laws governing the banking sector in China are:

(a)   The Law of the PRC on Commercial Banks, effective 1 July 1995.

(b)   The Law of the PRC on the People's Bank of China, effective 1995.

(c)   PRC Administration of Foreign-funded Financial Institutions, and its detailed Implementing Regulations, both effective 1 February 2002 (the FFI Regulations).

(d)   Administration of Representative Offices in China of Foreign-funded Financial Institutions Procedures, effective 18 July 2002.[12]

2-414   The most important law affecting foreign investors wishing to set up a banking business in China is the FFI Regulations.[13] The FFI Regulations seek to shift the basis of market-access and general banking supervision of foreign-funded financial institutions to more weighted and prudential-based standards that are in line with the Basle Accord. The FFI Regulations govern both banks and finance companies. Under the FFI Regulations, banks are allowed to offer a range of comprehensive banking services except the selling of mutual funds or unit trusts. Finance companies are also permitted to offer a wide range of services except that deposits accepted shall not be less than Rmb 1 million and the tenure shall not be less than three months. A noteworthy point is that the interest rates for lending and deposits are strictly determined by the People's Bank of China with the exception of foreign exchange loans and deposits that are above US$3 million. The interest rates for such foreign exchange loans and deposits may be independently set by the banks themselves.

Legal framework for securities companies

2-415   The relevant law on setting up joint venture securities companies is the Establishment of Securities Companies with Foreign Equity Participation (the Securities JV Rules) issued by the China Securities Regulatory Commission (CSRC) on 1 June 2002, effective on 1 July 2002. The salient features of the Securities JV Rules are as follows:

(a)   the foreign shareholder must have been operating a securities business in its country of incorporation for at least ten years;

(b)   the foreign shareholder must not have been sanctioned by any securities regulatory body or judicial department for the last three years;

---

12   This Regulation repealed the 1996 Administration of Representative Offices in China of Foreign Financial Institutions.

13   An excellent commentary on the FFI Regulations can be found in *China Law & Practice* April 2002, pp 26–30.

(c)   the securities regulatory body overseeing the foreign shareholder has signed a memorandum of understanding with the CSRC with respect to co-operation in securities regulation;[14]

(d)   the foreign shareholder has implemented risk control targets, a sound internal control system and enjoys a good reputation and achievement in the international securities market, and other prudential requirements;

(e)   the Chinese shareholder must be a domestically funded securities company that meets the requirements set out by the CSRC;[15]

(f)   the minimum registered capital of a joint venture securities company shall be Rmb 500 million;

(g)   the foreign shareholder may not hold more than one-third of the total equity of the joint venture;

(h)   if there is only one Chinese shareholder, he must be a domestically funded securities company, and shall hold at least one-third of the total equity of the joint venture; and

(i)   the permitted scope of securities businesses that a joint venture securities company may conduct is much smaller than that of the comprehensive-type domestic securities company. They are basically allowed to engage in underwriting 'A' and 'B' shares and bonds, dealing in 'B' shares as a broker and dealing in bonds as a broker and on its own account only.

Legal framework for fund-management companies

2-416   On 1 June 2002, the CSRC promulgated the Establishment of Fund Management Companies with Foreign Equity Participation Rules (Fund Management JV Rules) which became effective on 1 July 2002.[16] The Fund Management JV Rules constitute a limited invitation for foreign participation in the Chinese fund industry. They are, however, more generous than the Securities JV Rules in allowing foreign shareholders to be controlling shareholders although they hold less than 50% of the total equity and place no restrictions on business scope. The salient features of the Fund Management JV Rules are as follows:

(a)   a joint venture fund management company may be created by joint promotion by the Chinese and foreign shareholder, or by the acquisition of shares in an existing fund management company;

---

14   As of August 2000, the CSRC has signed such a memorandum of understanding with Hong Kong, USA, Singapore, Australia, the UK, Japan, Malaysia, Brazil, Ukraine, France, Luxembourg, Germany, Italy and Egypt.

15   This effectively means that foreign investors may not establish a joint venture securities company with another joint venture securities company.

16   An Official Explanation of the Rules can be found in *China Law & Practice* October 2002, pp 119–131 and a commentary on the Rules can be found in *China Law & Practice* July/August 2002, pp 35–40.

(b)   the foreign shareholder must be a financial institution in its country of location, have not received any 'serious punishment' from the securities regulatory authorities or judicial organs in the past three years;[17]

(c)   the foreign shareholder's country of location must have a 'perfected' securities law and whose securities regulatory authorities must have signed a memorandum of understanding with CSRC;[18]

(d)   the foreign shareholder must have a paid-up capital of not less than Rmb 300 million, the joint venture fund management company must itself have a registered capital of not less than Rmb 10 million, and each fund must raise no less than Rmb 200 million; and

(e)   the foreign shareholder is not allowed to hold shares in more than two fund management companies and can be the controlling shareholder in only one.

New Rules Open up 'A' share market to foreign institutional investors

2-417   The singular problem facing fund management companies is of course the dearth of securities and bonds that are available for investment to fund managers in China. This problem has been partially resolved with the promulgation of the Administration of Securities Investments in China by Qualified Foreign Institutional Investors Tentative Procedures (QFII Procedures) by the CSRC and the People's Bank of China, effective from 1 December 2002.[19] The QFII Procedures allow certain types of institutional investors outside China that meet the relevant requirement to invest in the 'A' share and bond market and other financial instruments in China. Obviously, these institutional investors include fund managers, insurance companies, securities companies and commercial banks.

2-418   Only approved institutional investors and not foreign individuals are able to directly access the financial instruments market in China. Foreign individuals may, however, participate indirectly through products designed by the institutional investors. There are restrictions on the size of investments made by the institutional investors. The minimum investment limit is US$50 million while the maximum is US$800 million. Because of the

---

17   The term 'serious punishment' is unclear. Recently, Merrill Lynch agreed to pay US$100 million to settle claims by the New York State Attorney General on charges that its analysts acted improperly. Would Merrill Lynch be disqualified from entering the Chinese fund industry?

18   Terms like 'perfected laws' and 'the place where the foreign shareholder is located' are unclear from the Fund Management JV Rules.

19   An excellent commentary on the QFII Procedures can be found in *China Law and Practice* December 2002/January 2003, pp 14–20.

high entry level, smaller institutional investors are effectively kept out of the market. In addition, the percentage of shares held by a *single* institutional investor in a single listed company cannot exceed 10% of the total 'A' shares in that company and similarly the aggregate percentage of shares held by *all* the institutional investors in a listed company shall not exceed 20% of the total 'A' shares in that company. With such restrictions, it is unclear how the Chinese authorities can improve the corporate governance mechanism of its domestically listed companies through these institutional investors (as they had hoped) because such investors would be minority shareholders without much clout against the majority shareholder, which is usually the state.

2-419   According to the QFII Procedures, the institutional investors must fulfil the following requirements before they are qualified to participate in the financial market:

(a) **Fund managers**: a track record of five years or more, and managing assets of not less than US$10 billion in assets in the last accounting year;

(b) **Insurance companies**: a track record of 30 years or more, managing assets of not less than US$10 billion in securities assets in the last accounting year, and a paid-up capital of US$1 billion;

(c) **Securities companies**: a track record of 30 years or more, managing assets of not less than US$10 billion in the last accounting year, and a paid-up capital of US$1 billion; and

(d) **Commercial banks**: no track record required but must be managing assets of not less than US$1 billion, and its total assets must rank within the top 100 banks in the world.

In addition to the above, the institutional investor must have a stable, healthy financial position and good credit rating, risk monitoring indicators that conform to the requirements set out by the securities regulator in the country where it is located, appropriately qualified professional employees, a sound corporate governance structure and internal control mechanism, and located in a country or region that has a sound legal and regulatory system and whose securities regulator has entered into a memorandum of understanding with the CSRC. The institutional investor must also not have been punished or penalized by the securities regulator of the country or region in which they are located in the preceding three years.

2-420   Most importantly, the institutional investor must entrust an commercial bank in China, called a custodian, to hold its assets and conduct securities trade through a securities company in China. It is unclear if foreign-invested joint venture securities companies may qualify as custodians, although the QFII Procedures permit branches of foreign commercial banks with more than three years of operating experience in China and who meet the various qualifying criteria to act as custodians. The QFII Procedures lay down detailed rules on the appointment, qualifications and approvals of custodians. Separate rules are issued by the China Securities Depository and Clearing Corporation Limited to govern the registration and settlement of securities trading by the custodians.

2-421 The procedure to seek qualification as an approved institutional investor is simple. The applicant submits a standard application form[20] and a set of documents to the CSRC through the custodian. The documents to be submitted include the qualification criteria, the draft custodian agreement between the institutional investor and the custodian, audited accounts for the last three years, and a letter of undertaking not to withdraw the funds within a restricted period. The CSRC then has 15 working days to reject or approve an application. If approved, the CSRC issues a securities business investment permit to the institutional investor. Armed with the permit, the institutional investor then applies to the State Administration of Foreign Exchange through the PRC custodian to have its investment limit approved. The State Administration of Foreign Exchange has 15 working days to approve or reject the application. If approved, the State Administration will issue a Notification of the Investment Limit and a Foreign Exchange Registration Certificate to the institutional investor.

2-422 The range of securities available for investment by the institutional investor are as follows:

(a) shares listed in the domestic stock exchanges except for foreign investment, or 'B' shares listed on the stock exchange;

(b) treasury bonds listed on the domestic stock exchange;

(c) convertible bonds and corporate bonds listed on the domestic stock exchange; and

(d) any other financial instruments approved by CSRC.

2-423 There are lock-in periods to prevent the remittance of the profits and principal to the offshore institutional investor. Even after the lock-in periods expire, each outward remittance cannot exceed 20% of the total principal and each must be made at one-month or three-month intervals. In summary, the QFII Procedures thus represent a limited liberalization of China's securities and bond markets.

---

20 The CSRC published a standard application form on its website http://www.csre.gov.cn on 30 November 2002.

Insurance sector

Legal framework for PRC insurance sector

2-424 By April 1998, Shanghai and Guangzhou had approved 11 foreign-funded insurance businesses, including ten branches of foreign insurance companies and one sino-foreign jointly funded insurance company. In addition, scores of insurance and reinsurance companies from all over the world have opened more than 180 representative offices and liaison offices in China.

2-425 The legal framework governing the PRC insurance sector is as follows:

(a) The PRC Insurance Law, effective 30 June 1995.

(b) The PRC, Administration of Foreign-funded Insurance Companies Regulations (Insurance Regulations), effective 1 February 2002.[21]

(c) Administration of Insurance Brokerages Provisions, effective 1 February 2002.[22]

(d) Administration of Insurance Agencies Provisions, effective 1 February 2002.

(e) Administration of Insurance Assessors Provisions, effective 1 February 2002.

(f) The Establishment of Reinsurance Companies (Reinsurance Companies Rules), effective 17 September 2002.

2-426 The salient features of the aforementioned regulations are as follows:

(a) the Insurance Regulations provide that a foreign-funded insurance company may be an equity joint venture insurance company, a wholly foreign-owned insurance company and a foreign insurance company branch in China (foreign-funded insurance companies);

(b) the foreign shareholder must have more than 30 years' experience in the insurance business, have established a representative office in China for over two years, and have a total year-end net asset value of not less than US$5 billion in the year preceding the application;

---

21 An English translation can be found in *China Law & Practice* February 2002, pp 39–47.

22 The new Brokerages Provisions supplement the 1999 People's Bank of China, Administration of Insurance Brokerages Provisions (Trial Implementation).

(c)   foreign-funded insurance companies, brokerages and agencies may only establish limited liability companies. They cannot establish joint stock insurance companies unlike domestic insurance brokerage houses and insurance agencies. The significance is that foreign-funded insurance companies, brokerages and agencies may not tap into the equity markets of China;

(d)   the minimum registered capital of foreign-funded insurance companies is Rmb 200 million;

(e)   the minimum registered capital for foreign-funded insurance brokerages is Rmb 10 million, whereas that of insurance agencies is Rmb 500,000;

(f)   foreign-funded insurance companies may conduct open or closed securities investment fund management businesses on China's stock exchanges;

(g)   foreign-funded insurance companies may not simultaneously conduct both life and non-life insurance business; and

(h)   a long time-frame (nearly two years) for approval by the China Insurance Regulatory Commission (CIRC).

2-427   Under the Reinsurance Companies Rules, the CIRC may approve applicants to set up a life, non-life or general reinsurance company. Approved applicants may conduct inward and outward reinsurance business within China, and international reinsurance business. Foreign-funded reinsurance companies may not participate in the statutory reinsurance business.[23] The Rmb 200 million capitalization requirement also applies to foreign-funded reinsurance companies. By and large, foreign-funded reinsurance companies are governed by the same regulations that govern foreign-funded insurance companies. When China acceded to the WTO, geographic or quantitative restrictions on the number of reinsurance licences issued to foreign insurers were lifted.

Infrastructure and public utilities sector

Classified as 'encouraged' FDI

2-428   In recent years, the Chinese government has encouraged foreign investment in the construction and operation of transportation infrastructure facilities such as public wharves and berths, highways, independent bridges and tunnels. China has also allowed foreign investors to construct civil airports and flight areas, including runways, taxi ranks and parking aprons. The relevant law is the

---

23   Under China's WTO commitments, statutory re-insurance will be phased out within four years after accession.

Foreign Investment in Civil Aviation Provisions promulgated on 21 June 2002, effective on 1 August 2002.[24]

2-429   The Catalogue classifies different aspects of infrastructure and public utilities projects under the 'prohibited', 'restricted' and 'encouraged' categories respectively. The construction and operation of thermo-electric cogeneration power stations, natural gas power stations and hydro-electric power stations fall within the 'encouraged' category. The construction and operation of nuclear power stations require the Chinese party to have controlling interests. Similarly, the construction and operation of comprehensive water conservancy hubs, railway main-line networks and branch lines, local railway and bridges, tunnels and ferry facilities, civil airports and air transport companies require the Chinese partner to have controlling interests.

Exploitation of oil and gas resources

2-430   Foreign investors who are interested in exploiting offshore oil and gas resources must co-operate with the China National Offshore Corporation, the only entity licensed to undertake such activities. Similarly, the China National Petroleum Corporation is the only Chinese entity authorized to exploit onshore oil and gas resources jointly with foreign investors. The relevant regulations promulgated by the State Council are the Exploitation of Offshore Oil Resources in Co-operation with Foreign Parties Regulations issued on 30 January 1982 (amended on 23 September 2001) and the Exploitation of Onshore Oil Resources in Co-operation with Foreign Parties Regulations issued on 17 October 1993 (amended on 23 September 2001). FDI in these areas are subject to a bidding process which is governed by the PRC Invitation and Submission of Bids Law promulgated in August 1999 and effective on 1 January 2000.

Foreign participation in the construction industry

2-431   On 27 September 2002, the Ministry of Foreign Trade and Economic Co-operation (MOFTEC) and the Ministry of Construction issued the long-awaited Administration of Foreign-invested Construction Enterprises Provisions that allow for the first time, a wholly foreign-owned construction company to undertake work in China. Previously, foreign participation in the construction sector was approved on a project-by-project basis.[25]

---

24   An English translation can be found in *China Law & Practice* September 2002, pp 90–94.

25   An excellent discussion of the Provisions can be found in *China Law & Practice* December 2002/January 2003, pp 124–126.

FOREIGN-INVESTED ENTERPRISES (FIE)

Types of investment vehicles

EJV, CJV and WFOE

2-501   Under China's foreign investment legal regime, three types of vehicles are traditionally available to foreign investors who wish to invest in China. They are the equity joint venture (EJV), co-operative or contractual joint venture (CJV) and the wholly foreign-owned enterprise (WFOE). In the mid 1990s, two additional types of investment vehicles were made available to foreign investors through the promulgation of the Chinese Company Law. They were the joint stock company with foreign investment or what can be loosely termed as foreign investment company (FIC) and the holding company (HC). Table 3 below sets out an incomplete breakdown of the different types of FIEs registered between 1984 and 2001.

Table 3: Breakdown of the Number of EJV, CJV, WFOE and Shareholding Companies Between 1984 to 2001

Year	EJV	CJV	WFOE	Shareholding Companies
mid 1984	362	1,372	–	–
1989	9,000	7,000	1,004	–
1995	12,606	3,201	7,695	
1996	12,628	2,849	9,062	
2001	8,895	1,589	15,640	11

2-502   As at September 1995, there were 153,537 EJVs, 37,080 CJVs and 54,549 WFOEs. In recent years, the number of WFOEs established by foreign investors far exceeds the number of EJVs and CJVs.

Approval jurisdiction and procedures

Authority to approve

2-503   Generally, local governments are authorized to approve investments of up to US$30 million. In view of the Chinese government's drive to open up and develop the central and western regions, they have authorized the provincial Commission of Foreign Trade and Economic Co-operation (COFTEC) to approve investments exceeding US$30 million. Table 4 sets out the approval jurisdiction of the various government bodies in China.

Table 4: Approval Jurisdiction

Total Investment (US$)	Location	Approval Authority
Over $100 m	PRC	State Council
$30 m to $100 m	PRC	SPC and MOFTEC
more than $30 m	central and western regions, 'encouraged' and 'permitted' projects	Provincial COFTEC
less than $30 m	coastal provinces, autonomous regions, centrally-administered municipalities, SEZs	Local Planning Commission and COFTEC
less than $10 m	other PRC areas not mentioned above	Local Planning Commission and COFTEC

Legend: SPC – State Planning Commission (renamed as State Development and Reform Commission)
MOFTEC – Ministry of Foreign Trade and Economic Co-operation
COFTEC – Local Commission of Foreign Trade and Economic Co-operation

Approval procedures

2-504   The Implementing Regulations of the joint venture laws generally provide that a joint venture is subject to examination and approval by MOFTEC or its local COFTEC.[26] Upon approval, MOFTEC or COFTEC issues an Approval Certificate. If the approval is obtained from the local commissions, then COFTEC upon approving the joint venture must notify MOFTEC for the record, and MOFTEC issues the Approval Certificate. Within 30 days of obtaining approval, the joint venture must apply for registration with the State Administration of Industry and Commerce (SAIC)[27] or its local and regional bureaus. The SAIC then issues a business licence. The business licence is important for tax registration and access to essential utilities and other services.

2-505   The Chinese partner must submit to MOFTEC or COFTEC a project proposal and preliminary feasibility study on the joint venture. Upon obtaining approval of the project proposal, the Chinese and foreign parties then proceed to undertake further work on the feasibility study and negotiate and sign a joint venture contract and articles of association. Figure 1 outlines the approval procedures and

---

26   In the latest restructuring of the Chinese government, the State Economic and Trade Commission (SETC) and MOFTEC have been amalgamated into the Ministry of Commerce. This will reduce overlap of jurisdiction between the two bodies, reduce red tape and create a more level playing field for both Chinese and foreign companies operating in the Chinese market.

27   The SAIC is equivalent to Singapore's Registry of Companies and Businesses.

time taken by the relevant authorities to approve the various stages of the project.

Establishment of EJV, CJV and WFOE: The legal requirements

Parties to a FIE

2-506   According to the joint venture laws, the foreign party may be a company or enterprise or other economic organizations formed under the laws of the foreign country and registered as a legal entity. They may also be individuals. In contrast, the Chinese party must be a legal entity, which may be a Chinese company or enterprise, or state-owned enterprise, collective enterprise, private enterprise or other economic organizations formed under the laws of China and approved by the relevant department in charge and registered as a legal entity.

Minimum requirements for establishment for EJV

2-507   Article 3 of the EJV Law states the basic policy requirement that EJVs must be able to promote the development of China's economy through the raising of scientific and technological levels.

Figure 1: Procedure for Approval

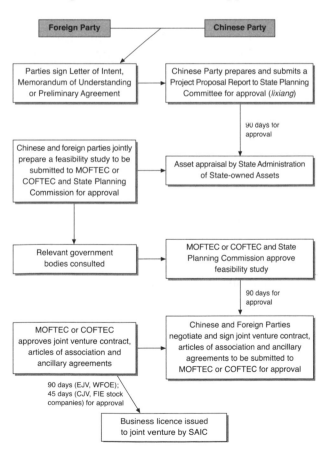

Applicants for an EJV must meet one or several of the following requirements:

(a)   they shall adopt advanced technical equipment and scientific management to help increase the variety, improve the quality and raise the output of products and save energy and materials;

(b)   they shall provide technical innovation so as to bring about quicker returns and bigger profits with less investment;

(c)   they shall help expand China's export base and help to earn foreign exchange; and

(d)   they shall help the training of technical and managerial personnel, ie technology transfer.

When approval will not be granted for EJV

2-508   Article 5 safeguards the interests of the Chinese by stipulating that joint ventures will not be granted approval upon any of the following conditions:

(a)   the joint venture is detrimental to China's sovereignty;

(b)   it violates Chinese law;

(c)   it does not conform with requirements for the development of the Chinese economy;

(d)   it causes environmental pollution; and

(e)   there is obvious inequality in the agreement and articles of association signed between the parties, thus impairing the rights and interests of one party.

Similar conditions apply to CJV

2-509   The CJV Law and Implementing Regulations do not provide any detailed rules for minimum requirements save to say that CJVs must be export-oriented or use advanced technology. Article 9 of the 1995 Implementing Regulations provides that a CJV that violates any of the following conditions shall not be approved:

(a)   where the sovereignty of the state and public interests are harmed;

(b)   where national security is jeopardized;

(c)   where environmental pollution is caused; and

(d)   where other laws and administrative regulations, or the state's industrial policy is violated.

Special conditions for WFOE

2-510   Article 3 of the WFOE Law provides that the establishment of WFOEs shall help the development of China's national economy; and they shall use advanced technology and equipment; and market all or most of their products outside China. This requirement to be export-oriented has since been removed because of WTO requirements for national treatment.

2-511 The WFOE Law further states that foreign investors shall not establish WFOEs in the following industries:

(a) the press, publishing, radio broadcasting, television or the cinematographic industries;

(b) domestic commerce, foreign trade and insurance;

(c) post and telecommunications; and

(d) other industries for which the Chinese government prohibits the establishment of WFOEs.

It is to be noted that some of the above-mentioned industries are now open to foreign investors in view of China's commitments under the WTO. Detailed provisions such as article 9 of the CJV Implementing Regulations (cited above) are also found in the WFOE Implementing Regulations.

2-512 It is to be reminded that the Catalogue is the best source of information to verify if one's area of investment falls within the 'encouraged', 'permitted' , 'restricted' or 'prohibited' category.

Organisation, structure and management

Form of organization: Limited liability entities

2-513 Both the EJV Law and WFOE Law provide that EJVs and WFOEs are limited liability companies. This means that the investors enjoy limited liability according to the amount of capital subscribed by them. On the other hand, CJV entities may be a legal entity, in which case they are limited liability companies, or they may be entities without the status of a legal person. If they are limited liability companies, the investors shall enjoy limited liability according to the capital subscribed by them. In the case of a CJV without legal person status, the investment made or co-operation conditions shall be owned by the parties individually. However, they may also be owned in common, or partly owned individually and partly in common as the parties may agree. Property accumulated by the CJV in the course of business shall be owned in common by the parties.

Management: Board of directors

2-514 For convenience, an EJV and CJV with legal person status shall be discussed together. A CJV without a legal person status and a WFOE will be treated separately later. The highest authority of an EJV or CJV with legal person status shall be the board of directors. The board of directors shall have at least three members. The distribution of seats on the board of directors is determined by the parties through consultation. Either party may appoint the Chairman of the board. If the Chinese side appoints the Chairman, then the Vice-Chairman must be appointed by the foreign party. For EJVs, the term of office of the directors is four years. For CJVs, the term of office is determined by the parties and stated in the articles of association but each term shall not exceed three years. The directors may serve consecutive terms if renewed.

Board of directors' meetings

2-515   The board of directors shall convene at least one meeting each year. Interim meetings may be convened if proposed by one-third or more of the directors. The quorum for board meetings is two-thirds of the directors who are present. If the directors are unable to attend meetings, they may send a proxy. The CJV Implementing Regulations further provide that board resolutions must be adopted by more than half of all the directors (article 28). Article 28 further provides that if a director fails to attend a meeting without legitimate reasons and appoint a proxy, he shall be deemed to have attended such meeting and abstained from voting.

Delegation of authority to managers

2-516   The Chairman of the joint venture shall be the legal representative of the company. Both EJVs and CJVs shall establish a management office comprising one general manager and several deputy general managers responsible for the day-to-day operations of the joint venture. These general managers may be either Chinese citizens or foreigners. These managers are agents of the joint venture and represent the joint venture in its external dealings with outside parties. They are appointed by the board of directors and may also be dismissed for graft or serious dereliction of duty.

Joint management committee in a CJV

2-517   A CJV without legal person status shall establish a joint management committee. Members of the joint management committee are analogous to directors, and enjoy the same rights and obligations as directors. All the provisions governing the board of directors of a CJV with legal person status apply *pro tanto* to a joint management committee of a CJV without legal person status.

WFOE

2-518   As regards WFOEs, there are no detailed provisions on its organizational structure or board of directors. Presumably the foreign investors are free to decide whatever organizational form they want for their WFOE. At this stage, it is pertinent to note that provisions of the PRC Company Law may apply to WFOEs insofar as they do not contravene the WFOE Law and its Implementing Regulations.

Registered capital and investment contribution

2-519 The registered capital of a joint venture refers to the investment amount actually registered with the SAIC. It represents the total amount of actual investment subscribed by the parties to the joint venture, and does not include either third party or shareholder loans, or other forms of external financing. Table 5 below sets out the ratio of registered capital and total investment for EJVs.

Table 5: Registered Capital/Total Investment Ratio for EJV

Total Investment Amount (US$)	Registered Capital/Total Investment
Up to $3 million	at least 7:10 (30% debt)
$3 m to $10 m	at least 1:2 (50% debt)
$10 m to $30 m	at least 2:5 (60% debt)
Over $30 million	at least 1:3 (70% debt)

Time schedule for capital contribution

2-520 The relevant laws also spell out a time schedule for contribution of capital by the parties. Parties may agree to contribute their capital contributions in one lump sum or by instalments. If capital is contributed in one lump sum, then the entire amount must be paid within six months of the issuance of the business licence. If the registered capital is to be paid in instalments, then the first instalment shall not be less than 15% and shall be paid within three months of the issuance of the business licence. The time schedule for the payment of the remaining instalments is set out in the table below (see Table 6 below).

Table 6: Time Schedule for Payment of Registered Capital

Total Registered Capital (US$)	Time Limit
$500,000 or less	One year
$500,000 to $1 million	One and a half years
$1 million to $3 million	Two years
$3 million to $10 million	Three years
$10 million and above	Negotiable

Capital contribution in cash or in kind

2-521 The joint venture laws generally provide that parties to the joint venture or WFOE may contribute their capital in cash or in kind.

The latter may include personal property, real property or technology, equipment and industrial property rights. It is common for the Chinese party to contribute land use rights as capital, and the foreign party to contribute technology and equipment as capital. The contribution of technology as capital shall not exceed 20% of the total investment. The contributions in kind are valued and given a currency value. They are stated in the joint venture contract and articles of association.

2-522   The new Regulations of the PRC on the Administration of Technology Import and Export (New Technology Regulations) were issued by the State Council on 10 December 2001, effective 1 January 2002.[28] For the first time, technology is freely imported or exported unless it infringes articles 16 or 17 of the PRC Foreign Trade Law. In other words, it adopts a negative list approach. The Regulations repealed the 1985 and 1987 Technology Regulations issued by the State Council. All previous approval proceedings for the import and export of technology are now abolished. Instead a contract registration system is implemented. The import of technology that is restricted under article 16 shall undergo a two-stage approval process with MOFTEC and SETC (now the Ministry of Commerce).

Matters that require unanimous voting

2-523   The following decisions require unanimous voting in an EJV or CJV:

(a)   amendments to the articles of association;

(b)   termination or dissolution of the joint venture;

(c)   increase, reduction or assignment of the registered capital of the joint venture;

(d)   merger, division or change in the form of organization of the joint venture; and

(e)   all other matters which the parties agree shall be decided by unanimous voting.

In a CJV, a mortgage of assets also requires unanimous voting. This does not seem to be required in an EJV.

Termination and dissolution

2-524   The duration of an EJV or CJV is determined by agreement between the parties subject to the approval of the relevant authorities. The term of an EJV is generally between 10 and 30 years. In practice,

---

28   An English translation of the Regulations and a commentary can be found in *China Law & Practice* February 2002, pp 56–65 and pp 36–38 respectively.

a 50-year duration has been approved. No term of operation is spelt out in the CJV laws for CJVs. Both the EJV Law and CJV Law and their Implementing Regulations provide that an EJV or a CJV may be dissolved in any of the following circumstances:

(a) expiration of term of co-operation;

(b) inability to continue operations due to heavy losses;

(c) inability to continue operations due to heavy losses caused by *force majeure*, making it impossible to continue to operate;

(d) where one, several or all of the Chinese and foreign parties fail to perform their obligations under the contract and articles of association of the joint venture, making the joint venture impossible to continue to operate;

(e) any other cause of dissolution as provided by the contract and articles of association of the joint venture; and

(f) if the joint venture is ordered to be closed down as a result of a violation of laws or other administrative regulations.

In the case of (d) above, the breaching party must compensate for the losses suffered by the other party as a result of his breach of contract.

Differences between an EJV and CJV

Distribution of profits

2-525 Generally, a CJV is more informal and flexible. The investors of a CJV can share profits in any way they desire unlike an EJV where the profits must be shared proportionately to the investors' original capital investments. In addition, profits in a CJV can be distributed in kind whilst in an EJV, only cash dividends are allowed.

CJV has no registered capital

2-526 Originally, there was no concept of a registered capital in a CJV. It was more like a partnership and the terms and conditions were often referred to as 'terms of co-operation'. The 1995 CJV Implementing Regulations, however, used the phrase 'registered capital' in relation to a CJV with legal person status. 'Registered capital' is defined as the 'sum of the capital contributions subscribed by each party as registered with the SAIC'. A CJV with legal person status is thus very much like an EJV. It is a limited liability company and the investors are generally accepted to have limited liability. Not so for a CJV without legal person status. In the latter, the co-investors pool their assets and resources together without creating any independent legal person. There is thus no limited liability for the investors of a CJV without legal person status. CJVs are popular in mining and infrastructure projects.

Early recoupment of capital in CJV

2-527   A distinctive feature of a CJV is that the investors, usually the foreign investor, are allowed an early recoupment of capital. A MOFTEC Explanation (MOFTEC, Problems Concerning the Establishment of Companies With an Investment Nature by Foreign Investors Explanation) dated 22 October 1996 states that an early recoupment of capital can take place in three forms:

(a)   where the CJV contract provides for an increase in the proportion of gains to be distributed to the foreign party;

(b)   where the recovery of investment is made prior to the payment of income tax; and

(c)   where there is an accelerated depreciation expense for fixed assets.

2-528   It is further provided that should the early return of capital to the foreign investor cause a reduction of capital in the CJV, the foreign investor must provide a bankers' guarantee for a corresponding amount in order to ensure the solvency of the joint venture.

Technology Licensing

2-529   On 10 December 2001, the State Council promulgated the New Technology Regulations which became effective on 1 January 2002.[29] The New Technology Regulations is significant in that it sets out a unified regime for the importation and exportation of technology, including the licensing of technology by foreign companies to Chinese companies and FIEs, and *vice versa*. In other words, foreign investors that contemplate licensing technology to their Chinese subsidiaries should ensure that their technology is not prohibited or restricted from importation. Similarly, foreign investors that are thinking of setting up R&D facilities in China have to ensure that the technology developed should not be prohibited or restricted from being exported out of China.

2-530   Basically the New Technology Regulations establish a unified system to enable a free and fair system of importation and exportation of technology. Technology can be freely imported or exported out of China unless it is prohibited or restricted by article 16 or 17 of the Foreign Trade Law. Under article 16 of the Foreign Trade Law, technology may be restricted if (a) it threatens state security or public interest; (b) it is needed to speed up the development of a particular domestic industry; (c) its import needs to be restricted to safeguard the state's international financial status and international payment

---

29   An English translation can be found in *China Law & Practice* February 2002, pp 56–65. A commentary of the New Technology Regulations can be found in *China Law & Practice* February 2002, pp 36–38.

balance; or (d) the restriction is based on an international treaty or agreement to which China is a party. Similarly, technology will be prohibited from being imported or exported if (a) it will endanger state security or public interest; (b) it endangers people's lives or health; (c) it will destroy the ecological environment; or (d) it is prohibited by an international treaty to which China is a party.

2-531 On 20 December 2001, the MOFTEC and SETC jointly issued the List of Technologies That are Prohibited or Restricted from Being Imported and Exported, which is a non-exhaustive list enumerating the types of technologies that are prohibited or restricted from being imported and exported. This list is crucial to foreign investors who deal with technology in their China investments.

2-532 The New Technology Regulations repealed earlier regulations on technology licensing. Under the New Technology Regulations, technology contracts that are not prohibited or restricted no longer need to be approved by the authorities. It has to be registered on the Internet (http://info.ec.com.cn) and submitted to MOFTEC but registration is for record purposes only. However, application for approval is needed for the importation of technology that falls within the 'restricted' category. The relevant approving authorities are MOFTEC and SETC.

OTHER FORMS OF FOREIGN INVESTMENT

Compensation trade

2-601 The early forms of co-operation with foreign investors took the form of compensation trade. In this arrangement, the Chinese enterprises purchase technology, equipment or raw materials from the foreign investors on credit, and pay off the principal and interest by instalments or on deferred terms using the products produced instead of cash.

Processing and assembling operation

2-602 A form of co-operation whereby the Chinese party processes and assembles products from raw materials and components supplied by the foreign party. The processed and assembled products are then exported by the foreign party. The Chinese party are compensated the processing and assembling costs.

Representative offices

2-603 Foreign investors seeking to establish a 'presence' in China may wish to set up a representative office. A representative office in China is not a separate legal entity but is an extension of its parent company. Such representative offices may only engage in 'non-direct and non-profit making business activities'. Applications must be submitted to the local COFTEC and the relevant government authority in charge of that particular industry such as the Ministry of Information, People's Bank of China, China Insurance Regulatory Commission or Ministry of Justice.

2-604 It is not difficult to obtain permission to establish representative offices. Lawyers keen on setting up representative offices in China should refer to the Administration of Representative Offices of Foreign Law Firms in China Regulations for the relevant minimum conditions and procedures.[30]

CONCLUSION

2-701 This chapter begins with stating the policy imperatives that led China to adopt the 'open door' policy in 1979. It then traces the development of the foreign direct investment legal regime from 1979 to the present day. A keen observer would quickly note that China's laws and regulations cannot be properly understood without looking at the wider social, economic and political ideology that underpin those laws. From mere policy declarations, the specific joint venture laws, ie the EJV, CJV and WFOE, have evolved into a more liberalized, systematic and consistent body of laws. The nuts and bolts of these laws are discussed in detail in this chapter to give the reader more insight into these laws. With the emergence of the PRC Company Law, more choices are now open to foreign investors, and the late 1990s saw a proliferation of M & A activities in China. The next chapter will contain a discussion of the relevant laws governing M & A activities in China as well as an outline of the various types of M & A transactions that are currently permitted in China.

REFERENCES AND FURTHER READING

Books

Laurence Brahm and Li Dao Ran, *The Business Guide To China* (Butterworth-Heinemann Asia, 1996).

Zeng Huaqun, *Chinese Foreign Investment Laws – Recent Developments Towards a Market Economy* (World Scientific and Singapore University Press, 2000).

---

30 An English translation of the Regulations and a commentary can be found in *China Law & Practice* September 2002, pp 37–49 and October 2002, pp 33–36.

Articles

Chen ChunLai, 'The Evolution and Main Features of China's Foreign Direct Investment Policies' (1997) China Program Working Papers Series, Chinese Economies Research Centre, School of Economics, The University of Adelaide, Australia.

Geoffrey Nicoll, 'The Future of the Ventures Law in China' (1997/98) 4 *Canberra Law Review* 103.

Zhao Xudong, 'The Ventures Laws and the Corporations Law in China – Comparisons, Conflicts and Suggestions for Reform' (1997) 4 *Canberra Law Review* 81.

CHAPTER 3

Mergers and Acquisitions in China

Tan Lay Hong

INTRODUCTION

Regulatory framework

3-101   Merger and Acquisition (M & A) activities have proliferated in China in recent years. Under China's current laws, foreign investors are allowed to purchase a stake in a Chinese domestic enterprise, eg a state-owned enterprise (SOE), a company with state-owned interests (SOC) or a collectively-owned enterprise; or a Chinese limited liability company or joint stock company; and a foreign-invested enterprise (FIE) through an equity purchase or asset acquisition.

3-102   The early legal framework for absorbing foreign capital was established by the joint venture laws discussed in chapter 2. Those specialized laws constitute a discrete system of law governing the setting up of sino-foreign joint ventures in the PRC especially in greenfield projects. The system has matured over the last 20 years and posed little difficulty to foreign investors. In 1994, a new regime was created by the seminal PRC Company Law.[1] In recent years, the Chinese authorities have passed the following specific measures to facilitate the absorption of foreign capital into China using the corporate form vehicle:

(a) Several Questions Concerning the Establishment of Foreign Investment Companies Limited by Shares Tentative Provisions, 10 January 1995 (FIC Provisions);

(b) The Establishment of Companies with an Investment Nature by Foreign Investors Tentative Provisions, 4 April 1995 (Holding Company Provisions);

(c) Changes in Equity Interest of Investors in Foreign Investment Enterprises Several Provisions, 28 May 1997 (FIE Restructuring Provisions);

---

1   The Company Law of the People's Republic of China was promulgated by the National People's Congress on the 29 December 1993 and was made effective on the 1 July 1994, (1993–94) 4 *China Current Laws* No 3, pp 5–43.

(d) Asset Reorganization by SOE Using Foreign Investment Tentative Provisions, 14 September 1998 (SOE Asset Acquisition Provisions);

(e) Merger and Division of FIE Provisions, 1 November 1999 (M & D Provisions);

(f) Interim Provisions on Domestic Investment by FIE, 25 July 2000 effective on 1 September 2000 (FIE Investment Regulations);

(g) Notice Regarding the Transfer of State Shares and Legal Person Shares of Listed Companies to Foreign Parties, 4 November 2002 (Transfer of State and Legal Person Shares Notice);

(h) The Tentative Provisions on the Use of Foreign Investment to Restructure SOE, effective 1 January 2003 (SOE Restructuring Provisions); and

(i) Measures for Acquisition of Domestic Enterprises' Shares and Assets by Foreign Companies (Acquisition of Domestic Enterprises Provisions), effective 12 April 2003.

3-103 In the early 1990s, China formally set up the equity markets to attract foreign capital. The main stock exchanges are the Shanghai and Shenzhen Stock Exchanges. As is common in China, the securities markets developed along bifurcated lines: 'A' and 'B' shares. 'A' shares are domestic shares that are issued and traded on the stock exchange by Chinese nationals, whilst 'B' shares are Rmb denominated shares traded in foreign currency by foreign investors. In addition, there are the 'N' and 'H' shares listed by Chinese companies in overseas stock exchanges such as New York and Hong Kong respectively. All these shares are held by individual and institutional investors and are traded on the stock exchanges. In contrast, other kinds of shares such as the state-owned shares, legal person shares and employee shares cannot be bought/sold or transferred at all.

EXAMPLES OF M & A ACTIVITIES IN CHINA

Case 1: Private placement share purchase in an unlisted joint stock company

In early 1993, the Ministry of Foreign Trade and Economic Co-operation (MOFTEC) specifically approved the first private placement share purchase by foreign investors of an unlisted joint stock company, Guangxi Yuchai Machinery Co Ltd. The acquisition was carried out before the promulgation of the Company Law and the FIC Provisions. At that time, MOFTEC encouraged the acquisition in accordance with its draft, but unpublished, version of the FIC Provisions. Apparently, MOFTEC contemplated the possibility of a joint stock company issuing 'foreign [capital] shares' which were distinguishable from 'B' shares. Five foreign investors collectively through their offshore holding companies signed a share contract to which they acquired newly issued common stock representing 51% of the shares of Yuchai. The transaction is now encapsulated in article 22 of the FIC Provisions.

Case 2: Purchase of state-owned shares in a listed company

In July 1994, the Nimrod Group of companies, a US registered private investment and industrial management firm, acquired 25.4% of Chinese state-owned shares in Sichuan Guanghua Chemical Fibre for Rmb 73.5 million. The acquisition was approved by the State Administration of State-owned Assets (SASOA) on 17 July 1994. Some six months later, the China Securities Regulatory Commission (CSRC) suspended the trading of Guanghua's shares on the Shanghai Stock Exchange on the grounds that the transfer was illegal. The suspension was lifted after the CSRC found that it had no firm grounds to impugn the acquisition.

Case 3: Purchase of unlisted legal person shares of a listed company

In August 1995, Japanese firms Isuzu Co and Itocho Corp acquired an existing 40.02 million legal person shares of minibus maker Beijing Light Bus Co Ltd, giving them a combined 25% stake in the Chinese company. The legal vehicle used was article 22 of the FIC Provisions – which allows a joint stock company to convert its shares into 'B' shares. The transaction was similar to a conversion of a state-owned or collectively-owned enterprise into a joint stock foreign investment company (FIC).[2] It was approved by the CSRC and MOFTEC. SASOA's approval was not obtained even though the acquisition involved the transfer or assignment of legal person shares to a foreign investor.

---

2   Articles 18 and 19 of the FIC Provisions governed such conversions.

Case 4: Purchase of 'B' shares in a listed company

In September 1995, Ford Motor Co purchased a 20% stake in Jiangxi Jiangling Motors Corp by acquiring 80% of (approximately) 25% new issue of 'B' shares by Jiangling Corp. The purchase was approved by the CSRC. A waiver was obtained from the relevant authorities to allow Ford to acquire more than 15% of the new issue. Other examples of this type of acquisition include the Atlantic Richfield Co's purchase of 'H' shares of Zhenhai Refining & Chemical Co Ltd and the purchase of Harbin Power Equipment Co Ltd's 'H' shares by ABB Asea Brown Boveri.

Case 5: Purchase of the assets of state-owned enterprises

In March 1998, Eastman Kodak Co announced its billion dollar deal to establish a manufacturing presence in the world's fastest growing economy. In the deal, Kodak purchased the assets of two Chinese SOEs, Xiamen Fuda Photographic Materials and Shantou Era Photo Materials Industry Corp for a sum of US$380 million. The asset purchase was conducted through a new FIC called Kodak (China) Co that is 80% owned by Kodak and 20% owned by Fuda and Shantou Era. The deal also included the transfer of the assets of a third troubled company, Wuxi Aermei Film & Chemical Corp to Kodak (Wuxi) Co that is 70% owned by Kodak and 30% owned by Wuxi Aermei. Kodak assumed none of the debts or liabilities of the state-owned firms.[3]

TYPES OF M & A TRANSACTIONS IN CHINA

3-201 The ensuing paragraphs will focus on M & A activities in China with reference to the different types of target companies, namely, where the target company is a SOE, SOC or collectively-owned enterprise; where the target company is a FIE; and where it is a Chinese listed company.

---

3   A list of recent M & A transactions can be found in the *China Economic Review* at http://www.chinaeconomicreview.com/subjects]acquisitions_and_mergers.htm# Acquisitions%20and%20mergers.

Case 1: Where the Target Company is a SOE or SOC

Purchasing a direct stake in a SOE, SOC or collectively-owned enterprise

3-301 A foreign investor may directly purchase a stake in a SOE, SOC or collectively-owned enterprise. Approvals are needed from the State Economic and Trade Commission (SETC). Generally, the SETC Circular issued in 1995 provides that projects involving large SOEs or existing plants of 'extra-large' scale have to be approved by SETC and the department in charge of the domestic enterprise. Projects above US$100 million have to be approved by the State Council while those below US$30 million may be approved locally. The local approvals must be sent to SETC for the record. For projects between US$30 million and US$100 million, approvals must be obtained from the local economic commission and SETC. After such approvals are obtained, MOFTEC and its local agencies will then approve the joint venture contract and articles of association.

Asset reorganization in a SOE

Definition of an asset reorganization

3-302 In order to facilitate the state sector reform, the SETC issued the SOE Asset Acquisition Provisions on 14 September 1998. Under these Provisions, an 'asset reorganization by SOEs using foreign investment' refers to three types of situations:

(a) SOE using foreign capital to merge with other domestic enterprises;[4]

(b) SOE using foreign capital to supplement its working capital; and

(c) SOE using foreign capital to repay its debts.

Minimum conditions for restructuring

3-303 Article 3 provides that in restructuring the assets of a SOE, the following principles must be adhered to:

(a) strictly comply with the June 1995 Guidelines for Directing Foreign Investment and Investment Catalogue (amended in 1998 and 2002);

(b) make proper arrangement for employees who will be trimmed off so as not to cause any damage to their legal rights;[5]

---

4 An example is the Kodak deal.
5 This was probably enacted in response to the Kodak deal where former Fuda workers protested outside the Xiamen government's offices to demand compensation for having been dumped in the recruitment for the new Kodak plants.

(c)   protect the interests in state-owned assets and prevent any loss of state-owned assets; and

(d)   safeguard the interests of creditors so that bank debts will not be evaded.

3-304   The last principle enumerated above shows that an asset deal in China is quite different from the usual asset deal in more developed countries. In the developed countries, the purchaser may purchase the entire assets and undertaking of the target company without assuming any of the debts and liabilities except in respect of encumbered assets. In fact, an asset deal is sometimes preferred for this very reason. To safeguard the purchaser, warranties and representations are usually extracted from the seller or a third party to the effect that the purchaser does not assume any debt or liability that is not disclosed in the contract documents. In China, the purchaser would have to involve the target company's creditors in the negotiation process to ensure that any undischarged debts or liabilities owing to these creditors will be repaid or compounded to their satisfaction in order to obtain a clean title to the assets. This is even more crucial in China as the 'paper trail' is often sketchy and incomplete.

Approvals

3-305   As regards approval limits, the SOE Asset Acquisition Provisions basically follow those stated in the 1995 SETC Circular. The payment of the acquisition price also follows the MOFTEC and State Administration of Industry and Commerce (SAIC) Supplementary Rules issued on 29 September 1997, ie the foreign investor must make its capital contribution in full within three months of the issuance of the business licence, unless it has to be postponed due to extraordinary circumstances. In such an event, the postponement has to be approved by the relevant authorities and at least 60% of the total contribution shall be made within six months and the remaining 40% within one year of the issuance of the business licence.

Restructuring a SOE and SOC with foreign capital

Definition of a SOE or SOC restructuring

3-306   The 1995 SETC Notice and 1998 SOE Asset Acquisition Provisions have been fleshed out by the recent SOE Restructuring Provisions which were jointly issued by the SETC, Ministry of Finance, the SAIC and State Administration of Foreign Exchange on 8 November 2002, effective 1 January 2003. The three regulations have significant overlaps but it is unclear whether the earlier regulations have been repealed by the latest SOE Restructuring Provisions.[6]

3-307   The SOE Restructuring Provisions list out five forms of restructuring:

(a)   restructuring a SOE into a foreign invested enterprise (FIE) by the sale of all or part of the state-owned interests to the foreign investor;

(b)   restructuring a SOC into a FIE by the sale of all or part of the state shareholdings to the foreign investor;

(c)   domestic creditors transferring or selling debts owed by a SOE to the foreign investor (debt-equity swap);

(d)   restructuring a SOE or SOC into a FIE by the sale of assets to the foreign investor who either alone or jointly with the seller of the assets establishes a FIE; and

(e)   restructuring a SOE or SOC into a FIE by way of a capital increase or the issue of new shares to the foreign investor.[7]

Minimum conditions

3-308   In restructuring a SOE or SOC, the following principles shall be adhered to:

(a)   abiding with state laws and regulations such as the Investment Catalogue;

(b)   promoting the optimal deployment of state-owned capital;

(c)   emphasizing the introduction of advanced technology and management experience that improves corporate governance and promotes industrial upgrading;

(d)   adhering to the principles of fairness, openness, impartiality and good faith, preventing the loss of state-owned assets, protecting the claims of banks and creditors, and the lawful interests of staff and workers, and the interests of foreign investors; and

(e)   promoting fair competition and preventing monopolization of the market.

---

6   It is becoming quite common for Chinese legislators to indicate expressly in a new legislation whether previous legislation or regulations concerning the same subject-matter have been repealed. The SOE Restructuring Provisions does not, however, indicate if the 1995 SETC Notice and 1998 SOE Asset Acquisition Provisions have been repealed.

7   Items (c), (d) and (e) overlap with the SOE Asset Acquisition Provisions.

Procedures to be followed

3-309   The owner of the state-owned interests or shares or creditor of the target enterprise or company shall carry out the following processes or procedures:

(a)   obtain the relevant consents such as shareholder's agreement and creditor's agreement;

(b)   conduct a financial audit and asset appraisal on the target enterprise or company to determine the acquisition price;

(c)   formulate an appropriate plan to settle the staff and workers including the payment of compensation and retrenchment benefits and social insurance premiums;

(d)   arrange for a succession of the target enterprise or company's claims and debts;

(e)   where the restructuring is effected through a sale of assets, the owner of the state-owned interests or shares must conduct an open competition bidding method to select the appropriate foreign investor; and

(f)   execute an assignment agreement containing the relevant terms and conditions.

3-310   The SOE Restructuring Provisions set out a detailed approval process that follows quite closely the previous approval process.

3-311   A new feature of the SOE Restructuring Provisions provides that the acquisition price may be in cash or 'other lawful property rights remitted from overseas'. Such property rights would presumably include intellectual property rights and technology. It is also stated that the capital contribution may take the form of net Rmb profits or other lawful property rights obtained from other FIEs established by the foreign investors in China.

Case 2: Where the Target Company is a FIE

Buying into FIEs – changes in the equity interest

Definition of a 'change in equity interest'

3-401   Prior to the FIE Restructuring Provisions, the foreign partners of FIEs were not able to assign their registered capital to a third party or dissolve the joint venture without the unanimous consent of the Chinese party. Thus the foreign partners of unprofitable joint ventures, or those whose relationship with the Chinese partner had turned sour, or those who simply wished to dissolve or sell their PRC investments had to work closely with their Chinese partners and authorities to negotiate a friendly exit. The FIE Restructuring Provisions issued by MOFTEC and SAIC on 28 May 1997 were therefore much welcomed by foreign investors in China. Under the

FIE Restructuring Provisions, 'changes in equity interests of investors in FIEs' refer to two types of events:[8]

(a)   changes that occur in the investors of a FIE; and

(b)   changes that occur in the shares of capital contributions of the investors in a FIE.

3-402   The FIE Restructuring Provisions list seven specific events that denote a 'change in equity interests' of a FIE:

(a)   where the equity interest is transferred through an agreement between the investors of the FIE;

(b)   where an investor transfers its equity interest to its affiliate or another assignee with the consent of all other investors;

(c)   where the registered capital is adjusted through an agreement between the investors in the FIE resulting in a change in the equity interests of all the investors;

(d)   where an investor pledges its equity interest;

(e)   where an investor becomes bankrupt, is dissolved, abolished, closed down or dies and its successor, creditor or other beneficiary acquires the equity interest of such investor;

(f)   where an investor is merged or divided and its successor after the merger or division inherits the equity interest of such investor; and

(g)   where an investor fails to pay its capital contribution (including any co-operation conditions) as prescribed in the contract and articles of association and with the approval of the original examination and approval authority, the investor is replaced or the equity interest changed.

3-403   In event (g) enumerated above, article 15 provides that the non-breaching party may unilaterally apply to the original approving authority to replace the other investor or alter its equity interest. Such forced buy-outs were not previously available to the non-breaching party. In support, the non-breaching party has to provide documentary evidence that he has given notice to the breaching party to pay the capital contribution or perform the co-operation agreement but the breaching party has failed to do so.

Approval from original approving authority required

3-404   The FIE Restructuring Provisions stipulate that any 'changes in equity interest' of the investors of a FIE require the approval of the original examination and approval authority. It further declares that changes that are not approved by the relevant authorities shall be

---

8   Article 2 of the FIE Restructuring Provisions.

invalid. After approval, the FIE shall register the 'change in equity interests' with the SAIC. [9]

Documents to be submitted

3-405 Articles 9 and 10 of the FIE Restructuring Provisions set out the formalities that must be adhered to when an equity interest in a FIE is assigned to the other investors or a third party. The documents that must be submitted to the approving authority are as follows:

(a) the application for change in the equity interest;

(b) the original joint venture contract and articles of association (and subsequent amendments);

(c) the approval certificate and business licence;

(d) the resolution of the board of directors approving the change;

(e) the list of members on the new board of directors; and

(f) the equity interest assignment agreement.

Where the equity interests involve state-owned assets

3-406 If the equity interest of a Chinese investor using state-owned assets is changed, an asset appraisal report by an authorized agency and a confirmation from the SASOA or its local counterparts of the valuation are required.[10]

Terms in the assignment agreement

3-407 Amongst other things, the assignment agreement shall state the purchase price for the assigned equity interests, stipulate the time limit for settlement of the price, the rights and obligations of the assignee, liability for breach of contract and the governing law.[11]

Payment of acquisition price

3-408 The time limit for settlement of the purchase price is governed by the supplementary rules issued by MOFTEC and SAIC on 29 September 1997. In other words, the acquisition price must be paid in full within three months of the issuance of the business licence. With government approval, payment may be delayed but at least 60% shall be paid within six months, and full payment within one year of the issuance of the business licence.

---

9   Article 3 of the FIE Restructuring Provisions.
10 Article 8 of the FIE Restructuring Provisions.
11 Article 10 implicitly provides that the parties to the agreement may choose a governing law other than Chinese law even though the original joint venture contract has to be governed by Chinese law.

Acquisition must comply with the Investment Catalogue

3-409   In the light of the Provisions, foreign investors contemplating a purchase of equity interest in a FIE or looking to buy all or part of the equity interest of the Chinese partner has to consider a few things. Firstly, article 4 provides that the acquisition shall not infringe the Investment Catalogue. Thus, a foreign investor may not buy the entire equity interest of a FIE where the Catalogue provides that a WFOE is not allowed in that sector.[12] However, where the FIE falls within an industry where a WFOE is *restricted*, a foreign investor may purchase the entire equity interest subject to MOFTEC's approval.[13] Again, where the state is required to hold a controlling interest or dominant position, a foreign investor may not purchase such interests in a FIE as will result in it holding a controlling interest or dominant position.[14]

Increase in foreign partner's registered capital

3-410   The registered capital of both the foreign and Chinese investor of the FIE may undergo 'adjustments' because the FIE needs more capital. Or perhaps the parties may have deliberately deflated the initial registered capital to qualify for local approvals and subsequently need more cash. As the Chinese side is often cash-strapped and cannot contribute proportionately, the foreign party may thus inject more capital into the FIE. This would invariably result in a dilution of the Chinese partner's equity interest. The FIE Restructuring Provisions state that the foreign partner may not do so if the dilution results in the Chinese side losing control in industries where foreigners are not allowed a dominant or controlling share. In addition, if the foreign partner occupies a majority stake as a result of the increase in capital, MOFTEC will check that the equity transfer agreement contains terms to protect the Chinese party as the minority shareholder.

Global restructuring exercise by foreign partner

3-411   Firstly, it is now made clear by the FIE Restructuring Provisions that foreign partners in a FIE who transfer their equity interest to an affiliate or holding company in a global restructuring exercise, require the Chinese partner's consent as well as approval from the original approval body.[15] The procedural technicality can be easily averted by the foreign partner writing into the original joint

---

12   Article 4 of the FIE Restructuring Provisions. Article 4 further provides that if the change in equity interest results in the FIE becoming a WFOE, the provisions of the WFOE laws must be complied with. Basically, a WFOE must use advanced technology and equipment or be export-oriented, see article 3 of the WFOE Law, Implementing Rules.

13   Article 7 of the FIE Restructuring Provisions.

14   Article 4 of the FIE Restructuring Provisions.

15   Article 2 of the FIE Restructuring Provisions.

venture contract express terms for the Chinese partner's consent and waiver of any pre-emptive rights it may have in such an event. Also the term should provide that the Chinese party would cause the directors appointed by it to vote in favour of such a transaction. However, the strategy only secures the Chinese party's consent and the foreign investor will have to face the additional hurdle of obtaining the approval of the original approval body to such restructuring.

3-412   Secondly, an offshore sale or merger of the foreign partner may require the Chinese authority's approval. MOFTEC officials have confirmed that if the transaction results in amendments to the joint venture contract, articles of association, business licence or other corporate documents, approval is required. In other words, unless the name of the foreign partner is changed, no approval is required even if the shareholders of the foreign entity are changed.

3-413   A good example is the merger of Ciba-Geigy and Sandoz in April 1996 to form the world's second largest drug company. In the merger, the specialty chemical businesses from both merged companies were hived off to form Ciba Specialty Chemicals. Ciba-Geigy had been very active in China and had established a holding company to hold stakes in a number of joint ventures. Sandoz, in contrast, had a low-key profile in China. In the restructuring, Ciba-Geigy's holding company was transferred to Ciba Specialty Chemicals and with it the joint ventures it controlled in China. The Chinese had difficulty understanding what had taken place but the transaction was smoothly approved by MOFTEC. Ciba-Geigy's merger took place before the Provisions were enacted; thus the very lack of established procedure or legal framework sped up the whole process.[16] In the light of the FIE Restructuring Provisions, Ciba-Geigy would have to submit the host of documents listed in article 9 of the FIE Restructuring Provisions and seek the approval of the original approving authority.

3-414   More importantly, article 14 provides an exit option to the Chinese partner in a 'Ciba-Geigy-type' merger that was previously not available. If the Chinese partner does not agree to continue operations, an application may be made to the approval body to terminate the FIE and liquidate the enterprise. Conversely, if it is the foreign side that does not wish to continue operations, it may not liquidate the enterprise but shall transfer the equity interest to the Chinese partner or a third party. Like most Chinese legislation, article 14 is skewed in favour of the Chinese partner. It presents a danger to foreign investors undertaking any global restructuring of their business as a disgruntled Chinese partner could conceivably seize the

---

16 'International Mega-deals Leave Authorities, Partners Powerless' *China Joint Venturer* March 1997, pp 18–21 at p 20.

opportunity to throw a monkey wrench to obstruct the effort unless his requests are met. Fortunately, Ciba-Geigy's merger took place before the Provisions were enacted.

Conversion to a wholly domestic-owned enterprise

3-415   Lastly, the Chinese party may want to buy out the foreign partner, thereby converting the FIE into a wholly domestic-owned enterprise. The FIE Restructuring Provisions sanction such a conversion. However, article 5 provides that the foreign partner may not sell down to a point where its interest drops below 25%. Thus, the change must either result in a wholly domestic-owned enterprise or a sino-foreign joint venture, not something in between.

Mergers and divisions of FIEs

What types of transactions are affected?

3-416   The M & D Provisions apply to the following types of transactions:

(a)   a merger or division of an equity joint venture (EJV), co-operative joint venture (CJV) with legal person status, wholly foreign-owned enterprise (WFOE) and a joint stock company with foreign investment; and

(b)   a merger between FIEs and certain Chinese domestic companies.

3-417   The Chinese domestic companies to be merged must either be limited liability companies or joint stock companies established under the PRC Company Law. They would include SOEs incorporated as limited liability companies or joint stock companies. The M & D Provisions do not allow a FIE to merge directly with an SOE or collectively-owned enterprise.

Meaning of 'merger'

3-418   The term 'merger' means either 'merger by absorption' or 'merger by new establishment'. In the former, company A admits company B into its fold, and after the merger, company A survives but company B is dissolved. In the latter, two or more companies merge to establish a new company, and each company to the merger is dissolved. The term 'division' means either 'division by continuation' or 'division by termination'. The former means that a company is split into two or more companies, and the original company continues operation with one or more new companies established. The latter means that a company is broken up into two or more companies, and the original company is dissolved whilst two or more new companies are established. The merger and division of companies shall conform to the relevant laws and to the principle of voluntariness, equality and fair competition. The merger and division of companies shall not harm the public interest or the lawful rights and interests of creditors.

Merger with a Chinese domestic enterprise

3-419   Where a FIE is merged with a Chinese domestic enterprise, the resultant entity is a Chinese domestic company, not a FIE. A merger with a Chinese domestic enterprise in an industry will not be allowed if foreign investment is prohibited in that industry. Examples of such industries are the broadcasting and power grid industries. The M & D Provisions openly proscribed the Chinese-chinese-foreign merger that was rampant in the telecommunication sector.[17]

Resultant entity entitled to preferential treatment

3-420   The merger or division shall not result in the equity interest of the foreign partner falling below 25%. The merged or divided FIE may continue to enjoy the preferential treatment as FIEs so long as the proper consents, approvals and registration procedures are complied with.

Compliance with Investment Catalogue, etc

3-421   A merger and division of a FIE shall comply with the Investment Catalogue. It cannot take place if the original investors have not paid their capital contributions in full or provided their co-operation conditions in full in accordance with the contract and articles of association, and if such a company has not commenced production or business. The foreign investor shall hold at least a 25% stake in the resultant merged company. Lastly, parties to the merger or division must also guarantee that employees will be fully employed or receive reasonable compensation.

Approvals from the authorities

3-422   The approval of the original examination and approval authority is needed in a merger by absorption of a FIE. In a merger by new establishment, the approval from the authority at the location of the new company must be obtained. If the company to be merged is a FIC, the merger or division must be approved by MOFTEC. If the merger or division involves a listed company, the approval of the CSRC is required. Detailed rules on obtaining approval, calculating registered capital, contents of merger and division agreement and documents to be submitted to the approving authorities are laid down in the M & D Provisions.

---

17   The telecommunications sector is now in the 'encouraged' category.

3-423   Approvals from the relevant authorities are needed when the merger or division leads to a change in industry or business scope of the resultant entity.

Formalities and procedures

3-424   Briefly, the process of merger or division takes four stages:

(a)   Initial application and preliminary approval.

(b)   Notification of creditors.

(c)   Formal approval of merger or division.

(d)   Registration matters.

3-425   An application is made to the original examination and approving authority for permission to merge or divide. The authority has 15 days to make a decision. If no reply is forthcoming from them, it is assumed that approval is granted. If the reply is negative, the applicant may appeal to a higher-level authority who must make a decision within 30 days whether to allow the merger or division.

3-426   A preliminary approval must be given within 45 days of receiving the application documents. If the merger will result in a monopoly or domination of the industry by the merged company, MOFTEC has up to 180 days to make a decision.

3-427   Upon receiving the preliminary approvals, the applicant must notify the creditors within 10 days and also issue three press announcements in the provincial newspapers within 30 days. The scheme to deal with the debts shall appear in the notice and the press announcement. Creditors have between 30 to 90 days to respond to the merger or division plans. The creditors may demand that the debt inheritance proposal be modified, claim full repayment or demand corresponding security from the company.

3-428   Formal approval is normally given after the creditors' approval. Within 30 days of the formal approval, the merged or divided company shall register with the SAIC for a new business licence. Within 30 days of receiving the new business licence, the merged or divided company shall notify all creditors and debtors of the merger or division, make announcements in the newspapers and register with all the relevant authorities such as the tax authorities, customs, land administration and foreign exchange authorities.

Case 3: Where the Target Company is a Chinese Listed Company

3-501   M & A activities in listed companies are relatively uncommon in China. The following paragraphs highlight the only type of M & A activity concerning listed companies that is currently permitted in China.

Purchase of state shares and legal person shares in a Chinese listed company

3-502 The Transfer of State and Legal Person Shares Notice 2002 permits the purchase of unlisted state shares and legal person shares of Chinese listed companies by foreign investors, thus lifting the previous ban imposed in 1995.[18]

3-503 The transfer of state and legal person shares to foreign investors shall comply with the following conditions:

(a) the foreign investor shall comply with the Investment Catalogue;

(b) the foreign investor shall have comparatively strong operations and management capabilities, be financially strong, and have the ability to improve the corporate governance and promote the continued development of the listed company;

(c) the transfer shall be conducted by the method of public bidding;

(d) if the transfer involves a restructuring of the target company, the approval of the SETC shall be obtained; if it involves the management of state-owned shares, the approval of the Ministry of Finance must be obtained; and any other major matters must be referred to the State Council;

(e) the CSRC's provisions regarding the take-over of listed companies and disclosure of information by listed companies shall apply;

(f) the foreign investor shall make payment of the acquisition price in a freely convertible currency or may use Rmb profits derived from other investments in China; and

(g) the foreign investor is subject to a mandatory holding period of 12 months after full payment of the entire acquisition price.

3-504 The resultant entity is not a FIE and is ineligible for preferential treatment.

Take-over of listed companies

3-505 On 28 September 2002, the CSRC issued the Administration of the Take-over of Listed Companies Procedure, effective on 1 December 2002, to regulate the take-over of Chinese listed companies. However, the regulation governs the take-over by Chinese parties only. Under current PRC law, foreign investors are still not able to acquire publicly traded shares via the stock exchange. Thus current regulations only allow the acquisition of unlisted state and legal person shares by foreign investors according to the procedures laid down in the aforementioned Transfer of State and Legal Person Shares Notice 2002.

---

18 An example of such an acquisition was Isuzu Co and Itocho Corp's acquisition of 40.02 million legal person shares in minibus maker Beijing Light Bus Co Ltd.

Case 4: Where the Target Company is a Domestic Enterprise

3-601   On 7 March 2003, MOFTEC and the State Administration of Taxation and the SAIC jointly promulgated the Interim Provisions on the Acquisition of Domestic Enterprises by Foreign Investors (Acquisition of Domestic Enterprises Provisions), effective 12 April 2003. The scope of the Acquisition of Domestic Enterprises Provisions is far-reaching and covers all domestic enterprises except FIEs.[19] In other words, the Provisions apply to direct acquisitions of SOEs, companies with state share-holdings, collective and private enterprises as well as the acquisition of Chinese listed and unlisted companies by foreign investors. The troublesome point about the MOFTEC Acquisition Provisions is that it is unclear how they will interface with the abovementioned rules and regulations as there are no express provisions repealing the earlier rules and regulations.

Four types of acquisition structures

3-602   The Acquisition of Domestic Enterprises Provisions set out four types of acquisition structures. The first two are referred to as share acquisitions and the last two as asset acquisitions. They are as follows:

(a)   a foreign investor purchases shares of registered capital of the target enterprises, which is converted into a FIE;

(b)   a foreign investor subscribes for the contribution of an increased amount of registered capital of the target enterprise, which is converted into a FIE;

(c)   a foreign investor establishes and capitalizes a FIE, which uses the capital to buy assets from the target enterprise and continues the operation of the business related to those assets; and

(d)   a foreign investor buys assets from the target enterprise and uses the assets as the foreign investor's capital contribution to a FIE, which continues the operation of the business related to those assets.

3-603   The Acquisition of Domestic Enterprises Provisions do not apply to a share acquisition in a FIE. It, however, applies in an asset acquisition of a FIE. The foreign acquirer may be a foreign enterprise or individual, or a holding company established in China by a foreign investor.

3-604   The Acquisition of Domestic Enterprises Provisions expressly state that acquisitions should adhere to the principles of equality and reasonableness, equal consideration and good faith, and not lead to excessive concentration, restrict competition, disrupt social and

---

19   The Provisions, however, apply if it is an asset acquisition of a FIE.

economic order, or harm the public interests. More importantly, the government will be concerned with issues such as retrenchment of employees and any potential anti-monopolistic effects of the acquisition.

Minimum conditions to be met

3-605   Most of the general rules governing foreign investment will apply, including the limitation on scope of business and foreign ownership outlined in the Investment Catalogue. The debt-equity ratios also apply as well as the minimum registered capital that the foreign investor must hold.

3-606   The acquisition price must be determined by a licensed appraisal firm in China using internationally accepted valuation methods. The acquisition price must be paid in foreign currency, or subject to approval by the State Administration of Foreign Exchange, shares or lawfully acquired Rmb. The payment of the price is subject to the same regulations as those governing FIEs.

3-607   The target enterprise in an asset acquisition shall give notice to its creditors about any impending acquisition and the creditor shall have the right to demand security from the target enterprise as a condition for the acquisition moving ahead.

Approvals

3-608   Approvals for an acquisition must be obtained from MOFTEC or the provincial-level COFTEC. If the target enterprise is a listed company, approval from the CSRC must be sought. Share acquisitions involving state-owned equity interest require the approval of the SETC and the special rules governing the valuation of state-owned assets or shares.

Anti-trust regulation

3-609   The Acquisition of Domestic Enterprises Provisions, for the first time, provide that special approvals must be sought from MOFTEC and SAIC in the following circumstances:

(a)   any party to the acquisition has an operating revenue from the China market in excess of Rmb 1.5 billion in the year of acquisition;

(b)   the foreign investor has acquired more than ten domestic enterprises in the same industry or related industry in the past year;

(c)　any party to the acquisition has a market share in China of 20% or more;

(d)　the post-acquisition FIE would achieve a market share exceeding 25% as a result of the acquisition; or

(e)　other circumstances where MOFTEC or SAIC believes that the acquisition would lead to excessive market share, or seriously impede market competition or economic security.

3-610　In applying the tests, the foreign investor and its affiliates are treated as an aggregate. The MOFTEC and SAIC shall render a decision within 90 days of receiving all the required documents from the foreign investor. The Acquisition of Domestic Enterprises Provisions also contain anti-trust rules that apply to offshore acquisitions that have monopolistic effects in China.

FOREIGN INVESTMENT USING THE CORPORATE VEHICLE

Foreign investment companies limited by shares (FIC)

Establishing a FIC

3-701　Foreign investors were not able to establish Western style companies with limited liability in China until 1995 when MOFTEC promulgated the FIC Provisions.[20] Briefly, the FIC Provisions allow foreign investors to establish foreign investment companies limited by shares (FIC) with Chinese partners. Such FICs are legal persons and their shareholders are liable to the company to the extent of the shares subscribed by them.[21] The quantum of foreign shareholding shall be at least 25% of the company's registered capital. Pursuant to the Company Law, the FIC Provisions provide that companies set up under its aegis can use either the 'promotion' or 'share offer' method.

20　Prior to the FIC Provisions, the Standards for Companies Limited by Shares Opinion (15 May 1992) issued by the State Commission for Restructuring of the Economic System (now renamed the High Level Business Discussion Organ under the State Council) provided that upon approval, MOFTEC would issue a certificate to a joint stock company with foreign shareholdings of more than 25% of its equity interests. Such a company will be subject to the laws and regulations governing FIEs. The FIC Provisions were specifically promulgated to flesh out the sketchy legal regime and article 25 further provides that 'any matters not specifically covered by these provisions shall be governed by the Company Law'.

21　Joint stock companies (*gu fen you xian gong si*) are to be contrasted with limited liability companies (*you xian ze ren gong si*) under the Company Law. In a limited liability company, the shareholders' shares are expressed as a percentage of the registered capital and the number of shareholders shall not exceed 50. There are restrictions on the transfer of shares by shareholders and a right of pre-emption by other shareholders. The limited liability company is akin to the closely held enterprise in the US or the 'Gmbh' in Germany whilst the joint stock company resembles the publicly traded corporations in the US or the 'AG' in Germany.

The 'share offer' can be either public offers or private placements. Article 21 of the FIC Provisions even allows the FIC to issue 'B' shares to the public subject to the approval of the CSRC.[22]

Conversion of FIEs into FICs

3-702 The FIC Provisions further provide the legal framework for the conversion of an existing FIE into a joint stock FIC. To do so, the existing FIE must have attained three consecutive years of profitability and have obtained the approval of MOFTEC and the local authorities. In such cases, it is the investors of the original enterprise who will act as the promoters of the new FIC, not the existing enterprise. In other words, the new FIC will not be the subsidiary of the existing FIE. The FIE will be dissolved. With the approval of MOFTEC, FIE status[23] could be obtained for such restructured joint stock companies if the foreign equity participation is at least 25%.

Conversion of SOEs into FICs

3-703 Even an existing SOE or collectively-owned enterprise may convert into a joint stock FIC if they can find a foreign party to subscribe to at least 25% of the registered capital of the new FIC. Also, they must have been in operation for at least five years and show a record of profitability for the last three years. Where an existing SOE converts into a FIC using foreign capital, an overlapping appears to occur with the SOE Restructuring Provisions. It is unclear how the two provisions will work out in practice.

Exit mechanism for FICs

3-704 On 16 August 2002, MOFTEC issued the Issue Regarding the Conversion of Non-listed Foreign Investment Shares of Foreign-invested Companies Limited By Shares to Tradable 'B' Shares Supplementary Circular to guide the conversion of unlisted foreign investment shares into tradable 'B' shares by FICs. Foreign-invested companies limited by shares that were incorporated under the Relevant Issues Concerning the Establishment of Sino-foreign Companies Limited by Shares (issued by MOFTEC in 1992) may also apply to convert their shares. To qualify for conversion, the shareholders of the unlisted foreign investment shares shall have held the shares for one year, and upon conversion, they will have to hold the shares for another year.

---

22 The Chinese Securities Regulatory Commission is the executive arm of the State Council Securities Policy Commission. These two bodies were established in late 1992 to regulate the securities industry in China.

23 FIE status is important for the various preferential tax and other policies that FIEs enjoy.

Holding companies

Minimum conditions for establishment

3-705   On 4 April 1995, MOFTEC promulgated the Holding Company Provisions. Prior to the Provisions, foreign investors formed holding companies using the WFOE Law.[24] The Provisions allow a foreign investor to either by itself or through its own offshore subsidiaries[25] establish a PRC holding company. To qualify, a foreign investor must have good credit standing and satisfy the following conditions:

(a)   a total asset value of no less than US$400 million[26] in the year preceding the application, have established FIEs in China with a capital contribution of more than US$10 million of the actual registered paid-up capital and have had three or more investment projects[27] approved; or

(b)   have established ten FIEs or more engaged in production or infrastructure projects with a capital contribution of more than US$30 million of the actual registered paid-up capital.

3-706   Where the holding company is established with a Chinese partner, the Chinese partner must have a total asset value of no less than Rmb 100 million. The minimum registered capital of a holding

---

24   An example is the wholly-owned Itochu (China) Holding Co set up in September 1993 by the Japanese conglomerate Itochu with a capital investment of US$36 million, see 'Itochu and Mitsubishi: Unclear Interests' *Business China* 27 October 1997, pp 6–7 and 'More Detail on Holding Companies' *China Law & Practice* 11 April 1994, pp 17–18.

25   Article 1 of the Holding Company Provisions allows foreign investors to use their wholly-owned offshore subsidiaries as vehicles to establish PRC holding companies. On 16 February 1996, MOFTEC issued a set of Explanations (MOFTEC, Problems Concerning the Establishment of Companies with an Investment Nature by Foreign Investors Tentative Provisions) to clarify that the parent company of such offshore subsidiaries must satisfy the qualifying conditions laid down in article 2 of the Holding Company Provisions; see *China Law & Practice* May 1977, pp 44–48. Furthermore, the parent company must provide two guarantees: (a) to guarantee the payment of the registered capital by the offshore subsidiary to the holding company; and (b) after the establishment of the holding company to guarantee the payment of the investment by the holding company to the underlying enterprises and also the transfer of technology by the parent group to the underlying enterprises.

26   A MOFTEC Opinion dated 5 November 1996 clarified that the US$400 million benchmark can include the assets of the corporate group as a whole but one member of the group must be designated to act as the party forming the holding company.

27   The same MOFTEC Opinion also clarified that the three projects can be of any size and level of governmental approval and if one of the projects is particularly large, this requirement may be relaxed; see 'Is MOFTEC Imposing Stricter Controls on the Approval of Foreign Investments' *China Law & Practice* May 1997, pp 31–35 at p 33.

company shall not be less than US$30 million.[28] Where two or more foreign investors are applying to set up a PRC holding company, at least one of them must hold a majority interest and satisfy the conditions laid out above.

3-707 Article 5 permits a holding company to invest in sectors such as industry, agriculture, infrastructure and energy that are encouraged by the state. In addition, MOFTEC issued an Opinion[29] (MOFTEC Opinion) stating that the total amount invested in other enterprises (the underlying enterprises) shall not exceed ten times the holding company's registered capital.

Scope of activities that holding companies may engage in
3-708 Secondly, they may provide selected services to their underlying enterprises as follows:

(a) assisting or acting as agents for the underlying enterprises in the purchase of machinery, office equipment, raw materials and spare parts required for production by the enterprises and in the sale of products inside and outside China;

(b) balancing foreign exchange amongst the underlying enterprises under the supervision of the exchange control authorities;

(c) assisting in the employment of staff for underlying enterprises, providing technical training, marketing and consultancy services to the underlying enterprises;

(d) assisting the underlying enterprises to raise loans and providing guarantees;

(e) since August 1999, holding companies are allowed to invest in or establish a non-manufacturing entity with legal person status whose business scope may include research and development of new products and high technology;

(f) since August 1999, holding companies are, subject to certain requirements, allowed to sell, either as an agent or by means of distribution inside or outside the PRC, the products manufactured by the underlying enterprises, or export commodities that it purchased in China that are not subject to PRC export quotas or export licences, ie engage in trading activities; and

---

28 The requirement under article 4 of the Holding Company Provisions that the capital contributions shall be paid up within two years after the issue of the business licence may also be relaxed under extenuating circumstances upon MOFTEC's approval.
29 'MOFTEC, Directing of the Examination and Approval of Foreign Investment Enterprises Opinion', 5 November 1996, *China Law & Practice* May 1997, pp 11–17.

(g)   since August 1999, holding companies are allowed to provide services such as transportation or warehousing for the underlying enterprises.[30]

3-709   Holding companies that wish to carry out trading activities and provide transportation or warehousing activities to their underlying enterprises must hold 10% or more equity in the latter enterprises. In addition, the actual amount of the registered capital of the holding company must be paid in full and shall be more than US$30 million.

3-710   On 31 May 2001, MOFTEC issued a second set of Supplementary Rules to further liberalize the scope of activities that may be undertaken by holding companies in China. They are as follows:

(a)   provide technical training to third parties other than their underlying enterprises;

(b)   purchase and integrate products of their underlying enterprises and other enterprises for domestic and international distribution;

(c)   conduct trial sales of the same or similar non-quota products imported from their parent companies before commissioning of their underlying enterprises; and

(d)   sponsor foreign-invested companies limited by shares, ie joint stock companies and hold non-listed shares in these companies.

3-711   Because of the huge capital outlay needed to establish holding companies in China and the restricted scope of activities that they are allowed to be engaged in, foreign investors have often side-stepped the Holding Companies Provisions.

FIEs establishing subsidiaries

3-712   On 25 July 2000, the MOFTEC and SAIC jointly promulgated the Interim Provisions on Domestic Investment by FIE (FIE Investment Regulations), effective on 1 September 2000. These Provisions allow a FIE to establish a new limited liability company or joint stock company (ie subsidiaries) or buy an equity interest in an existing Chinese domestic enterprise (collectively referred to as investee companies).

3-713   The FIE Investment Regulations probably replaced the earlier 1995 SAIC Administration of the Registration of Foreign Investment

---

30   Items (e), (f) and (g) are provided under the Supplementary Rules issued by MOFTEC on 24 August 1999, which can be found in *China Law & Practice* October 1999, pp 23–24. A commentary on the Supplementary Rules can be found in *China Law & Practice* October 1999, pp 19–22.

Enterprises as Company Shareholders or Sponsors Several Provisions although they do not expressly provide so.

3-714 The FIE Investment Regulations expressly exclude an investment made in China by a FIE holding company. Direct investments by FIE holding companies are governed by the Holding Company Provisions. Joint investments between a foreign investor and a FIE are also excluded and are governed by the foreign investment laws, ie the EJV and CJV laws.

Compliance with Investment Catalogue, etc

3-715 Domestic investments by FIEs must accord with the provisions of the Investment Catalogue. In addition, FIEs may only make such investments when their registered capital has been fully paid in, have become profitable and have been operating legally. The aggregate amount invested domestically by a FIE may not exceed 50% of its net assets. To encourage the reinvestment of distributable profts by the parent FIE in a subsidiary, it is provided that capitalized profits shall not count towards the net assets.

Approvals from the authorities

3-716 Where a FIE establishes the investee company in the 'encouraged' or 'permitted' category, approvals need only be obtained from the relevant branch of the SAIC of the place where the investee company is to be located. No MOFTEC or COFTEC approval is required. Within 30 days of the issuance of the business licence for the investee company, the FIE shall file for the record with its original approving authority.

3-717 Where the investment is to be made in the 'restricted' category, approvals have to be sought from the provincial level authority for foreign trade and economic co-operation, ie the provincial branch of MOFTEC. The provincial branch of MOFTEC shall then seek the opinion of the relevant branch of the industrial administrative department. Within ten days of the receipt of the opinion from the industrial administrative department, the provincial branch of MOFTEC shall then issue an official reply. With the official reply, the FIE shall then apply for registration of a business licence at the place of location of the investee company. Within 30 days of the establishment of the investee company, the FIE shall file for the record with its original approving authority.

Changes in scope of business

3-718 If a FIE invests its fixed assets, thereby changing the original scale of its operations or the contents of its business, approval must be obtained from its original approving authority. This is to prevent foreign investors from 'gutting already-approved projects' to invest elsewhere. Likewise, if the business scope of the investee company changes, the approval from the original approving authority shall be obtained. This is to prevent a FIE from investing in an 'encouraged' or 'permitted' industry (which only requires approval from the SAIC) and then changing it into the 'restricted' category.

FIE status

3-719   If a FIE invests in the central or western regions of China and the proportion of foreign investment in the registered capital of the investee company is not less than 25%, the investee company shall acquire FIE status and enjoy preferential treatment. The implication is that the FIE investments in other regions, and those in the central and western regions that have less than 25% foreign investment do not qualify as FIEs. In other words, the FIE's subsidiaries generally do not have FIE status. They are considered to be domestic companies.

Overlap with merger and division of FIEs

3-720   Where a FIE merges with a Chinese domestic enterprise through the purchase of equity or equity interests in the latter enterprise, it is unclear how the FIE Investment Regulations will interact with the M & D Provisions. This is particularly significant with regards to issues as to which authority approval should be obtained from and FIE status. Where the Chinese domestic company is a FIE, the FIE Restructuring Provisions will also apply.

BASIC MODELS OF M & A IN CHINA

Purchase of assets in SOE

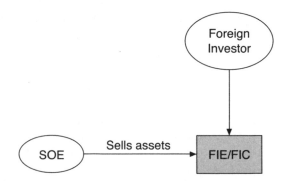

3-801   In this model, the foreign investor establishes a FIE or FIC and uses it as a vehicle to purchase assets of a SOE. The FIE or FIC may or may not assume the debts of the SOE. The relevant provisions of the SOE Asset Acquisition Provisions, the SOE Restructuring Provisions, the FIC Provisions and the MOFTEC Acquisition

Provisions apply. An example of this model is Eastman Kodak's acquisition of Xiamen Fuda Photographic Materials and Shantou Era Photo Materials Industry Corp.

Purchase of assets by foreign investor as capital contribution

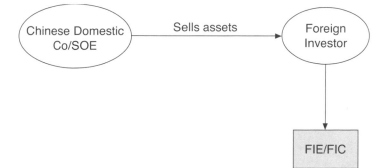

3-802 In this model, the Chinese domestic company which may be a limited liability company or joint stock company (ie company limited by shares) or a SOE sells and transfers the assets to a foreign investor who in turn pumps the assets into a newly established FIE or FIC. The transaction is governed by the FIC Provisions if the resultant entity is a FIC. If state assets are involved in the sale, a valuation from the SASOA is required, and the SOE Restructuring Provisions and the Acquisition of Domestic Enterprises Provisions will also apply. The payment for the assets must be made within three months of the issue of the business licence.

Purchase of equity in offshore investor

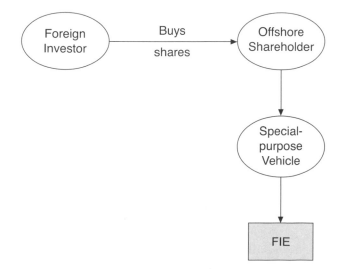

3-803 In this model, the foreign investor buys the shares of the offshore shareholder in the special purpose vehicle. No PRC government approval is required. The approvals of the Chinese joint venture partner and the board of directors are also not required.

Purchase of equity interest in onshore FIE

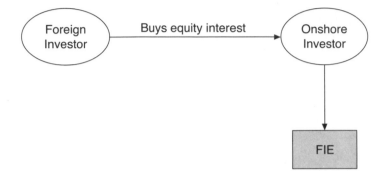

3-804 In this model, the foreign investor acquires the equity stake of the FIE. This acquisition transaction is governed by the FIE Restructuring Provisions as well as the Acquisition of Domestic Enterprises Provisions. The Chinese government approval is required. In addition, the consent from the other joint venture partner is required. The FIE board of directors must also give its consent. In acquiring the equity stake, the foreign investor assumes all the debts and liabilities of the FIE.

Purchase of equity interest in Chinese domestic companies

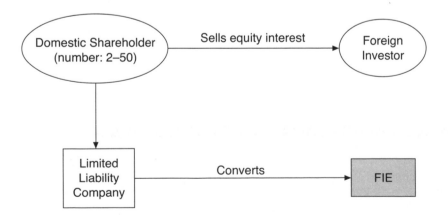

3-805 In this model, the foreign investor purchases an equity stake in a Chinese domestic limited liability company and converts the entity into a FIE. Under Chinese laws, a limited liability company may have between two and fifty shareholders. For the disposal of the equity stakes, the approval of the Chinese government is required. Internally, the transaction requires a simple majority vote from the other shareholders. Those who oppose the assignment shall purchase the equity stake to be assigned; and if such stake is not purchased, the assignment shall be deemed to have been agreed to. The Acquisition of Domestic Enterprises Provisions would apply to such an acquisition.

Purchase of equity in Chinese domestic companies

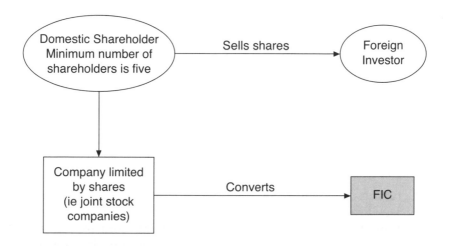

3-806 In this model, the target is a domestic joint stock company. Under the PRC Company Law, the minimum number of shareholders of a joint stock company is five. The transaction is governed by the FIC Provisions and the Acquisition of Domestic Enterprises Provisions. The foreign investor must buy at least 25% of all the issued shares, in order for the resultant entity to qualify as a FIC. The FIC's status is equivalent to a FIE and is entitled to all the preferential treatment that a FIE enjoys. The minimum registered capital of a FIC is Rmb 30 million. The shareholders must have held the shares for at least three years before they can transfer the shares to a foreign purchaser.

A COMPARATIVE ANALYSIS: FIE VERSUS M & A

3-901 This final section will examine the pros and cons of establishing a FIE as a greenfield investment as opposed to the M & A method of acquiring equity or assets of an existing Chinese enterprise such as a SOE, SOC or FIE, or the establishment of a FIC or a holding company.

Approvals

Easier to establish a FIE

3-902   A distinct advantage of establishing a FIE is that smaller joint ventures with a total investment of less than US$30 million can be approved by the local Commission of MOFTEC or the municipal or provincial government. This is a much simpler process compared to establishing a joint stock FIC or acquiring equity or assets of Chinese domestic enterprises, which must be approved by MOFTEC, in addition to approvals from its local counterparts and the municipal or provincial governments. It is also more difficult to establish a joint stock FIC because the conditions require the promoter, be it the foreign investor or the Chinese investor, to give details of its production, business, assets, liabilities and profits for the last three years. In contrast, foreign investors establishing a FIE would not face such difficulties. Needless to say, establishing a holding company is only open to sizeable foreign investors with total group assets of US$400 million and who have already established several FIEs in China.

3-903   Furthermore, buying into an existing FIE would require the approval of the original approving authorities in addition to approvals from MOFTEC, SAIC and other bodies such as the Ministry of Finance. Where the acquisition involves state-owned assets, the SASOA's approval must also be sought. These procedures are more cumbersome than establishing a FIE especially if the investment amount is less than US$30 million, not to mention that it is not always clear which authority's approval is required.

High minimum capital required for M & A activities

3-904   The minimum registered capital of a joint stock FIC and a holding company is US$30 million. No minimum capital requirement exists for establishing a FIE. Thus, smaller projects of less than US$30 million will usually take the form of a FIE and be approved locally.

Governing legal regime is uncertain

3-905   It is not always certain which legal regime governs the target company after a restructuring. For instance, if a FIE is restructured with foreign capital, or if the FIE establishes limited liability companies or joint stock companies as subsidiaries or merge with a Chinese domestic enterprise, which law is to apply to the resultant entity? Is it the joint venture laws or the Company Law of the PRC? This issue may be significant especially with regard to questions of capital payment or reduction and management structure.

Reduction of capital

3-906 Unlike a CJV, an EJV is not permitted to reduce its capital during the term of the joint venture.[31] Article 44 of the CJV Law, Implementing Rules provides that if the CJV contract gives the Chinese party ownership of all 'fixed assets' of the CJV upon its expiration, the foreign party may apply to recover its investment during the term of the co-operation.[32] Three methods are provided:

(a) a provision in the CJV contract to increase the proportion of gains to be distributed to the foreign party;

(b) recovery by the foreign party of its investment prior to the payment of income tax by the CJV subject to the approval of the authorities;

(c) accelerated depreciation expenses for the fixed assets subject to prior approval.

3-907 In contrast, articles 103 and 106 of the Company Law provide that shareholders may at a general meeting by a simple majority vote to reduce the company's registered capital. Hence, the capital of a joint stock FIC may be reduced with relative ease compared to an EJV that cannot reduce its capital or a CJV where an approval has to be sought from the relevant authorities for the early return of capital.

Management structure

3-908 In an EJV, the parties must establish a board of directors and a management office under a general manager to oversee daily management. The parties to a CJV may, however, set up a joint management committee instead of a board of directors and they have considerable freedom to structure the management as they deem fit. In contrast, in a joint stock FIC or where the resultant target company is governed by the Company Law, three levels of authority are represented: (a) the shareholders, (b) the board of directors; and (c) the board of supervisors. No directors, managers or person-in-charge of financial affairs are allowed to sit on the supervisory board. The supervisory board acts as 'whistle-blowers' when the management violates state regulations or the articles of association of the company. They are entitled to look into the company's accounts and ensure the financial health of the company.

3-909 More importantly, the FIE laws provide that if the Chairman is appointed by the Chinese side, then the Vice-Chairman has to be appointed by the other party. By contrast, the Company Law allows

---

31 Article 22 of the EJV Law, Implementing Regulations.

32 'Detailed Rules for the Implementation of the Sino-foreign Co-operative Joint Venture Law', 4 September 1995, *China Law & Practice* 1 November 1995, pp 18–32 at p 29.

the majority shareholder to appoint the directors and senior managers.[33] In cases of dispute between the parties, the Company Law enables the majority shareholder to decide on the matter by a simple majority vote unless the dispute concerns the merger or division or dissolution of the company or a proposed amendment to the articles of association. In such a case, a two-thirds majority vote is required. However, in a FIE (which is more of a consensual partnership), major disputes touching on amendments to the articles of association, the merger division or dissolution of the FIE and an increase or assignment of registered capital require the unanimous consent of the other directors. The result is that a foreign investor who has a majority shareholding in a FIC or a resultant target company that is governed by the Company Law is in a better position than the foreign investor in a FIE.

Exit options

3-910   Foreign shareholders of shares that are listed on the stock exchanges (like Ford) may readily dispose of their equity interest in the secondary market. In unlisted joint stock companies, the foreign shareholder may still transfer their shares without governmental approval or consent from the other shareholders. But if the transfer necessitates an amendment to the articles of association, then the consent of the other shareholders may be required if the foreign shareholder holds less than two-thirds majority. The only restriction is that promoters may not dispose of their shares within three years and directors, supervisors and managers may not sell off their shares during their term of office.

3-911   On 17 May 2001, MOFTEC issued a Circular (Questions Relevant to Foreign-Invested Companies Limited by Shares Circular) that permits FICs to publicly list their 'B' shares after obtaining approval from the CSRC and MOFTEC. The unlisted foreign investment shares that are to be listed shall have been held by the foreign investor for at least one year prior to listing.[34] After listing the 'B' shares, at least 10% of the total capital stock shall consist of non-floating shares owned by foreign investors. This effectively means that the FIC will lose its FIE status. FICs' rights to publicly list their foreign investment shares were given a further boost when the

---

33   Articles 103 and 106 of the Company Law.
34   This one-year holding period is probably instituted to arrest the rampant practice amongst foreign investors, particularly Hong Kong companies, who acquire major factories and other assets from Chinese enterprises partially on credit and at low prices, and then using the proceeds of subsequent public offerings to pay for the Chinese assets. Such bootstrap tactics are frowned upon by the Chinese authorities because there is no actual injection of capital by the foreign investor.

MOFTEC issued a Supplementary Circular on 16 August 2002 (Issues Regarding the Conversion of Non-Listed Foreign-Invested Companies Limited by Shares to Tradable B Shares Supplementary Circular) allowing for the conversion of unlisted foreign investment shares into tradable 'B' shares.

3-912   On the other hand, a unanimous decision of the board of directors is required to dissolve, assign the registered capital or merge the FIE with other entities.[35] This effectively means that the foreign investor cannot pull out without the blessings of the Chinese party. Also, the other party has a pre-emptive right to the assignment of the registered capital.[36] One possible exit mechanism is to install a 'put option' in the joint venture contract. This requires the Chinese party to buy out the foreign party's interest under certain specified conditions. When the conditions occur, the Chinese party will be in breach of contract if it does not buy out the other party. In this way, articles 23 and 36 of the EJV Law, Implementing Rules are effectively circumvented. Furthermore a non-breaching party may in the light of the FIE Restructuring Provisions unilaterally apply to the authorities to have the defaulting party replaced or the equity interest altered.

3-913   The gap seems to be closed by the issuance of the Foreign Investment Issues Relating to Listed Companies Several Opinions by MOFTEC on 5 November 2001 which governs the conversion of a FIE into a FIC for the purpose of publicly listing the foreign investment shares. The Several Opinions augment the Circular issued by MOFTEC on 17 May 2001 (mentioned above) and also alluded to the 16 August 2002 Supplementary Circular issued by MOFTEC.

Termination and dissolution

3-914   It is difficult to say conclusively whether it is easier for a foreign investor to dissolve a joint stock FIC or a FIE. As regards the former, article 106 of the Company Law provides that dissolution requires more than two-thirds majority vote at a shareholders' meeting. A foreign investor occupying a minority position of less than one-third share will be helpless against the Chinese party if he wishes to dissolve the FIC on, say, grounds that it is incurring losses or that the Chinese party is breaching his part of the bargain. The only way out is to provide clearly at the outset in the articles of association that the foreign shareholder has a right to dissolve the FIC in certain

---

35   Article 36 of the EJV Law, Implementing Regulations and article 29 of the CJV Law, Implementing Regulations.
36   Article 23 of the EJV Law, Implementing Regulations.

specified conditions.[37] If any of the conditions occur, then the foreign shareholder can dissolve the FIC and avert the 'two-thirds majority' rule.

3-915   As regards the latter, the FIE laws provide that a dissolution requires the unanimous consent of the FIE partners. A practice has widely grown that a unanimous vote of the board of directors is required to dissolve the joint venture, even if the foreign party obtains a judgment or arbitral award ordering dissolution of the joint venture. As a consequence, the foreign party who is faced with an unco-operative or even belligerent Chinese partner may be held in a deadlock. However, the law seems to have changed. A subtle recognition of the right of one party to dissolve the joint venture through obtaining a judgment or arbitral award to that effect is given in the recent liquidation procedures (FIE Liquidation Procedures) passed by MOFTEC on 9 July 1996. Article 5 of the FIE Liquidation Procedures states that the 'date of commencement of liquidation of a FIE shall be ... (*inter alia*) the date on which the contract for the FIE is terminated by the judgment of a people's court or the award of an arbitration institution'. This appears to imply that a FIE may be unilaterally terminated by one party if sanctioned by a Chinese court or arbitration body.

3-916   It must be noted that article 102 of the EJV Law, Implementing Regulations and article 48 of the CJV Law, Implementing Regulations also provide that one party to a joint venture may seek a dissolution on the grounds stated in the contract or articles of association. Hence, the foreign party can always seek to protect himself by careful drafting of the articles of association or joint venture contract in all cases.

CONCLUSION

3-1001   With the emergence of the PRC Company Law, more choices are now open to foreign investors, and the late 1990s saw a proliferation of M & A activities in China. The chapter discusses the relevant laws governing M & A activities in China as well as an outline of the various types of M & A transactions that are currently permitted in China. A comparative analysis of the alternative methods of entering the Chinese market, namely the traditional method of establishing a FIE versus the M & A method, is also made.

---

37   Article 190 of the Company Law provides that a company may be dissolved in the following three instances: (a) where the term of operation as specified in the articles of association expires or one of the conditions for dissolution as specified in the articles of association arises; (b) where the shareholders' meeting resolves to dissolve the company; and (c) where dissolution becomes necessary as a result of a merger or division of the company.

REFERENCES AND FURTHER READING

Books

Laurence Brahm and Li Dao Ran, *The Business Guide to China* (Butterworth-Heinemann Asia, 1996).

Zeng Huaqun, *Chinese Foreign Investment Laws – Recent Developments Towards a Market Economy* (World Scientific and Singapore University Press, 2000).

Articles

Chen Chunlai, 'The Evolution and Main Features of China's Foreign Direct Investment Policies' (1997) China Program Working Papers Series, the Chinese Economies Research Centre, School of Economics, The University of Adelaide, Australia.

Geoffrey Nicoll, 'The Future of the Ventures Law in China' (1997/98) 4 *Canberra Law Review* 103.

Tan Lay Hong, 'Mergers and Acquisitions in the People's Republic of China: An Emerging Legal Framework?' (2000) 28 *Asia Business Law Review* 14.

Zhao Xudong, 'The Ventures Laws and the Corporations Law in China – Comparisons, Conflicts and Suggestions for Reform' (1997) 4 *Canberra Law Review* 81.

CHAPTER 4

Chinese Company Law

Tan Lay Hong

INTRODUCTION

State-run economy

The traditional property rights system in state enterprises

4-101 The late Deng's seminal 'open-door' policy had undoubtedly brought in its wake a revolution in the system of enterprise ownership in China. The revolution engendered a rethinking of the political and economic underpinnings of the traditional Marxist theory of socialism. The traditional concept of socialism recognizes two forms of socialist public ownership: (a) ownership by the whole people or state ownership and (b) collective ownership, ie ownership by a group of individuals, usually peasants and workers in a collective. State ownership was the backbone of China's socialist economy and controlled the majority of all industrial sectors in China.[1]

4-102 The system was characterized by a high degree of centraliza-tion. The whole economy was directed by administrative commands from state executive units of the central government to the local governments. Enterprises were appendages of the state organs; their production was controlled by mandatory planning, materials and funds were allocated by the state, all products were priced, bought and sold by the state, and all profits went to the state which also shouldered all losses and unlimited liabilities of state-run enterprises. Under such a system, enterprises have neither legal personality nor independent property rights. The state itself is the sole owner of property.

4-103 The main shortcomings of this property rights system are as follows:

(a) The direct exercise of ownership rights by state organs mixed with the administrative relations between the state and enterprise created a situation where the state and enterprise

---

1　By 1985, state-run enterprises contributed 70.4% of China's industrial output; retail sales of commodities by state-run commercial enterprises had reached 40.4% of the total; the total fixed assets of all state-run enterprises amounted to Rmb 737.05 billion. The total number of state-run industrial enterprises is 90,700; see 3 *Zhongguo Jingji Nianjian* (China's Economic Yearbook) 19.

became indistinguishable and administrative methods interfered with the production activities of the enterprise. This curbed the vitality and vigour of enterprises.

(b)   The heavily centralized planning system led to the subordination of enterprises to the state government units, prevented beneficial economic associations between enterprises, and cut the links between socialized production and the commodity economy. The rule of 'specified funds for specific uses' (*zhuankuan zhuanyong*) prevailed, which meant that all funds allocated to state enterprises could only be used for the purposes specified by the state. As a result, there was unchecked construction, duplicate production and heavy financial losses for the state.

(c)   There was uncontrolled investment by the state as investors did not care about returns, and because enterprises had no independent property rights, they naturally neglected the gains and losses of their capital. Together, they caused a surge in basic construction, over-capacity and diminished the state's economic benefits.

(d)   As the state absorbed all losses and liabilities of the enterprises, the enterprises did not feel the pressure of competition and became sluggish in the security of the 'iron rice bowl' and the 'one big pot'. At the same time, because they handed over all profits to the state, they lacked the incentive to maximize economic efficiency. Chinese workers under an egalitarian wage structure lacked the zeal, initiative and creativity to maximize productivity and efficiency of the enterprises.

Reform of state enterprises

'Invigoration' of state enterprises

4-104   The early reformers therefore identified the invigoration of enterprises as the key to increasing socialized production and efficiency. This was achieved by expanding the autonomy of enterprises (*kuoda qiye zizhuquan*). As time passed, other steps were taken:

(a)   to decrease the tax rate from enterprises and concede profits to enterprises (*jiansui rangli*);

(b)   to carry out 'tax for profit' (*li gai sui*);

(c)   to implement the contract system (*chengbao zhi*); and finally to transform China's state enterprises into shareholding enterprises (*gufeng jingji*).

The contract and leasing system: separation of 'ownership' rights from 'operating' rights

4-105   The next wave of reform was thus aimed at changing the property rights relationship between the state and enterprises – 'the separation of "ownership" rights from "operating rights"'.[2] The Seventh Five-Year Plan provided that 'some small [state] enterprises may be contracted or leased to collectives or individuals for management'.

4-106   Under this system, state enterprises may be contracted or leased to a collective (which is often composed of the original employees of the state enterprise) which will have complete management rights and the right to retain all profits after paying over to the state an agreed amount set by contract or shares with the state its after-tax profits according to a pre-agreed formula. The state remains the owner of the original enterprise property but new assets and funds belong to the collective. Ownership rights[3] were split between the state as property owner and the collective as property manager. Although the amount of taxes and profits that were required to be turned over to the state were lower than state enterprises, the contracted enterprise, on the other hand, would be forced to use their own capital to complement any shortfall in taxes and profits. Such an arrangement gave enterprises complete 'operating rights' and provided them with incentives to take full responsibility for their profits and losses.[4]

COLLECTIVE ENTERPRISES

Origins and nature

4-201   From the late 1950s to the 1980s, the government choked off private enterprises but gave a significant role to collective ownership. Collectives operate primarily in the agricultural, services and light industrial sectors of the economy. They were not included in the state

---

2   The reform received its legitimacy at the Plenary Session of the Committee Party Central Committee on 20 October 1984 where ideologically the Communist Party endorsed the call for comprehensive economic reform by allowing ownership and management of state-owned enterprises to be appropriately separated.

3   Ownership rights are a 'bundle of rights' which includes the right to the income generated by the property, the right to transfer and dispose of the property, the right to control or manage the property and the right to trade these rights.

4   A fine example of the success of the collective contract system was the Capital Steel and Iron Corp which progressively increased its annual profits by 20% from 1979 to 1986 and in the span of seven years, the state received Rmb 582 million from the enterprise, representing a figure 1.6 times higher than the total amount the enterprise had contributed to the state in the last 30 years.

economic plan and were not subject to direct control by the central or provincial government. Most collectives are subject only to local government control and operate virtually as local state enterprises. Collectives differ in origin, type and structure. At one end of the spectrum are the large urban collectives which had been administratively absorbed by the local government and were often incorporated into the economic plan, whilst at the other end, rural and smaller urban collectives are more private in nature, independent and informal.[5] Many new collectives have also been formed from the conversion of small state enterprises into collectives.

4-202 But collective enterprises are a form of non-private ownership. Their assets are not owned by members of the collective individually; they are collectively owned. These rights are not transferable. The member cannot sell his rights, liquidate his anticipated future benefits into a present lump sum and he cannot continue to enjoy the rights after he leaves the collective. Early legislation provided for the separation of management from ownership, ie the qualification and rights of enterprise managers, autonomy of the enterprise in controlling production, hiring employees, entering into economic contracts and undertaking external trade and joint investment. At least 60% of the after-tax profits should be retained by the enterprise for reinvestment, technological upgrading or bonuses while the balance is paid to government agencies to assist in developing other collectives, improve worker education and collective welfare facilities. This traditional set of priorities in the use of collective profits reflects the public nature of collectives.

PRIVATE ENTERPRISES

Origins and nature

4-301 Private enterprises re-emerged in the 1980s as individual households (*getihu*) and gradually enjoyed legal protection under the Constitution. Subsequently, private firms (*siying jingji*) were also established. Under the law, the number of employees working in an individual household was limited to seven but in practice, more were

---

5   Township and village enterprises have rapidly emerged as a growing industrial force in China. In 1991, they accounted for around Rmb $18 billion or 25% of China's total export earnings from a low of 4.5% in 1984–85; see 'Reaping Rural Rewards' *The China Business Review* November–December 1992, pp 12–17. There are more than 23 million township enterprises in China with 80% located in rural township and villages. Between 1991–96, the export volume of this sector had grown at an average annual rate of 30%; see 'Booming Township Enterprises' *Beijing Review* 23 February–1 March 1998, pp 16–18.

employed. Only rural residents, unemployed individuals, operators of individuals and commercial households, retirees or discharged employees could set up a private enterprise and only in restricted lines of business.

4-302   To curb any tendency for capitalist exploitation and excesses, the rules stipulated that the salary of a director should not exceed ten times the average of staff wages. In addition, the enterprise should retain at least 50% of after-tax profits in a production development fund and exemptions from taxes were granted in respect of retained profits that were not distributed to the owners.

4-303   Private enterprises constituted serious ideological challenges to socialism as it raised issues of worker exploitation, profits and private ownership. The ideological difficulties were finally resolved at the Communist Party Central Committee in 1987. In typical communist rhetoric, the theory was advanced that China was in the 'primary stage of socialism' which began in 1950 and the main goal in that stage was to develop production to meet the material needs of the people. Public ownership must dominate but a private sector may contribute to production and employment that the state cannot provide. Jiang's 'three represents' theory has recently embraced the private sector of the economy into the Chinese Communist Party's (CCP) charter.

SOCIALIST MARKET ECONOMY

Third Plenary Session of the Chinese Communist Party
Policy Imperative

4-401   The watershed third Plenary Session of the Communist Party Central Committee on 14 November 1993 gave new impetus to the development of a socialist market economy with Chinese characteristics. As a matter of policy, it was decided that the publicly-owned sector should remain the mainstay of the economy but the government would strive for the simultaneous development of all other economic sectors as well. More importantly, a modern enterprise system must be established to function within a market economy and in which the property rights as well as rights and responsibilities of enterprises are clearly defined, and government administration and enterprise management is separated. The government's functions in economic management must be transformed from the role of enterprise owner to regulator/administrator; and a sound macro-economic control system underpinned by open market and competitive systems in all sectors of the economy must be implemented.

ENTERPRISE AUTONOMY AND THE DEVELOPMENT OF ENTERPRISE LAW

Breakaway from the Chinese Communist Party (CCP)

Erosion of CCP status in enterprises

4-501 Beginning in 1982, the Party committee's monopolistic power was gradually eroded to give the enterprises greater autonomy. Firstly, the 'general manager responsibility system' was reinstituted to transfer leadership of the enterprise from the Party committee to the general manager and to grant the latter complete control over management. The role of the Party committee in enterprises was reduced from a 'leadership' role to a supervisory function. Secondly, the general manager should not assume the position of Party secretary at the same time to ensure his independent status and need only periodically report his work to the Party committee.

4-502 Thirdly, the general manager is empowered to make his own independent decisions despite contrary views of the Party committee. This shift in the power base was neatly encapsulated in the 1988 PRC Industrial Enterprises Owned by the Whole People Law[6] (the Enterprise Law) where it is provided that the Party committee's leadership should take the form of ideological guidance rather than control over routine management activities. The Enterprise Law entrenches enterprise autonomy against government interference.

The Enterprise Law 1988

Separation of 'ownership' from 'management'

4-503 The tremendous success of experimental enterprises that implemented the separation of 'ownership' from 'management' finally heralded the Enterprise Law on 13 April 1988 after a long gestation period of about eight years.[7] Article 3 provides that state enterprises are to become commodity producers with profit-seeking motives to create wealth and meet the demand of the state plan and the market. This represented a fundamental shift from the traditional state ownership concept where state enterprises were appendages of state organs charged with the task of fulfilling state plans without any responsibility for profits or losses.

---

6   *China Law & Practice* June 1988, pp 35–50. The phrase 'enterprise owned by the whole people' historically refers to a state enterprise.

7   For a legislative history of the Enterprise Law, see Kenneth TK Wong and Zhonglan Huang, 'A Critical Analysis of the Law of the People's Republic of China on Industrial Enterprises Owned by the Whole People' (1990) 7 *Pacific Basin Law Journal* 180 at pp 181–186. Further see, 'Law and the Enterprise' *The China Business Review* March–April 1987 pp 38–42 for a brief discussion of the predecessor regulations.

Property rights structure

4-504   The property rights structure was clearly set out in the Enterprise Law. Article 2 provides that the 'property in enterprises shall be owned by the whole people', ie the state, but the state grants to the enterprise, in accordance with the principle of separating ownership from management, the right to operate and manage the property. This right includes the right to possess, use and dispose of the property. Article 6 implements the 'tax for profit' principle and articles 22 to 27 grant greater autonomy to the enterprises. They are entitled to request adjustment of mandatory plans,[8] decide on what products and how much to produce,[9] sell their products independently,[10] select independent suppliers of production materials,[11] fix the prices of non-controlled products[12] and contract with foreign businesses.[13]

4-505   Enterprises were implored to adopt management responsibility systems on a contractual or leasing basis.[14] They are allowed to determine suitable forms of wage and bonus distribution,[15] hire and dismiss employees in accordance with state regulations,[16] and decide on the type of organizational structure and staff strength they should have.[17] Further concessions are granted to the enterprise to allow them to lease or assign for value the enterprise's fixed assets,[18] exercise full control over depreciation funds and retain for reinvestment all profits in excess of a specified amount.[19]

Capitalization

4-506   The minimum amount of capitalization of state enterprises is not stipulated in the Enterprise Law but in separate legislation. Briefly, the circulating capital of manufacturing enterprises should not be less than Rmb 100,000; commercial enterprises with wholesale businesses should not be under Rmb 200,000 while those in retail trade should not be less than Rmb 100,000; and consultant service enterprises must not be under Rmb 50,000. No provisions, however, exist for the protection of capital for the benefit of creditors.

---

8   Article 23 of the Enterprise Law.
9   Article 22 of the Enterprise Law.
10   Article 24 of the Enterprise Law.
11   Article 25 of the Enterprise Law.
12   Article 26 of the Enterprise Law.
13   Article 27 of the Enterprise Law.
14   Article 2 of the Enterprise Law.
15   Article 30 of the Enterprise Law.
16   Article 31 of the Enterprise Law.
17   Article 32 of the Enterprise Law.
18   Article 29 of the Enterprise Law.
19   Article 28 of the Enterprise Law.

Internal governance: the factory (manager) responsibility system

4-507 The Enterprise Law expressly mandates the implemen-tation of the factory (manager) responsibility system.[20] It gives an extremely powerful managerial role to the factory director. Article 45 provides that the factory director 'shall occupy the central position in the enterprise', and shall direct the production, operation and management of the enterprise, and shall be the 'legal representative' of the enterprise.

4-508 The powers granted to the factory director are carefully balanced with administrative and legal restrictions and workers' rights. Firstly, factory directors are appointed or removed by the supervisory government department after considering the views of the workers' representative, or elected by the workers' congress with government approval.

4-509 Secondly, the law stipulates that enterprises shall carry out democratic management through the workers' congress or by other means,[21] and further declares that the workers 'enjoy the status of masters'.[22]

4-510 Administrative sanctions and in more severe cases, criminal liability are imposed on errant directors or leading cadres who cause losses to the enterprise due to their neglect or fault, or who abuse their powers for private gain or violate workers' interests.[23]

4-511 Quite clearly, the Enterprise Law transformed amorphous state enterprises into discrete economic units, each possessing and managing its own property and premises with an organizational structure and internal governance, having legal personality and capacity to assume civil liabilities and obligations and responsible for its own profits and losses. This property rights system and organizational structure were the inevitable springboard to the corporatization of state enterprises.

'CORPORATISATION' EXPERIMENT

Corporate shareholding system

World Bank proposal

4-601 As early as 1984, the World Bank proposed a shareholding system as a reform strategy for China's state enterprises. Under the

---

20 Article 7 of the Enterprise Law. Separate legislation already exists on the factory director responsibility system, viz the 1986 Regulations on the Work of General Manager of Industrial Enterprises Under the Ownership of the Whole People.
21 Article 10, Article 10 of the Enterprise Law.
22 Article 50, Article 50 of the Enterprise Law.
23 Articles 62 to 64 of the Enterprise Law.

proposal, the enterprises' assets were to be divided into shares and owned by several government departments.

4-602 This system aims to break up the single ownership system and implement a multi-ownership system that would, *inter alia*, fulfil the following objectives:

(a)   improve the efficiency of a public ownership system;

(b)   specialize government administration through a board of directors;

(c)   separate the government's social and political goals from those of enterprises; and

(d)   build self-management and self-restraint mechanisms within the enterprise.[24]

The World Bank proposal provoked great interest in theoretical circles. Extensive debates raged as experimental shareholding systems in various forms were implemented in state and collective enterprises throughout the country.[25]

Modern enterprise system

4-603 The year 1993 was a watershed in the process of transition from state enterprises into corporations. The third Plenary Session of the Communist Party Central Committee on 14 November 1993 propounded a significant ideological development to take the 'separation of ownership from management concept' to a higher plane – the modern enterprise system. It is a system akin to the Western concept of a corporation.

---

24   World Bank, *Zhongguo Changqi Fazhan De Wenti Yu Fang'an Zhu Baogao* [A major report on the problems and patterns for long-term development in China] (1985) and World Bank Experts on China's Enterprise Reforms, *Zhongguo Fazhan Yu Gaige* [Development and Reform in China] vol 10, 1987.

25   For a chronological history of the debates surrounding the shareholding system and stock markets, see Andrew Xuefeng Qian, 'Riding Two Horses: Corporatizing Enterprises and the Emerging Securities Regulatory Regime in China' (1993) 12 *Pacific Basin Law Journal* 63 at pp 72–85. Extensive debates on the theoretical and ideological aspects of the shareholding system can be found in the following articles: 'CRES Advocates Shareholding System for State Enterprises' *Joint Publication Research Service JPRS-CAR-93-033* 18 May 1993, pp 22–23; 'Theoretical Issues Surrounding Stocks, Bonds' *JPRS-CAR-92-070* 14 September 1992, pp 26–27; 'State Commission Outlines Shareholding System' *JPRS-CAR-92-059* 3 August 1992, pp 34–39; 'Article on Joint-Stock Companies, Stock Market' *JPRS-CAR-92-079* 21 October 1992, pp 20–27; 'Report Examines Joint-Stock System' *JPRS-CAR-89-011* 7 February 1989 pp 13–18; 'Thoughts Related to the Trial-implementation of the Shareholding System in Shanghai' *JPRS-CAR-89-052* 24 May 1989, pp 29–33 and 'From Contract System to Share System – Transformation of the Enterprise Operational Form and Property Organization Form' *JPRS-CAR-88-059* 26 September 1988, pp 9–13.

4-604 Firstly, the property rights relationships are more clearly defined. The investors (including the state) are the owners of the enterprise, and enjoy limited liability in proportion to their share of capital investment, are entitled to dividends, to take part in strategic decisions affecting the enterprise and to choose the managers. Secondly, the enterprises as legal entities possess all rights over the assets pooled from the investors and independently assume civil obligations and liabilities. They are to be responsible for their own profits and losses, pay taxes to the government and enhance the value of their assets. Most importantly, it was decided that state enterprises should experiment with the corporate system. Various corporate forms were postulated; from wholly state-owned companies to limited liability companies or limited liability stock companies and partnerships.

4-605 Secondly, the 1993 amendments to the Constitution changed all references of state-run enterprises to state-owned enterprises, a phrase that better describes the new operating mechanisms and the relationship between the state and the enterprise. Thirdly, the shareholding experiment culminated in the national corporation law. The Company Law of the People's Republic of China (the Company Law) was finally promulgated by the NPC on 29 December 1993 and became effective on 1 July 1994.[26]

1995 reform of state-owned enterprises

State-owned sector problem

4-606 Despite the numerous measures taken to invigorate state enterprises, problems remained. The state-owned sector continued to carry a heavy debt and social burden, and most state enterprises had weak internal management systems aggravated by continual interference from government officials. Various mechanisms were thus employed to address the state sector problems. For example, Rmb 140 million loans which were borrowed by Chongqing Iron and Steel Co from public finance were transformed into national capital through the Chongqing Municipal. The Tangshan Alkali Factory divided its Rmb 935 million debt (owing to the state, provincial and municipal government) into national capital and became a limited liability company held by diverse investors, and its asset-liability ratio dropped from 91.5% to 60%. To hive off its social burden and redundant workers, the Taiyuan Iron and Steel Co gradually transferred its elementary and middle schools to the local government and reduced its Rmb 30 million (in 1994) expenditure related to these schools by 20% every year.

---

26 (1993–94) 4 *China Current Laws* No 35.

Corporate restructuring

4-607   The reform of state-owned enterprises took centre-stage in 1995. The State Council approved 100 enterprises to pilot the modern enterprise system, 18 cities to introduce the programme to optimize capital structures, 57 enterprise groups and three state-holding companies were selected as experimental units. More than 2,000 enterprises in various localities participated in the effort to establish a modern enterprise system.

4-608   These enterprise groups were exhorted to merge on a trans-regional and trans-industry scale to combine industrial production with technological development and trade.[27] Even China's state farms went corporate.[28] On the other hand, some small state-owned enterprises have been transformed into co-operative shareholding companies with diversified ownership structures.[29]

4-609   Rough statistics suggest that the implementation of the modern enterprise system has proceeded at a rapid rate. From 3,220 joint stock companies in 1991, the figure increased exponentially from 3,600 to 9,000 between 1995 and 1997.[30] Successful transformation of small state-owned enterprises into shareholding co-operative companies where the employees purchased the enterprises' entire assets and liabilities in return for shares have also taken place in several cities like Shanghai, Shandong and Sichuan.

CONCEPT OF A LEGAL PERSON IN CHINA

Origins of legal person concept

4-701   The idea of legal personality was not legally accepted in China until the adoption of the Civil Code (1929) of the Republic of China. The Communist take-over in 1949 resulted in the abolition of almost all Nationalists laws and legal theory save for a few surviving concepts

---

27   For example, China's biggest shipping conglomerate was recently formed from five regional companies with combined assets of US$3 billion, 413 big ships and sales that reached US$771 million in 1996. In a trans-industry merger, four petrochemical and fibre companies merged to form China's largest manufacturing base for fibre, petrochemicals and fertilizer with profits of US$398 million in 1996; see 'New M & A Opportunities in China' *China Law for Business*, August 1998.

28   'China's State Farms Go Corporate' *The China Business Review* November–December 1994, pp 28–31.

29   'Enterprise Ownership with Chinese Characteristics' *Beijing Review* 15–21 September 1997, pp 9–12. A co-operative shareholding system means that all employees in an enterprise buy out its production assets in the form of holding shares, eg a Ybin County brewery in Sizhuan divided its accumulated state assets worth Rmb 3.28 million into Rmb 350,000 worth of shares held by the state, Rmb 1.01 million stock held by all employees and Rmb 1.92 million shares held by individual employees.

30   'Joint-stock system: A Way to Invigorate State Enterprises' *Beijing Review* 23–29 March 1998, pp 19–21 at p 19.

such as the 'legal person' concept. Article 5 of a 1950 Measure (Temporary Measures Concerning the Conclusion of Contracts between State Organs, State Enterprise and Cooperatives) provides that 'a contract or deed must be concluded between legal persons represented by their responsible persons'. But the meaning and implications of a legal person were left undefined. For the most part of the Communist regime until the 1980s, the notion of a legal person was attacked as a bourgeois legal concept.

Revival of legal person concept

The Economic Contract Law 1981

4-702   The Economic Contract Law (ECL) was the first law to use the term 'legal person'. However, the term was used as a matter of convenience to define the capacity of business organizations to enter into contracts. Under Chinese law, only legal persons may enter into contracts, not individuals. The law did not grant enterprises who are legal persons any significant independence and autonomy. In fact, the ECL used the term 'unit' (*danwei*) rather than 'legal person' (*faren*) to refer to various economic organizations. Chinese lawyers and legislators were still unfamiliar with the notion of legal person at that time.

Provisional Regulations Concerning State Industrial Enterprises 1983

4-703   This 1983 State Council Regulation was promulgated in the wake of the state enterprise reform of the 1980s described above. It provides that state industrial enterprises are:

> '... legal persons. Their directors are the representatives of the legal persons. Enterprises shall exercise, in accordance with the law, the right to possess, use and dispose of the state assets which the state authorizes them to manage and administer, shall independently engage in production and operation, shall bear the responsibility to which the state prescribes, and shall independently initiate and defend legal proceedings in the court'.

4-704   As such, the Regulations not only assumed the legal person status of state enterprises, but also actually set out the principal characteristics of an enterprise legal person. In 1984, the CCP in a Party Decision endorsed the idea of making state enterprises legal persons.

The General Principles of Civil Law (GPCL) 1986

4-705   In the GPCL, the term 'legal person' is used in contrast to 'citizens' or 'natural persons'. Of the 156 articles in the GPCL, 18 articles are devoted to the notion of the 'legal person'. Article 37 provides that a legal person shall:

(a)   be established in accordance with the law;

(b)   possess the necessary property or funds;

(c)   possess its own name, organization and premises; and

(d)   have the ability to independently bear civil liability.

4-706   Any entity that meets the above requirements can become a legal person. State enterprises are automatically granted legal person status. Collective enterprises with proper qualifications may also become legal persons. Under the joint venture laws, a foreign invested enterprise (FIE) is an enterprise legal person except a co-operative joint venture (CJV) without legal person status. According to the GPCL, even official organs, institutions and social organizations such as trade unions that meet the basic requirements can be legal persons. Political parties are, however, not included in the notion of a legal person.

Nature of legal personality

Limited capacity

4-707   The GPCL basically defines a legal person as an 'organization' (*zuzhi*). In dealing with organizations, the question of capacity often crops up. The question of capacity is related to the issue of whether a legal person has its own 'mind'. The Chinese subscribe to the 'organ' theory.[31] According to this theory, a legal person can enjoy legal rights and execute legal acts through its organ. The 'organ' (*jiguan*) means either 'an individual or a collective body that, in accordance with the law or articles of association, is able to represent the legal person in its external relations with others in the course of its business operations'. The acts of the organ are thus seen as the acts of the legal person. The 'organ' of a Chinese legal person is the 'legal representative' (*fading daibiaoren*), defined as the person with the responsibility to exercise authority on behalf of the legal person, in accordance with the law or articles of association. The legal person is bound by the acts performed by its legal representative within its business capacity.

4-708   Under Chinese legal theory, the corporate personality created by law is merely a 'legal fiction' (*falu nizhi*). Thus, the mind of the legal person is just a metaphor, not a reality. Being a legal fiction, a legal person must necessarily have limited capacity.

---

31   A theory contrasting to the organ theory is the agency theory. Under the agency theory, the legal person being an artificial entity created by the law does not have its own mind or capacity to act. Therefore, its activities have to be carried out through its agents such as its directors and employees. This theory is generally adopted by Western countries, but finds no support in China.

4-709 Indeed, Chinese law has developed very strict limited capacity rules regarding enterprise legal persons. Enterprise legal persons must have clearly stated objectives and approved by the relevant government departments. Unlike companies in Western legal systems, Chinese enterprise legal persons may not have unlimited purposes or unlimited capacity. In fact, an enterprise applying for more than one major business objective is unlikely to gain approval for registration.[32] In Chinese law, an enterprise must have a strictly stated 'business coverage' (*jingying fanwei*) and specific 'business pattern' (*jingying fangshi*), ie the way through which the approved businesses will be carried out. Thus, an enterprise engaged in retailing business cannot do wholesale business. Any act or transaction which is not consistent with the business coverage or business pattern of the enterprise is void.

4-710 The legal personality of enterprises generally comes into existence only when a business licence is issued. The enterprise is not allowed to engage in business operations before the issue of the business licence. Hence, there are no problems with pre-incorporation contracts in China.

Acts of the legal representative

4-711 Under article 42 of the GPCL, a legal person must act within the limits of its business capacity. But in reality, sometimes, the organ as an independent body may perform illegal acts. These illegal acts may be within or outside the business capacity of the legal person. Is the legal person bound by such acts? The GPCL provides that a legal person should be unconditionally responsible for the business activities of its legal representative as well as its other personnel. This means that the legal person is liable for *all* acts committed by its legal representative, including illegal acts. Therefore, there appears to be a contradiction between the limited capacity rule (ie that legal persons are only liable for acts conducted within its business scope and coverage) and liability for acts outside this capacity. The result is that a legal person is not able to perform illegal acts but is nevertheless made liable for illegal acts performed in its name. One main policy consideration that is used to support this proposition is the need to protect third parties who have contracted with the legal representative. It is to be noted that the legal person is not only liable for acts of its legal representative, it is also liable for the acts of its

---

32 A SAIC Circular issued in July 1989 (Circular Concerning Several Issues Regarding Approving Business Capacity) provides that an enterprise may have one main business and several other collateral businesses, but not vice versa.

'other personnel'. This is because a legal person bears a duty of care and supervision towards its personnel, and thus should be responsible for their acts.

4-712   The 'organ' theory and the notion of the legal representative are carried over into the Company Law 1993.

Legal personality and property rights

Different property rights structure for different enterprises

4-713   Under Chinese law, a system of varying property rights structure exists for different enterprises. As mentioned above, state enterprises have a unique property rights structure. In other words, even though 'ownership' is separated from 'management', the enterprise does not own the property it manages. It is the state that directly owns the property.

4-714   On the other hand, a *de facto* two-tier property rights structure exists for collective enterprises. Article 48 of the GPCL provides that 'collective enterprises as legal persons shall bear civil liability with respect to the property which the enterprises *own*'. In other words, a collective enterprise as a legal person enjoys the property ownership rights but the collective which invested in the first place to establish the enterprise is also entitled to ownership rights over the property of the enterprise. There are two layers of property rights ownership.

4-715   What is the property rights structure of FIEs? It is clear under the joint venture laws that the investors own the capital contribution to the joint venture whilst the FIE owns the property of the joint venture. This brings FIEs in line with Western-style corporations. It is also stated in the joint venture laws that the investors enjoy limited liability in accordance with the capital subscribed by them.[33]

4-716   The question whether the 'shareholders' of state and collective enterprises enjoy limited liability is difficult to answer. Presumably, the same policy argument may be advanced that in order for the reform of Chinese state and collective enterprises to be successful and to break the 'iron rice-bowl', the state or collective as owner of the enterprise should enjoy limited liability. But in practice, 'soft budget' constraints may cause the state to absorb all the losses of the enterprise.

---

33   Further analysis on the concept of limited liability in China can be found in Chuan Roger Peng, 'Limited Liability in China: A Partial Reading of China's Company Law of 1994' (1996) 10 *Columbia Journal of Asian Law* 263.

THE COMPANY LAW

Legislative history

4-801 China's Company Law was designed to restructure state enterprises on international capitalist models and to legitimate a much smaller private sector. The primary purposes of the law are as follows: (a) to restructure the organization and management of state-owned enterprises by establishing the modern enterprise system; (b) to protect the lawful rights and interests of companies, shareholders and creditors; and (c) to promote the development of the socialist market economy. The Company Law superseded provisional corporate regulations of the central government and two municipalities.[34]

4-802 Commentators have contended that the Company Law represented the gradual process of 'legalization', ie the replacement of the traditional emphasis on policy and propriety with codified law and legal institutions in China. In this process, Chinese legislators frequently draw upon the legislative experiences of foreign countries and are keen to adopt international business practices. For example, the Company Law provides for stock with par value and dividends, shareholders with limited liability, pre-emptive rights and the power to elect directors, and directors with fiduciary duties and power to appoint officers.

4-803 Western corporate models are welded with traditional concepts of Chinese law to produce a Company Law with distinctly Chinese characteristics. These special features include the 'legal representative', the extraordinary grant of extensive powers to shareholders and the 'board of supervisors' to oversee the board of directors and the right of workers to determine corporate policy. Finally, the Company Law relies primarily on administrative sanctions rather than on derivative or personal actions by shareholders to seek redress for misconduct by company officers that cause loss to the company and/or the shareholders.

---

34 At the central level, the Opinion on Standards for Limited Liability Companies and Companies Limited by Shares, 15 May 1992 issued by the State Commission for Restructuring the Economic System (now known as the High-Level Business Discussion Organ under the State Council) (1992) 6 *China Law & Practice* No 69. At the local level, the Shenzhen Municipality, Companies Limited by Shares Tentative Provisions, 17 March 1992 and the Shanghai Municipality, Companies Limited by Shares Tentative Provisions, 18 May 1992. Discussions on these early corporate regulations can be found in Preston M Torbert, 'China's Evolving Company Legislation: A Status Report' (1993) 14 *Northwestern Journal of International Law & Business* 1 and Matthew D Bersani, 'Privatization and the Creation of Stock Companies in China' (1993) 3 *Columbia Business Law Review* 301.

Types of companies

4-804   To be incorporated, the company must first be registered. Registration requires the approval of the relevant government authorities subject to the ability of the company to meet certain stringent prerequisites.[35]

4-805   There are three corporate forms under the Company Law: (a) a limited liability company[36] (*you xian ze ren gong si*); (b) a company limited by shares (*gu fen you xian gong si* – hereinafter referred to as a joint stock company); and (c) a wholly state-owned company. The first is akin to the closely held enterprise in the US or the 'GmbH' in Germany whilst the second resembles the publicly traded corporations in the US or the 'AG' in Germany. The third type of company means a limited liability company invested in and established solely by an organization or department authorized by the state to make investments.

WHOLLY STATE-OWNED COMPANIES

4-901   Article 64 of the Company Law provides that companies that produce special products or are engaged in a special line of business as determined by the State Council shall be structured as wholly state-owned companies.

4-902   The highest decision-making body in a wholly state-owned company is the board of directors, not the shareholders' meeting. However, important matters such as the merger, division, dissolution, increase or decrease of capital and the issue of company bonds must be decided by the organization or departments that establish the company, ie the shareholders.

4-903   The board of directors shall be empowered to make the following decisions:

(a)   make decisions on the business plans and investment plans of the company;

(b)   work out the proposed annual budgets and financial accounts of the company;

---

35   The authority responsible for approving registration is the State Adminis-tration of Industry and Commerce and its local branches. It is referred to as the Company Registry in the Company Law.

36   The Chinese term 'limited liability company' must not be confused with the same term used in American legislation. In America, it refers to a form of business organization that qualifies for certain tax benefits that partnerships normally enjoy while retaining the corporation's protection of investors; it is not considered incorporated and possesses extensive discretion to structure its own internal governance.

(c)   work out the profit distribution plans and plans for making up losses of the company;

(d)   work out plans for the increase or reduction of capital;

(e)   draft plans for the merger, division, restructuring and dissolution of the company;

(f)   decide on the company's internal management structure; and

(g)   engage or dismiss the senior managers of the company.

4-904   The board of directors shall compose of three to nine members, who shall be appointed by the organization or department that establishes the company. Each term of office of the directors shall be three years. The members of the board of directors shall include representatives of the staff and workers, who shall be democratically elected. The board of directors shall have one Chairman who shall be the legal representative of the company. There may be a Vice-Chairman, if necessary. The board of directors shall engage a general manager to manage the day-to-day affairs of the company. If approved, a member of the board of directors may concurrently serve as the general manager.

4-905   To prevent conflict of interest situations, article 70 prohibits the Chairman, Vice-Chairman, director or general manager of a wholly state-owned company from serving as a responsible person in another limited liability company, joint stock company or any other business organization.

4-906   On 25 December 1999, the Standing Committee of the National People's Congress (NPC) amended the Company Law to introduce supervisory boards for wholly state-owned companies. These supervisory boards are to take over the functions of supervision and control from the shareholders. The supervisory boards are to comprise of persons appointed by the State Council or by departments authorized by the State Council, and representatives of the company's workers. They shall have at least three members, and these members may attend the board of directors' meetings as non-voting members. Directors, managers and persons in charge of the financial affairs of the company are barred from serving concurrently as members of the supervisory boards.

LIMITED LIABILITY COMPANIES AND JOINT STOCK COMPANIES

Conditions for establishment

4-1001   The prerequisites for establishing a Chinese company are stringent by Western standards. The company must have its own name, organizational structure and articles of association with a fixed place of business and the necessary facilities. In addition, it must possess sufficient funds and workers in accordance with state regulations, as well as in proportion to the scale of the company's operations. More importantly, it must have the ability to bear civil liability independently and have a scope of business that conforms with the provisions of state laws, statutory regulations and policies.[37]

4-1002   Unlike Western countries, a Chinese company is created or registered not by right, but by approval. The Ministry of Foreign Trade and Economic Co-operation (MOFTEC) and the State Administration of Industry and Commerce (SAIC) will examine the substantive validity of all the application documents and acts of incorporation. The SAIC will not approve the application unless it is satisfied with the procedural and substantive validity of the information in the documents including the company name, business purpose, qualification of the legal representative, directors and supervisors. Any later changes to the registered information are only effective upon the approval of the relevant registration authorities. In other words, incorporating a company is not a suffrage but a privilege subject to the discretion of the relevant authorities.

Form and structure

4-1003   The limited liability form is suitable for smaller corporations with two to fifty shareholders. It may not publicly offer its stock. On the other hand, a joint stock company is typically larger than a limited liability company. It may have any number of shareholders and may distribute stock either by the 'promotion method' or the 'public offer method'.[38] In the former, the promoters purchase all the shares by subscription; in the latter, the company offers shares to the public but the promoters must subscribe for at least 35% of the stock.[39]   The number of promoters, except for state-owned enterprises restructuring into joint stock companies, shall not be less than five.[40] Promoters generally must be legal persons (excluding wholly foreign-owned enterprises or Chinese private enterprises) or authorized government departments.[41]

4-1004   Shareholders enjoy limited liability in proportion to the amount of their capital contributions and the company is liable for its own debts to the extent of all its assets.[42]

---

37   Articles 19 and 73 of the Company Law.
38   Article 74 of the Company Law.
39   Article 83 of the Company Law.
40   Article 75 of the Company Law.
41   The main functions of the promoters are to organize the establishment of the company and to act as 'deep pockets' in the event problems are encountered; see article 97 of the Company Law for the liabilities of promoters.
42   Article 3 of the Company Law.

Registered capital

4-1005   The 'first to contribute' principle is a distinctly Chinese characteristic adopted by the Company Law. The Company Law stipulates that the investors have first to pay in full their capital contribution before they can apply to the company registry to register the company.[43] This practice departs from Western practice where registration usually precedes payment of capital. It was opined that the principle was necessary to protect creditors' interests and possibly to discourage 'fly by night' operators.[44] It is, however, contended that the principle should be seen against the backdrop of stringent prerequisites for incorporation in China rather than in isolation as efforts on the part of legislators to protect creditors. Together they form part of the wider strategy aimed at reforming the state sector through rescuing large and viable state-owned enterprises from the brink of bankruptcy and turning them around into profit-making business entities whilst leasing, contracting or selling off the smaller ones to private operators.[45] Thus, only viable state-owned enterprises of sizable financial strength and operation, and possessing sufficient fixed assets will satisfy the prerequisites for incorporation and obtain the authorities' approval for corporatization.

4-1006   This argument is reinforced by the relatively high minimum registered capital (which is the paid-up capital) required of Chinese companies.[46] For limited liability companies, it ranges from Rmb 500,000 to Rmb 100,000 depending on the line of business, whilst joint stock companies require a minimum registered capital of Rmb 10 million.[47] The minimum registered capital of listed companies is Rmb 50 million.[48]

4-1007   Capital contribution may be made in cash or in kind and must be verified by an authorized investment verification organization.[49] If intellectual property rights are contributed as

---

43   Articles 27 and 94 of the Company Law.
44   'First to Contribute Doctrine Delays Adoption of International Standards' *China Law & Practice* 25 June 1996, p 25.
45   'Report on the Work of the Government' delivered at the First Session of the 9th National People's Congress on 5 March 1988, *Beijing Review* 6–12 April 1988, pp 9–24 at p 16–18.
46   In Singapore, for example, the minimum paid-up capital is S$2.00.
47   For a company engaged in production and operation, the minimum registered capital is Rmb 500,000; a company engaged in wholesale of commodities, the minimum registered capital is Rmb 500,000; a company engaged in commercial retailing, the minimum registered capital is Rmb 300,000; and for a company engaged in technology development and consulting services, the minimum registered capital is Rmb 100,000.
48   Article 152(2) of the Company Law.
49   Such appraisal work is usually carried out by an accounting firm; see the Administration of the Registration of Company Registered Capital Tentative Provisions promulgated by the State Administration of Industry and Commerce on 18 December 1995, *China Law & Practice* June 1996, No 5, p 30.

capital, they shall not exceed 20% of the total registered capital.[50] After the registered capital has been paid in full, the company applies for registration.[51]

Maintenance of capital

4-1008 In China, there is no general doctrine for the maintenance of capital for the protection of creditors.[52] But rudimentary rules are present. Two provisions exist which may arguably be used to support the existence of such a doctrine. Articles 34 and 93 provide that shareholders, promoters and subscribers shall not withdraw their capital contribution after the registration of the company. However, it may be equally argued that these provisions are intended to prevent government officials and cadres from converting state capital to their private use through the joint-stock vehicle.[53] Article 81 thus provides that in restructuring state-owned enterprises into joint-stock companies, it shall be illegal to convert state-owned assets into shares and sell them off at unreasonably low prices or distribute them *gratis* to individuals.

Reduction of capital

4-1009 A reduction of capital is permitted with a two-thirds majority vote by the shareholders. But no court sanction is required.[54] In respect of joint stock companies, article 149 specifically prohibits the company from acquiring its own shares except for the purpose of reducing its capital or merging with other companies. Neither shall the company accept its own shares as security for a loan. For cases of reduction of capital or merger with another company, the Company Law provides for creditors of the company to be notified to enable them to claim full repayment of the debts or obtain suitable guarantees.[55] The reduction of capital and merger are the only clear instances where creditors are protected under Chinese law.

---

50 Articles 24 and 80 of the Company Law.
51 For convenience, this practice is termed as the 'first to contribute' principle; see above n 44.
52 For a general discussion of this doctrine, see Paul L Davies, *Gower's Principles of Modern Company Law* (Sweet & Maxwell, 1997) chapter 11.
53 In a recent incident, the Taiyuan Small Commodities Wholesale Market established by the Shanxi Jin'an Chemical Plant illegally converted into a joint stock company and issued some of its assets in the form of shares to individuals. The relevant authorities investigated the illegal conversion and found that the market's assets (worth some Rmb 2.15 million) were state assets and had been diverted out of the control of the state without proper authorization; see *China Daily* 2 June 1995, p 5.
54 In most common law jurisdictions, a reduction of capital requires court sanction; see Paul L Davies, *op cit*, chapter 28.
55 Articles 184 and 186 of the Company Law.

Distribution of profits

4-1010 Next, when might dividends be distributed? Generally, dividends must be distributed out of available profits to prevent a return of capital to shareholders.[56] Article 177 may arguably support this view. It stipulates that profits may only be distributed to shareholders out of the balance available after they have been used to make up the company's losses and allocations have been made to the statutory reserve and welfare funds. But it can be equally contended that this accords more with the objective of encouraging self-accumulation rather than for the protection of creditors. The company is obliged to contribute 10% of its profits annually to a reserve fund to be used for the purposes of expanding the company's capital and operations until the fund reaches 50% of its registered capital. The provisions are unclear and inchoate and thus cannot support a coherent doctrine of the maintenance of capital to protect creditors.

Dynamics of internal governance

4-1011 The main object of corporatization was to deepen the 'separation of administration from management' concept. It was intended to take the state sector reform a step further by converting the state from a sovereign with plenary powers to a corporate shareholder, so that the state's power of unbridled or *ad hoc* intervention in the affairs of business would be curtailed. Secondly, it hopes to redress the problem of managerial abuse and excesses under earlier legislation.

4-1012 Under the Company Law, the shareholders' meeting is declared to be the 'highest power organ' in the enterprise. Unlike the Enterprise Law which bestows managerial power solely on the factory director, managerial power under the Company Law is fragmented among the shareholders' meeting, board of directors, board of supervisors and the general manager.

4-1013 Shareholders of Chinese companies wield an extraordinary array of powers. They are entitled to call for meetings, to elect and dismiss directors and members of the supervisory board, set their salaries and consider their reports. They have the right to inspect financial reports, to decide on the issuance of additional shares and to vote on fundamental changes such as mergers, dissolution and liquidation.[57] In addition, shareholders in China possess managerial powers well beyond those of their Western counterparts. They are entitled to decide the policy of management, business and investment

---

56 Paul L Davies, *op cit*, chapter 12.
57 These rights are comparable to those given to shareholders in common law jurisdictions.

plans, approve the budget and the plan of distribution of profits and recovery of losses and the issuance of company bonds.[58]

4-1014   China adopted the two-tier board structure consisting of the board of directors and supervisory board. The model is closest to the German one. The board of directors enjoys the usual gamut of managerial powers comparable to its Western counterpart.[59] A limited liability company may have three to 13 directors on its board. Where the company is formed by two or more state-owned enterprises, it must have on its board representatives democratically elected by its workers.[60] Small limited liability companies may have a single executive director instead who may double up as the manager.[61] Each term of office is three years.[62] A joint stock company may have between five and 19 directors on its board.

4-1015   The board's powers are in theory held in check by the supervisory board which is supposed to be the watchdog over management. In addition, the board must obtain workers' input before making certain decisions affecting their welfare. Only large limited liability companies and joint stock companies need to establish a supervisory board.[63] First, the supervisory board polices the directors and managers to ensure that they carry out their duties in accordance with the articles of association and state laws and regulations. They have the right to inspect the financial affairs of the company, propose the holding of special and interim shareholders' meetings and instruct directors or managers to rectify any act harmful to the interest of the company.[64] Its members may attend meetings of the board of directors in a non-voting capacity. The supervisory board shall compose of at least three members, each with a term of three years, comprising representatives of the shareholders and workers in a ratio to be determined by the articles of association.[65]

4-1016   Second, the workers theme prevalent in the Enterprise Law persists into the Company Law, *albeit* on a 'softer' note. Workers have no voting rights although a company must 'hear the opinions' of the

---

58   Articles 38 and 103 of the Company Law. One commentator has opined that the extensive powers accorded to Chinese shareholders are consistent with the overall approach to reforming state-owned enterprises, which is that the state as the largest shareholder will exert ultimate control of the productive enterprises; see Robert C Ark and Minkang Gu, 'China Incorporated: The First Corporation Law of the People's Republic of China' (1995) *Yale Journal of International Law* 273 at pp 274–275.

59   Articles 46 and 112 of the Company Law.

60   Article 45 of the Company Law.

61   Article 51 of the Company Law.

62   Articles 47 and 115 of the Company Law.

63   Articles 52 and 124 of the Company Law.

64   Articles 54 and 126 of the Company Law.

65   Articles 52 and 124 of the Company Law. The German model prescribes that between one-third and one-half of the supervisory positions must go to workers.

workers and their unions before making any decision affecting their personal interests such as wages, welfare benefits, labour insurance and major issues concerning production and operation.[66] Workers and their unions may attend directors' meetings but in a non-voting capacity. If a company is formed by two or more state-owned enterprises, the board of directors must include democratically elected workers' representatives.[67]

4-1017 Directors, supervisors and managers owe fiduciary duties to the company. The Company Law provides that they shall abide by the articles of association, faithfully perform their duties and protect the interests of the company. They shall not take advantage of their positions to seek private gains for themselves.[68] They shall not misappropriate company funds, accept bribes or appropriate company assets as their own or disclose any company secrets. To prevent any conflict of interest situations from arising, directors and managers shall not engage in the same line of business as their company's, nor shall they conclude any contracts or business with the company unless it is provided in the articles of association or approved by the shareholders' meeting.[69]

FROM ENTERPRISES TO CORPORATIONS 'WITH CHINESE CHARACTERISTICS'

'Corporate veil' concept

4-1101 The 'corporate veil' concept of the company as a distinct legal person in its own right, separate and distinct from its shareholders and even from its directors, and with its own rights and obligations underpin the entire basis of company law in most common law jurisdictions. It is the exception, rather than the rule, for this corporate veil to be pierced so that shareholders and directors can be held personally liable for what the company has done. This notion of artificial personality is only partially adopted in China. First, under the Enterprise Law, state-owned enterprises are not true legal persons. The Company Law bridged this gap by providing that a company enjoys the rights and liabilities of a legal person in regard to its property.[70] It bestows true corporate legal personality on Chinese companies. It also provides that shareholders enjoy limited liability in proportion to their capital contributions.

---

66 Articles 55 and 56 of the Company Law.
67 Article 45 of the Company Law. The number of such worker directors is unclear.
68 Article 59 of the Company Law.
69 Article 61 of the Company Law.
70 Articles 4 and 5 of the Company Law.

4-1102   But the 'corporate veil' rhetoric is not relevant in China as it is a common theme in the Company Law to hold shareholders, promoters and officers who are directly responsible for breaches of the Company Law personally responsible for the wrongful acts.[71]

'Legal representative'

4-1103   The Company Law weaves the distinctively Chinese concept of the 'legal representative' (*fading daibiaoren*) into the Western doctrine of corporate personality to create another channel of corporate responsibility. The legal representative is usually the Chairman of the board of directors or the President, or the executive director in smaller limited liability companies. Under Chinese law, the legal representative is authorized to act and contract on behalf of the company and binds the company to his acts.[72] He is like an agent. Most importantly, the legal representative is liable to administrative penalties for the company's misconduct, as for example where the company conducts its business beyond its authorized scope, conceals facts from the authorities, or hides property to evade the repayment of debts.[73] He is, however, not personally liable for the debts of the company but may face administrative sanctions as mentioned above and even criminal prosecution if the offence constitutes a crime.

Stringent capital requirements

4-1104   Stringent capital requirements exist for the formation of a company in China. Basically, capital contributions must have been paid in full before the company can be registered to commence business. There is no general principle of maintenance of capital for the protection of creditors. Rather capital is protected to encourage self-accumulation and prevent illegal pilfering by cadres. Third, management power is fragmented among the shareholders, board of directors, supervisory board and the workers. The dynamics of such a power structure is unclear although one commentator has suggested that the board of directors would wield the lion share of the management powers with the supervisory board and workers playing passive roles.[74]

---

71   Articles 208 to 214 of the Company Law.
72   Article 43 of the General Principles of the Civil Law of the PRC.
73   Article 49 of the General Principles of the Civil Law of the PRC.
74   Willaim H Simon, 'The Legal Structure of the Chinese "Socialist Market Enterprise"' (1996) 21 *The Journal of Corporation Law* 267 at pp 290–291.

CRITICAL PROBLEMS

Deadlock

Conflicts between shareholders

4-1201 Suppose Z company, an equity joint venture (EJV) in China, has two shareholders: Mr Wang who holds 60% of the registered capital and Mr Hong who holds 40% of the registered capital. Mr Hong wants to transfer his interest to a third party but Mr Wang does not agree. As a result, Mr Hong instructs his directors not to attend the company's board meetings. Because of this, the company cannot validly hold its board meetings as it cannot attain the two-thirds quorum. As a result, the board of directors cannot validly pass any resolution. Can Mr Wang or Mr Hong unilaterally petition to dissolve the company in the face of this deadlock?

4-1202 It is common to find in Western legal systems a right for shareholders to petition the court to resolve a deadlock on the grounds of oppression, or a fraud committed on the company. In China, no such right is to be found in the joint venture laws or in the Company Law.

Shareholder's or director's failure or refusal to co-operate

4-1203 Article 43 of the Company Law provides that minority shareholders holding one-quarter or more of the voting rights, or one-third or more of the directors or supervisors may call for interim shareholders' meetings. If the board, dominated by the controlling shareholder, *expressly* refuses to call the meeting or simply fails to respond to the proposal for a meeting, the minority shareholder may enforce this statutory right in court. But the right is simply to convene a meeting. During the meeting, a deadlock would still occur. What then are the rights of the minority shareholders? Clearly, they have no right to unilaterally petition for a dissolution of the company.

4-1204 In respect of FIEs, article 35 of the EJV Implementing Regulations provides that a board of directors' meeting may be held only if two-thirds of the directors are present. This enables a shareholder to sabotage board meetings by a simple refusal or failure to attend the meetings. This would cause a deadlock as the board of directors is the highest authority for an EJV. There is no provision for a shareholders' meeting. This shortcoming has been addressed in the CJV Implementing Regulations. Article 28 provides that a director must attend a meeting or appoint a proxy. If he fails to do either of the two things, he shall be presumed to have attended the meeting and abstained from voting. This solves the two-thirds quorum requirement for board meetings. But the problem still remains for EJVs.

Deadlock in a share transfer

4-1205   Under the joint venture laws, a transfer of registered capital to a third party is subject to the unanimous consent of the other party to the joint venture. What is the position if the other joint venture partner refuses to consent to the transfer or simply ignores the transferring party's notice for consent? There is simply nothing that the transferring party can do in the circumstances. He is caught in the deadlock.

4-1206   The Company Law, contemplating such a situation, provides that shareholders that disapprove of a proposed transfer shall purchase the capital to be assigned. If such capital is not purchased, the transfer shall be deemed to have been agreed to (article 35). This would solve the deadlock alluded to above. But this provision itself creates problems: firstly, under what price and conditions shall the dissenting shareholder purchase the capital? Secondly, what if more than one shareholder disagree with the proposed transfer? Are the dissenting shareholders to purchase the capital in equal portions, or *pro rata*, ie in accordance to the ratio of their capital contributions? Thirdly, can article 35 apply to an EJV caught in a deadlock in the context of a share transfer? Article 18 of the Company Law provides that the Company Law shall apply to limited liability companies with foreign investment. But where the joint venture laws have different provisions, those different provisions shall apply. It is unclear whether article 23 of the EJV Implementing Regulations which calls for a unanimous consent for an assignment of registered capital to a third party is a *different provision* so that it applies to the exclusion of article 35 of the Company Law. Or can we argue that article 35 of the Company Law should apply *vide* article 18 of the Company Law?

Protection of minority interests

4-1207   Can a minority shareholder in a limited liability company stop a majority shareholder from undertaking any actions that may cause harm or jeopardize his interests? The answer is in the negative.

4-1208   The Company Law contains no provisions for the protection of minority shareholders. In this regard, the joint venture laws fare better. In a joint venture, the directors are appointed to the board by the investing parties in accordance with the ratio of their capital contributions. Directors vote by head (ie each has a single vote) not by the number of shares they represent. The board of directors is the highest authority for the joint venture. Thus, in this sense, the minority shareholder's rights and interests are protected. In contrast, minority shareholders do not have a right under the Company Law to appoint a minimum number of directors to the board of directors or board of supervisors. Thus, the board of directors would be dominated by directors representing the majority shareholders. Even at the highest authority, ie the shareholders' meeting, voting is conducted by the number of shares held by the shareholder, not by head. Thus, a majority shareholder will again dominate the shareholders' meeting. The Company Law does not address this problem.

Directors' fiduciary duties

4-1209 As mentioned earlier, directors owe fiduciary duties to the company. These fiduciary duties are comparable to those established under Western legal systems. But the problem is that the Chinese legal system lacks a body of laws and practices to determine the operating standard for fiduciary duties. For example, what is the standard of 'loyalty' and 'honesty' required under Chinese laws? In contrast, Western legal systems have developed a body of well-reasoned case law on the standards and ambits of a director's fiduciary duty to the company.

Limited business purpose

4-1210 Under Chinese law, the business purpose, coverage and pattern must be clearly stated in the business licence. This means that if a company in China whose registered business purpose is in the manufacture and sale of soft drinks, wants to diversify its business operations to selling beer, it cannot do so even if it can effect a change in the articles of association. This is in sharp contrast to corporations in Western legal systems where they can engage in any 'lawful business' as set out in the articles of association. And these articles of association are often couched in general terms. In China, a limited business purpose must be selected at the time of incorporation. Broad and general business purposes are not allowed in China, and registration will be refused.

4-1211 This practice harks back to the planned economic era, where a factory or company functioned as a unit of a larger system, and was therefore only authorized to act within a very narrow area. A company was intended to play its assigned role rather than to pursue profits. But in a market-oriented economic system, this rigidity will not only produce uncertainty in business transactions and impede a company's autonomy of contracts, but it will also affect a company's ability to maximize its profits.

An unco-operative legal representative

4-1212 Under Chinese law, if a legal representative disagrees with the decision of the board of directors, can the board of directors go ahead with the necessary resolutions and authorize the Vice-

Chairman to deal on behalf of the company? The answer is a resounding no.

4-1213   Unlike Western corporations, where the directors or an officer of the corporation may act on behalf of the corporation, a Chinese company may only act through its legal representative. In China, a legal representative is a natural person authorized by the law (not by the board of directors or shareholders) to act on behalf of the company and bind the company. In other words, once a person is properly appointed as the Chairman of the board of directors, he automatically becomes the legal representative if he is approved by the SAIC. He has the authority to bind the company even in the face of an opposing resolution by the board of directors or shareholders. This gives the shareholder who has the authority to appoint the Chairman of the board of directors tremendous power and advantage over the other shareholders. Presumably the majority shareholder would have the right to appoint the Chairman and if so, the legal representative of the company.

4-1214   The legal representative concept may work well in a state-owned enterprise where the state is the sole owner, and there are no unequal shareholders' rights to contend with. But in a market-oriented economic system where companies ought to be controlled by the shareholders according to their ratio of registered capital contribution, the legal representative concept is unworkable. There appears to be a legislative trend to dilute the legal representative concept in China. In recent legislation, the terms 'responsible person' and 'directly responsible persons' have been used.

Certificates of capital contribution

4-1215   Under the 'first to contribute' principle, the registered capital of a Chinese company must be actually and fully contributed to the account of the company before the SAIC issues the requisite registration approval. This is different from the 'stated capital' of companies in many Western countries. Under the joint venture laws, the joint venture partners have a time schedule to contribute their registered capital. This has been discussed in chapter 2.

4-1216   The problem that arises is that in China, it is easy to obtain a false 'Certificate of Capital Contribution Examination'. This Certificate, which must be issued by a qualified accounting institution, has been routinely issued for a fee even when the accounting firm has not verified the company's bank records. Secondly, in spite of the prohibition against withdrawal by shareholders of their capital contributions after registration of the company, it is common practice in China that investors withdraw their capital contributions after obtaining registration and the company is left to rely on loans.

Distribution of profits

4-1217 In China, profits may only be distributed to shareholders out of the 'accumulated retained earnings'. In other words, after-tax profits may not be distributed to shareholders. Under the Company Law, a company is required to contribute 10% of its profits to a reserve fund annually to be used for the company's expansion until the fund reaches 50% of its registered capital. In addition, the company must also contribute 5% to 10% of its profits into a 'mandatory public welfare fund'. Under the joint venture laws, allocations must be made to a 'reservation fund', an 'employee bonus and welfare fund' and an 'enterprise development fund', with the percentages to be decided by the board of directors.

4-1218 These mandatory fund contributions fetter the share-holders' autonomy to distribute profits, reinvest or repatriate their investments. In fact, it is the common complaint of foreign investors that they face difficulty in repatriating their profits and investments out of China to their home country.

Restrictions on foreign investors' ability to establish wholly-owned subsidiaries

4-1219 Can a wholly foreign-owned enterprise (WFOE) in China, due to its expanding business, incorporate wholly-owned subsidiaries in other major cities in China? Again, the answer is in the negative, although it is commonly practised by multi-nationals and permitted in most countries.

4-1220 Under Chinese law, a WFOE is a domestic Chinese company. To establish a limited liability company, the WFOE has to partner another shareholder. This is because the Company Law does not allow a company to be invested by a single shareholder unless it is a wholly state-owned company. No official legislative explanation has ever been offered for this quirk in the Company Law. One possible reason is that the NPC is afraid of Chinese nationals or companies misusing the limited liability vehicle to commit fraud.[75]

4-1221 Clearly, the solution lies in educating the Chinese populace about the legal implications of terms such as 'Co', 'Ltd' and so on, rather than a blanket prohibition against formation of such companies by Chinese nationals and companies, which unfortunately include a WFOE, EJV or CJV. The legal impediment will stymie China's bid to win big and strong multi-nationals to invest within its shore.

---

75 It was found that in the early days of the 'open door' policy, some unscrupulous Chinese businessmen had used the labels 'Co' and 'Ltd' to commit fraud as these labels used to signify in the planned economic era that the company was owned by the state and were thus symbols of trustworthiness.

FORMALITIES AND PROCEDURES

4-1301   Finally, we will look at some practical issues that should be considered by the foreign investor registering a company in China, such as the protection of business names and the use of signatures, seals and powers of attorney.

Business names

Right to use a business name

4-1302   Chinese law provides that a legal person enjoys the right to use a business name after it has been examined, approved and registered. The 1991 Administration of the Registration of Enterprise Names Provisions established a first-to-file system whereby prior registration of a business name would block the subsequent registration of the same or similar business name.

4-1303   On 8 December 1999, the SAIC issued the Administration of Registration of Enterprise Names Implementing Procedures (the 'Procedures') (effective 1 January 2000) to unify the guidelines for business name registration.[76] The Procedures prescribe the formalities for the registration of business names in China. As far as FIEs are concerned, the SAIC had suspended the registration of the foreign language name of the FIE. The Procedures reaffirm the position that FIEs need not seek approval for the registration of their foreign language name. The FIE must, however, seek approval for registration of its Chinese name. If the foreign language name of the FIE is a trade or service mark, it would be prudent to register them as such in China.

Minimum conditions for registration

4-1304   The Procedures stipulate that a business name shall compose of:

Administrative Region + Trade Name + Industry + Organization.

FIEs often seek to omit the relevant administrative region from their business name to signify the company as an international rather than a local Chinese company. Such omission is permitted if approved by the SAIC. To obtain such approval, the FIE must have been approved by the State Council, be registered with the SAIC and has a registered capital of not less than Rmb 50 million.

4-1305   The Procedures further prohibit the use of words such as 'China', 'National', 'State' or 'International' unless the enterprise is

---

76   An English translation of the Procedures and a commentary can be found in *China Law & Practice* April 2000 pp 34–45 and 31–33 respectively.

established by the State Council. The only exception is when a WFOE uses the word 'China' in the body of its name.

4-1306 The rest of the provisions in the Procedures are concerned with establishing the rules for the registration of business names as well as setting out a procedure for challenging registrations of the same or similar names.

Signatures, seals and powers of attorney

4-1307 Although contracts in China can be made orally, it is always preferable to ink the contract in writing when dealing with Chinese entities. It is common in China for a legal person such as an EJV, CJV, WFOE or a foreign invested limited liability company or joint stock foreign invested company to acquire and use a company seal when executing any formal documents.

4-1308 To have a seal made, the legal person must apply to the registration organ. The registration organ only permits an enterprise to make one legal person seal. Chinese regulations provide that the leaders of the legal person shall strictly supervise the application for and use of seals. A Supreme Court Explanation (1987) entitled Explanations Concerning Application of the Economic Contract Law in Deciding Economic Contract Disputes provides that even though a person does not have a formal power of attorney and does not possess the qualifications of an authorized agent, the other contracting person may view him as an authorized agent by his act of signing the contract with the legal person seal.

4-1309 It is further provided that the legal representative of a legal person shall register his handwritten signature with the registration organ. Upon registration, the legal representative shall be authorized to sign any documents on behalf of the legal person.

4-1310 Legal persons may also empower certain persons to sign contracts or documents on its behalf by virtue of a power of attorney. Chapter IV section 2 of the GPCL lays down the basic rules governing the relationship between a principal and an agent. These rules will apply when a legal person such as a FIE appoints an agent to perform acts on its behalf through a power of attorney.

CONCLUSION

4-1401 It is again clear that China's corporation laws cannot be understood without looking at the broader social, economic context and political ideology that underpin the development of those laws. A cursory comparison between the Chinese Company Law and Western company laws would show similarities at the surface, but a deeper analysis would leave one to conclude that China's Company Law is indeed uniquely Chinese, what one would term as 'with Chinese characteristics'. Thus, concepts of legal personality, limited liability, registered capital, maintenance of capital, fiduciary duties and so on have to be understood in the light of China's socialist legal tradition even though some of these concepts may have been borrowed from the West.

REFERENCES AND FURTHER READING

Books

Feng Chen, *Economic Transition and Political Legitimacy in Post-Mao China: Ideology & Reform* (State University of New York Press, 1995).

Paul L Davies, *Principles of Modern Company Law* (Sweet & Maxwell, 1997).

Nigel Graham Maw and Alison Alsbury (eds), *Maw on Corporate Governance* (Dartmouth Publishing Co Ltd, 1994).

Wang Guiguo, *Wang's Business Law of China* (Butterworths Asia, 1996).

Articles

Robert C Ark and Minkang Gu, 'China Incorporated: The First Corporation Law of the People's Republic of China' (1995) 20 *Yale Journal of International Law* 273.

Matthew D Bersani, 'Privatization and the Creation of Stock Companies in China' (1993) 3 *Columbia Business Law Review* 301.

Howard Chao and Yang XiaoPing, 'The Reform of the Chinese System of Enterprise Ownership' (1987) 23 *Stanford Journal of International Law* 365.

Daniel C K Chow, 'An Analysis of the Political Economy of China's Enterprise Conglomerates: A Study of the Reform of the Electric Power Industry in China' (1997) 28 *Law and Policy in International Business* 383.

TingMei Fu, 'Legal Person in China: Essence and Limits' (1993) 41 *The American Journal of Comparative Law* 261.

Chuan Roger Peng, 'Limited Liability in China: A Partial Reading of China's Company Law of 1994' (1996) 10 *Columbia Journal of Asian Law* 263.

William H Simon, 'The Legal Structure of the Chinese "Socialist Market Enterprise"' (1996) 21 *The Journal of Corporation Law* 267.

Preston M Tobert, 'China's Evolving Company Legislation: A Status Report' (1993) 14 *Northwestern Journal of International Law and Business* 1.

Wang Liming and Liu Zhaonian, 'On the Property Rights System of the State Enterprises in China' (1989) 52.3 *Law and Contemporary Problems* 19.

Kenneth T K Wong and Zhonglan Huang, 'A Critical Analysis of the Law of the People's Republic of China on Industrial Enterprises Owned by the Whole People' (1990) 7 *Pacific Basin Law Journal* 180.

Guanghua Yu, 'The Relevance of Corporate Governance Studies for China' (1997) 8 *Australian Journal of Corporate Law* 49.

Anyuan Yuan, 'Foreign Direct Investments in China – Practical Problems of Complying with China's Company Law and Laws for Foreign-Invested Enterprises' 20 *Northwestern Journal of International Law and Business* 475.

Jim JinPeng Zhang and Jung Y Lowe, 'Foreign Investment Companies Limited by Shares: The Latest Chinese Organization for Major International Ventures' (2001) 21 *Northwestern Journal of International Law and Business* 409.

Zhao Zhongfu, 'Enterprise Legal Persons: Their Importance Status in Chinese Civil Law' (1989) 52.3 *Law and Contemporary Problems* 1.

Henry R Zheng, 'Business Organization and Securities Law of the People's Republic of China' (1988) 43 *The Business Lawyer* 549.

CHAPTER 5

Chinese Contract Law

Tan Lay Hong

INTRODUCTION

Historical background of Chinese contract law

5-101   Like many other areas of law in China, Chinese contract law was and continues to be shaped by the economic reform policy of the government. From the founding of the Republic in 1949 to the 'open-door' policy in 1979, China's contract law system was based on the planned model. The decision-making power for the production and allocation of resources and commodities was concentrated in the hands of the state, with the exception of certain currency-commodity goods and services.[1] Within such a planned system, the role of contract law was very limited.

5-102   Early PRC legislation on contract law subjected a great number of contracts to state planning with the exception of contracts for personal consumption items in cities and towns and for mutual assistance in the construction of houses in the rural communities. Such contracts were largely governed by custom.

5-103   Contract law development in the 1960s was just as bland. In addition, the Cultural Revolution (1966–76) precipitated the complete collapse of whatever rudimentary contract law system that could be said to exist then.

MODERN CONTRACT LAW OF CHINA

The Economic Contract Law 1981

Definition of an economic contract

5-201   Modern contract law in China can be traced to the seminal Economic Contract Law (ECL) that was passed by the National People's Congress (NPC) on 13 December 1981. The ECL espoused the concept of 'economic contract' (*jingji hetong*) which originated from

---

1   Although the state planned production of most end goods and services, certain goods and services were, however, not directly allocated to the individuals but were exchanged through the medium of money on the market.

the former Soviet Union. In contrast to economic contracts, there were the non-economic contracts, namely civil contracts (*mingshi hetong*). Civil contracts basically dealt with consumer transactions while economic contracts governed transactions relating to productive resources.

5-202   Article 2 of the ECL provided that an economic contract was 'an agreement between legal persons to fulfil certain economic goals and to determine the rights and obligations of both sides'. The scope of the ECL was narrow as it applied only to contracts made between legal persons such as firms, companies or corporations, and was intended to apply to contractual relationships among state-run enterprises, collective-run enterprises and joint-venture enterprises. The feature of state planning remained strong in the ECL.

Contracts governed by the ECL

5-203   Article 8 of the ECL enumerated a list of contracts that were governed by the law. They were contracts for purchase and sale, construction projects, processing and assembling, goods and transportation, electricity, storage, loans, property leases, property insurance and other economic contracts. The State Council further enacted a series of detailed regulations to supplement the ECL on these listed contracts.

5-204   As China accelerated its reform to become a more market-oriented economy, it became clear that the 1981 ECL was inadequate to cope with the rapid changes. Domestic private individuals and foreign investors were allowed to participate in the production process. For this reason, the ECL was substantially amended in 1993. The amendment enlarged the scope of its application to households, ie private enterprises. The ECL was amended to apply to a contract where both parties were either legal persons, other economic organizations, individual economic households (*getihu*) or rural lease-holding households (*nongchunchengbao jinnyunhu*). In addition, article 4, which provided that an economic contract shall meet the requirements of the state policy or plan, was deleted in the 1993 amendments. Article 7 which provided that any contract that is inconsistent with the state plan and policy shall be void, was also deleted.

5-205   Contracts that were not governed by the ECL included ordinary consumer contracts where a party acquires goods and services for personal consumption; foreign economic contracts where one of the parties is a foreigner; and technology contracts, where the subject-matter of the contract is the development, transfer, consultation or service of technology.

Planned model under the ECL

5-206 Despite the 1993 amendments, the ECL still possessed features of the planned economy. Economic contracts governed by the ECL were subject to severe governmental intervention (article 11). If an economic contract was intended to harm the state or society, the properties these parties had acquired or may have acquired under the contract would be confiscated and put into the state treasury.

5-207 The ECL eclectically adopted Western contract doctrines such as good faith and mutual assent. The ECL stressed the need for writing in contracts to prevent fraud and bad faith. It required that all transactions be in writing or evidenced in writing, except for face-to-face contracts that were to be completed at once.

5-208 Economic contracts had to be concluded in accordance with the laws and administrative regulations. Article 4 provided that no work unit or individual may use contracts to carry out illegal activities, disrupt the social and economic order, harm the state interest or the public interest or seek illegal revenues. In concluding an economic contract, the parties must implement the principles of equality and mutual benefit, and achieve agreement through consultation. No party may impose its will on the other party, and no work unit or individual may illegally interfere in the contract (article 5).

The General Principles of Civil Law 1986

What is a civil contract

5-209 On the other hand, civil contracts relate to personal consumption, barter, gifts, agency or trust. They were governed by the General Principles of Civil Law (GPCL) 1986. The GPCL contains only a few provisions on contract. Article 85 defines a contract as 'an agreement whereby the parties establish, change or terminate their civil relationship'. In other words, a contract is made when the parties carry out a civil act.

5-210 A civil act shall meet the following requirements (article 55):

(a)   the actor has relevant capacity for civil conduct;

(b)   the intention expressed is genuine; and

(c)   the act does not violate the law or public interest.

5-211 Unlike the ECL which emphasized the written form, a contract governed by the GPCL may be in oral or other form. Making a civil contract is a civil activity and shall meet the following requirements:

(a)   it shall be made and carried out in accordance with the principles of voluntariness, fairness, exchange of equivalent values, honesty and good faith;

(b) it must be in conformity with the law; or where there is no provision of law, the activities must be in conformity with state policy;

(c) civil activities must be in accordance with social morality. They must not harm the public interest, undermine the state plan, or disrupt the economic order.

List of civil contracts that are void

5-212 Article 58 sets out a list of civil acts (ie civil contracts) that are void:

(a) those performed by a person without capacity for civil conduct;[2]

(b) those performed by a person with limited capacity for civil conduct[3];

(c) those performed by a person against his true intentions as a result of cheating, coercion or exploitation of his unfavourable position by the other party;

(d) those that are performed through malicious collusion to injure the interest of the state, a collective or third party;

(e) those that violate the law or public interest;

(f) economic contracts that violate the state's mandatory plans; and

(g) those that are performed under the guise of a lawful act to conceal an illegal purpose.

Implied terms

5-213 The GPCL sets out some implied terms in article 88. Article 88 provides that if a contract contains terms that are ambiguous as to quality, time for performance, place of performance, or price, and the intended meaning cannot be determined from the other relevant terms of the contract, and if the parties cannot reach an agreement through consultation, the following provisions shall apply:

(a) If the quality requirements are unclear, state quality standards shall apply; if there is no relevant state standard, the generally held standards shall apply.

(b) If the time for performance is unclear, the debtor may at his convenience fulfil his obligations towards the creditor; the

---

2   Under the GPCL, a citizen over the age of 18 shall be an adult with full civil capacity for civil conduct. A person who has reached the age of 16 but not over 18 and whose main source of income is his own labour shall be regarded as a person with full capacity for civil conduct (article 11).

3   Under the GPCL, a minor over the age of 10 shall be a person with limited capacity for civil conduct. A minor under the age of 10 shall be a person with no capacity for civil conduct (article 12).

creditor may also demand at any time that the debtor perform his obligations, but sufficient notice shall be given to the debtor.

(c)   If the place of performance is unclear, and the payment is cash, the performance shall be effected at the place of residence of the recipient; if the payment is other than money, the performance shall be effected at the place of residence of the obligor.

(d)   If the price agreed between the parties is unclear, the state-fixed price shall apply. If there is no state-fixed price, the price shall be based on the market price or the price of similar products or to standard remuneration for similar services.

Rescinding a contract

5-214   Under the GPCL, a party to a contract shall have a right to request a people's court or an arbitration agency to alter or rescind (ie render null and void) the contract if he has seriously misunderstood the contents of the contract, or if the contract is obviously unfair to him (article 59). The former appears to echo the common law on mistake but the latter is clearly not part of any common law doctrine.

Breach and damages

5-215   Where one party is in breach of contract, the other party shall have the right to demand performance or the taking of remedial measures and claim compensation for his losses. The compensation sought shall be equal to the losses suffered by the other party. If both parties breach the contract, each party shall bear its respective civil liability. The innocent party shall have a duty to mitigate his losses.

5-216   The parties to a contract may agree to a liquidated damages clause in the contract or a method of assessing the damages caused by the breach.

The Foreign Economic Contract Law 1985

Scope of application

5-217   The Foreign Economic Contract Law (FECL) was adopted on 21 March 1985 to safeguard the lawful rights and interests of parties to an economic contract involving foreign interests and to promote the development of China's foreign economic relations. Promoting the state plan was thus not the aim of the FECL. A striking feature of the FECL is that it followed the common law system and the United Nations Conventions on Contracts for the International Sale of Goods, (CISG) 1980 quite closely.

5-218   There was no definition of a foreign economic contract in the FECL. Instead the FECL provides that it applied to 'economic contracts   concluded   between   enterprises   or   other   economic organizations of the PRC, and *foreign* enterprises, other *foreign* economic organizations or individuals'. PRC individuals could not be parties to a foreign economic contract. It is to be noted that contracts entered into between a sino-foreign joint venture and a Chinese domestic entity were governed by the ECL and not the FECL as such a joint venture is a Chinese entity once incorporated in China.

Types of contract governed by FECL

5-219   The scope of the FECL was so broad that it virtually encompassed all kinds of commercial activities with foreign entities. It applied to contracts for the sale and purchase of goods and equipment, joint venture enterprise contracts, co-operative enterprise contracts, contracts for the co-operative exploration and exploitation of natural resources, loan contracts, leasing contracts, technology transfer contracts, project tender contracts, processing and assembling contracts, labour contracts, contracts for scientific or technical consultancy or design services, guarantee contracts, insurance contracts, storage and warehousing contracts and agency contracts.

Emphasis on writing

5-220   Like the ECL, the FECL placed great emphasis on writing. Only written contracts were valid. Contracts could be concluded through an exchange of mail, telegram or facsimile. If one party required a confirmation letter to conclude the contract, the contract would be concluded only when the letter was signed by both parties. If the contract required governmental approval, then the contract will only be formed when the approval was granted.

Terms in a foreign economic contract

5-221   In general, the FECL provided that a foreign economic contract should contain the following terms:

(a)   the corporate or personal name, nationalities and principal places of business of each party;

(b)   the date and place of the contract's signature;

(c)   the type of contract and specification of the contract subject;

(d)   the quality standard and quantity of the contract subject; the place, time and mode of performance;

(e)   the price term or payment amount; the conditions for assignment of the contract;

(f)   liability for breach of contract;

(g)   dispute settlement clause; and

(h)   the language of the contract and its legal effect.

5-222   Extolling the freedom of contract as one of its primary objectives, the FECL allowed the parties to displace any of the above stated terms by agreement. This was to be contrasted with the ECL which provided that an economic contract shall have five major terms, namely, subject-matter; quantity and quality; price or compensation; the time period, location, form of performance; and liability for breach of contract. The listing of those five major terms in an economic contract had in practice been misunderstood as meaning that the absence of any of those terms rendered the contract invalid.

5-223   Like the ECL, the FECL espoused the principle of equality and mutual benefit, and achieving agreement through consultation. A foreign economic contract must abide by the laws and must not harm the state interest and the social and public interest of the PRC (article 4). Presumably, a contract for the importation of pornographic films and materials would be invalid according to this article.

Parties may choose a governing law
5-224   Unlike the ECL, the FECL allowed the parties to a contract to choose a governing law for the contract. If the parties have not chosen a governing law, the law of the country which has the closest connection with the contract applies. This is akin to the common law position. But there is a caveat – should the application of a foreign law violate the fundamental principles of Chinese law and the social and public interests of society, the foreign law shall not be applied and the corresponding Chinese law shall be applied. The issue that arises is what happens if there is no corresponding Chinese law, what law would the Chinese court or arbitration agency then apply? It is likely that internationally accepted norms and practices would be applied in view of articles 5 and 6.

Alignment with international practice
5-225   Under the FECL, it was provided that international treaties and practices that relate to contracts may be sources of foreign economic contract law. Article 5 provided that international practice may apply in case no provision is stipulated in Chinese domestic law. In cases of conflict between an international treaty (to which China is a party) and Chinese domestic law, the provisions of the international treaty shall apply except for clauses in respect of which the PRC has declared a reservation (article 6).

The Technology Contract Law 1987
5-226   The Technology Contract Law (TCL) was promulgated on 23 January 1987 and implemented on 1 November of the same year. The Implementing Regulations were passed on 15 March 1989 and

contained much more detailed regulatory mechanisms that supplemented the general rules in the TCL.

5-227 The TCL governed technology contracts between legal persons, a legal person and a citizen, and between citizens with respect to technology development, transfer, consultation and services. It did not govern technology contracts with a foreigner. Technology contracts between a Chinese domestic entity and a foreigner were governed by the FECL and special regulations such as the Administrative Regulation on Technology Import Contracts.

5-228 One of the important issues clarified by the TCL was that an employee of a state-run enterprise who invented a new technology without any connection to his job position or without utilizing the enterprise's facilities, should own the new technology.

5-229 The ECL, FECL and TCL formed the contract law regime of China until the promulgation of the Uniform Contract Law on 15 March 1999 by the NPC.

DEFICIENCIES OF THE OLD LAW

Old law inadequate for burgeoning market economy

5-301 The old contract law regime was promulgated to cope with China's modernization plans to create a more market-oriented economy whilst retaining adherence to socialist philosophy. But as marketization gathered pace, the inadequacy of the ECL became very obvious. Hence, the major amendments carried out to the ECL in 1993. But the core problem remains — that of using socialist conceptions of contractual function to apply to more market-oriented transactions was intellectually untenable.

5-302 The inadequacy of the old contract law regime is even more pronounced in view of China's accession to the WTO. There must now be a level playing field for all participants of the Chinese economy and national treatment must be granted to locals and foreigners alike. This requirement is starkly in contradiction to the old regime composed of the ECL, FECL and TCL that segregated contracts between locals from contracts between locals and foreigners.

Different textual issues in the old law

5-303 The different textual issues made the statutes difficult to reconcile. The ECL and TCL followed the civil law tradition closely while the FECL was skewed in favour of the common law tradition and the CISG. Thus, there existed a bifurcated regime of contract law in China which could be confusing to lawyers and laymen alike.

5-304   In addition, there were substantive incongruities between the three laws. The ECL and FECL covered economic contracts while the TCL did not define the term contract all. Presumably the definition found in the GPCL could be applied. In terms of formality, the ECL allowed oral contracts if its performance was immediate. But the FECL and TCL required contracts to be in writing in order to be valid. The GPCL that governed civil contracts between Chinese individuals allowed oral contracts. The ECL did not govern contracts made by individuals while the FECL allowed foreign individuals to contract under its aegis but not Chinese individuals. The GPCL and TCL allowed Chinese individuals to be parties to a contract. Thus, some gaps existed in the old contract law regime such as the legal basis for deciding disputes in a non-economic contract involving a foreigner. For example, when a foreign individual rented a house from a Chinese citizen, which law under the old regime would apply?

Contradictions and inconsistencies in the old law

5-305   There were many contradictions and redundancies in the old contract law regime. For example, the FECL stipulated that 'a party may temporarily suspend its performance if he has conclusive evidence that the other party is unable to perform' (the so-called suspended performance doctrine under the civil law system). The ECL did not have such a provision.

5-306   The GPCL stipulated that 'civil acts (including a civil contract) should follow the principles of voluntariness, fairness, equal compensation and *good faith*'. This requirement of *good faith* (which is a civil law doctrine) was absent in the ECL and FECL which only required contracts to be made on the principles of equality, mutual assent, consultation and agreement.

5-307   The basis for liability for breach of contract was also dissimilar under the three statutes. The ECL required the party in breach to be at fault before liability could be established while the FECL and TCL used a strict liability approach.

5-308   The abovementioned problems of inconsistencies existed in the old contract law regime because of the strong influence of the executive branch on legislation. Many laws as well as administrative regulations and rules have been drafted by ministries and departments of the State Council without regard to creating a unified legal structure. Each ministry and department was only concerned to protect its own turf and self-interest.

Lack of basic rules on contract formation

5-309   Despite the promulgation of the three laws to govern contracts made in China, there existed no rules on basic issues as such contract formation. There were no rules on offer and acceptance, or what was to distinguish an offer from an invitation to treat. These gaps in the laws were filled in by the courts and resulted in much discrepancy.

5-310 Similarly, the old laws lacked any legal rules on pre-contractual liabilities. For instance, it was quite common in China that one party might accidentally or maliciously cause damage to the other party even though no contract was signed in the end. Could the injured party claim compensation in quasi-contract or tort? It was unclear.

THE UNIFORM CONTRACT LAW 1999

Legislative history

5-401 Efforts to draft a uniform contract law in China began in earnest shortly after the 1993 amendments to the ECL. In September 1993, the Legislative Affairs Committee (LAC) of the NPC began debating on a uniform contract code. The LAC solicited input from legal academics and the various ministries at state and provincial level as well as from industry experts.

5-402 Based on these discussions, a formal 'Draft' was released publicly on 7 September 1998. The proposed uniform contract law was drafted to keep in line with some of the definitions under the GPCL. For instance, the contract relationship came to be described as one entailing 'civil rights and obligations' (*minshi quanli yiwu guanxi*) rather than a creditor-debtor relationship (*zhaiquan zhaiwu guanxi*) that epitomized the economic contract concept.

5-403 The final draft of the law was passed by the Second Session of the Ninth NPC on 15 March 1999 and came into effect on 1 October of the same year. For convenience, the law will be referred to as the Uniform Contract Law (UCL) in the remainder of this chapter.

Applicability of the UCL

5-404 On 29 December 1999, the Supreme People's Court issued the Interpretation Concerning Certain Questions on the Application of the Contract Law (Interpretation). The Interpretation clarified that as a general rule, the old law applies to contracts entered into *before* the promulgation of the UCL. The UCL applies to contracts made on or *after* its promulgation on 15 March 1999. Only when the old law does not have provisions on a legal issue would the UCL apply. There are, however, two exceptions: firstly, the UCL would apply to a contract made before the UCL came into force, if on an issue of performance, the contractually promised performance went beyond the date the

UCL came into force or when the performance period began after the entering into force of the UCL. Secondly, if an issue of validity of contract arises as regards a contract entered into before the UCL came into force and the old law invalidates such a contract whilst the UCL would validate it, the court must apply the UCL.

General format

5-405   The UCL contains 23 chapters and 428 articles, which are divided into three parts, namely the General Provisions (articles 1–129), Specific Provisions (articles 130–427) and Supplementary Provisions (article 428).

UCL as a uniform code

5-406   Article 1 of the UCL provides that the purpose of the law is to protect the lawful rights and interests of contracting parties, maintain social and economic order and promote socialist modernization. This essentially promotes the sanctity of contracts but within the broader context of socialist modernization. Article 2 defines a contract as 'agreements by which natural persons, legal persons and/or other organizations, as equal parties, establish, modify or terminate relationships of civil rights and obligations'. This provision adopts the GPCL's definition of a contract, and abolishes the distinction between a civil contract and an economic contract. More importantly, article 428 repealed the ECL, FECL and TCL; thus effectively abolishing the concept of a foreign economic contract, and creating a unified system of law. The UCL is a uniform code that is intended to form part of a prospective civil code.

Fifteen types of contracts governed by UCL

5-407   The Specific Provisions govern 15 types of specific contracts. They are contracts for the sale of goods, contracts for the supply of utilities, donation contracts (gifts), loan contracts, lease contracts, lease-finance contracts, processing contracts, construction project contracts, transportation contracts, technology contracts, bailment contracts, storage and warehousing contracts, entrustment contracts, commission agency contracts and brokerage contracts.

5-408   In this book, we will only look at the general principles of contract law as laid down under the General Provisions. The specific contracts will not be discussed.

Relationship with other laws

5-409   The UCL's relationship with the other laws such as the GPCL is unclear. For instance, which law should govern a contract made between Chinese citizens? The GPCL or the UCL? This question takes on significance when a contract is entered into as a result of fraud or coercion. Under article 58(3) of the GPCL, such a contract is rendered null and void. But under article 54 of the UCL, the contract is only voidable and the injured party has a right to petition the People's Court or arbitration agency to modify or rescind the contract.

5-410 Two obscure provisions in the UCL may throw some light on this issue although the provisions are problematic in themselves. Article 123 provides that 'if *other laws* make other provisions concerning a contract, those laws shall govern'. Article 124 further provides that 'if no express provision for a particular contract is made in the Specific Provision of this Law [UCL] or in other laws, the General Provisions of this Law [UCL] apply, and reference may be made to the Specific Provisions of this Law or the provisions of other law which most closely correspond to that contract'.

5-411 Article 123 is a problematic provision. Using the above example, it would appear that the GPCL would prevail over the UCL on the issue of voidability of a contract made as a result of fraud or coercion. But this would mean that the benefit of the improvements made in the UCL would not be available. It is ironic that the UCL which was heavily debated amongst academics, law enforcers and business people, and which purports to represent a unified legal regime for contract law should give way to an earlier 'non-specific' law.

5-412 Secondly, article 123 goes against the grain of a basic tenet in Chinese judicial practice that a subsequent law shall prevail over a previous law that contradicts the subsequent law. On the other hand, it may be argued that '*other laws*' meant specific laws so that only the provisions of a specific law would prevail over the UCL, ie the GPCL which is a general law will not prevail over the UCL. But if the position is indeed so, then article 123 is redundant as the relationship between a general law and specific law is well-established under Chinese judicial practice. In case of conflict or inconsistency between a general law and specific law, the specific law shall prevail.

5-413 Article 124 is another difficult provision. It provides in essence that the General Provisions of the UCL shall apply to a particular type of contract which is not dealt with in the Specific Provisions nor in any other laws. At first sight, this position is unassailable. But it appears from various sources that during the drafting of the UCL, successful lobby by state organs had resulted in specific contracts such as employment contracts, partnership contracts, deposit and settlement contracts and tourism contracts being kept out of the UCL. Seen in this light, would a Chinese court, nevertheless still apply the General Provisions of the UCL to a specific contract that had been lobbied out of the UCL?

FUNDAMENTAL DOCTRINES OF CHINESE CONTRACT LAW

5-501   Part I (articles 1–8) of the UCL lays down the fundamental doctrines of Chinese contract law. Four fundamental principles form the core of the UCL. They are: freedom to contract, equality, fairness, good faith and the fostering of contract transactions.

Freedom to contract

Voluntariness and legality

5-502   Under the rubric of freedom to contract, the UCL adopts the terminology of voluntariness and legality. Article 4 of the UCL provides that parties enjoy the legal right to voluntarily conclude contracts, and no work unit for individuals may illegally intervene therein. Article 3 further provides that contracting parties shall have equal status, and one party shall not impose his will upon the other party. This represents a significant progress and is of pivotal importance in China's transition to a market-oriented economy. These articles provide the legal means to resist intervention from the government and other administrative organs and embrace party autonomy.

Are contracts subject to government interference?

5-503   In the past, the freedom to contract doctrine was shunned by the Chinese government because it was an antithesis to communist ideology. It was unthinkable that state organs and individuals would have the freedom to enter into contracts. But in China's transition to a more market-oriented economy, it was realized that the government should encourage entrepreneurship, market transaction and competition. The history of the drafting of the UCL makes clear that the basic notion of freedom of contract is now accepted in China, although the term 'freedom to contract' was still eschewed by the authorities. There is a fear that the freedom to contract may mean something more than what the UCL intended in terms of the parties' right to make a contract. The LAC clarified that the freedom to contract referred primarily to party autonomy in making a contract and determining the terms of the contract. The concept is not absolute and generally constrained by article 7. Article 7 provides that when concluding and performing a contract, the parties shall comply with the laws and administrative regulations and respect public morals, and they may not disrupt the social and economic order or harm the public interest.

5-504   In other words, a contract must be entered into according to law. And only *unlawful interference* with the parties' freedom to contract is prohibited. This leaves a loophole large enough for any ingenious government authority (who wants to interfere with a contract) to drive a truck through.

Six aspects of 'voluntariness'

5-505   Nevertheless, most regard the term 'voluntariness'; as being equal to freedom to contract. There are six aspects to this doctrine under the UCL.

5-506   Firstly, the parties have the freedom to decide whether or not to enter into a contract. This potentially takes away the propensity of the Chinese authorities to interfere and exert undue influence on the parties' contracting power.

5-507   Secondly, the parties have the freedom to choose the other party to the contract, ie parties are free to choose their counterparts. This is important as it often happened in the past that the Chinese authorities would pre-arrange 'marriages' between the foreign investors and their domestic entities, particularly in merger and acquisition cases.

5-508   Thirdly, the parties have the freedom to determine the contents of the contract. Article 12 states that the parties shall determine the contents of the contract. It provides a list of eight items to make up the general contents of a contract. These terms include the names and domiciles of the parties, the subject-matter, the quantities, the quality, the price or remuneration, the time limit for, place and method of performance, liability for breach of contract and method of dispute resolution.

5-509   Fourthly, the parties are free to choose the contract form. Under article 10 of the UCL, the contract may be in writing, oral or other form. The term 'writing' includes electrically and electronically transmitted documents such as telegrams, telexes, facsimiles, electronic data interchange and e-mails. It would appear that electronic commerce is governed by the UCL.

5-510   Fifthly, the parties have the freedom to modify or terminate the contract. Article 77 provides that the parties may amend the terms of the contract by agreement. Article 93 similarly provides that the parties may terminate their contract by agreement. It is noteworthy that a modification of the contract under the UCL does not require consideration, unlike in most common law countries.

5-511   Sixthly, the parties have the freedom to choose the method for dispute resolution. There are four alternatives, namely, mediation, conciliation, arbitration and litigation. Most importantly, the parties are not required to seek mediation or conciliation as a first resort. They are merely encouraged to do so. Alternatively, the parties may choose to arbitrate their differences. Litigation is available as a last resort if there is no arbitration agreement or if the arbitration agreement is invalid.

Equality and mutual assent

Parties equally protected by law

5-512   Article 3 of the UCL provides that contracting parties have equal status, and one party may not impose its will upon the other. This article reflects the 'equality and mutual assent' precept under the ECL, which is now imported into the UCL. Equality means that the parties enter into the contract on an equal footing, and are entitled to equal protection of the law. Thus, the state has no right to impose its will on its counterpart. This article helps to reinforce the notion of a more limited role for the state in the economic sphere.

Consideration not required

5-513   Under the ECL, all contracts must be supported by an exchange of equivalent values. In other words, there must be sufficiency of consideration. But curiously, this requirement was left out in the UCL. As such, consideration is not required under the UCL.

Fairness

Unfair contracts are voidable

5-514   Article 5 of the UCL provides that the parties shall abide by the principle of fairness in determining the rights and obligations of the parties. Fairness is a concept relating to the moral values of a society as well as justice. Under article 59 of the GPCL, a contract that is obviously unfair to one party is voidable and the injured party may petition to the People's Court or arbitration agency to rescind the contract. This provision was, however, not present in the FECL and TCL. But an administrative regulation was issued on 19 October 1987 to extend this concept of avoiding a contract for unfairness to a foreign economic contract.

5-515   Article 54 of the UCL appears to adopt this doctrine as it stipulates, *inter alia*, that a contract that is 'clearly unconscionable to one party at the time of conclusion of the contract' is voidable. It is submitted that any contract that is unconscionable would obviously be unfair to one of the parties.

Hong Kong Co A v Chinese Import and Export Branch B
(Source: Duncan Webb, 'Towards a Contract Law of China: Some Salient Features' (1996) *Lloyd's Maritime and Commercial Law Quarterly* 245.)

A Hong Kong company agreed to purchase aluminium gauze from Branch B at a very low price. Branch B failed to perform the contract. When sued, Branch B argued that the contract had been signed by an inexperienced representative of the company by mistake, who quoted a price that was appropriate for steel gauze but not aluminium gauze. This led to manifest unfairness in the contract and Branch B should not be bound by it. Although Branch B did not succeed, it was quite clear from the judgment that an assertion of unfairness or disparity in price can be a ground for relief if good reasons are shown.

Good faith

Definition

5-516 Article 6 provides that the parties shall abide by the principle of good faith (*chengxin*) in exercising their rights and obligations. The doctrine of 'fairness' and 'good faith' are civil law concepts borrowed from the French or German law. Professor Wang Liming, who was one of the major drafters of the UCL, maintained that the principle of good faith extends to the performance of the contract as well as the formation of the contract. The principle of good faith, which literally means honesty and trustworthiness, requires the parties to conduct themselves honourably, to perform their duties in a responsible manner and not abuse their legal rights and to follow the law and common business practice.

5-517 The principle of good faith was adopted as it reflects China's traditional values under the influence of Confucianism and commercial ethics. It is also in keeping with the norms of international commercial practice. Secondly, the principle of good faith would help to foster commercial transactions. When parties abide by the principle of good faith, they will respect and execute their obligations. Even if their contract is deficient in some ways, they will endeavour to cure the defects and fulfil their obligations. It is believed that no matter how detailed and well-drafted a contract may be, a contract cannot be duly performed if the parties do not act in good faith. Conversely, if a contract is poorly drafted but the parties abide by the principle of good faith, the contract will be faithfully carried out.

5-518 Lastly, the principle of good faith will enable judges to fill in any legal loopholes or gaps, which will in turn help to develop China's legal system.

Good faith at contract formation

5-519 Even when a contract has not yet come into existence, the parties may have reached some preliminary agreement. They should thus observe some ancillary (*fusui*) duties. This encompasses the duty of loyalty. They should not, under the guise of making a contract, negotiate in bad faith in order to cause loss to the other party (article 42(1)).

> *A contract case*
> (Source: Wang Liming, 'China's Proposed Uniform Contract Code' (1999) 31 *St Mary's Law Journal* 7. Reprinted by permission of the copyright owner, St Mary's Law Journal.)
>
> In one case, a foreign investor negotiated with his Chinese partner to establish a joint venture. The parties signed a letter of intent. In a meeting, the foreign investor orally promised that if the infrastructure on a particular piece of land were ready, he would invest and sign the contract. However, after the Chinese partner had invested Rmb one million in the land for the infrastructure, the foreign investor refused to sign the contract without good reason. The foreign investor was sued for damages. The UCL would clearly provide a remedy in such circumstances.

Honesty and non-deception

5-520   In addition, they must adhere to the duty of honesty and non-deception. Article 42(2) provides that one party should not deliberately conceal an important fact relevant to the conclusion of the contract or provide false information to the other party. The sanction for a breach of article 42 is an order to pay damages to the injured party. It is clear that the common law doctrine of *caveat emptor* has no place in Chinese contract law.

Duty of confidentiality

5-521   Article 43 lays down the duty of confidentiality. It provides that trade secrets which are learned by a party during the course of negotiations may not be disclosed or improperly used, regardless of whether a contract was formed or not. If a party causes loss to the other party through the disclosure or improper use of such trade secrets, he shall pay damages to the other party.

Good faith during contract performance

5-522   Article 60 provides that the parties shall in good faith fully perform their obligations as agreed. They shall perform their obligations in accordance with the nature and objective of the contract and usage of trade, and adhere to the principle of good faith. In addition, the parties should observe various ancillary duties in the spirit of exercising good faith. For instance, if a contract is lacking in quality requirements for its subject-matter, the contractor should not, contrary to the principle of good faith, intentionally select and deliver goods and services of inferior quality.

Xinfeng Fertilizer Case
(Source: Duncan Webb, 'Towards a Contract Law of China: Some Salient Features' (1996) *Lloyd's Maritime and Commercial Law Quarterly* 245.)

A seller entered into a contract for the sale of 2,000 tons of fertilizer subject to the buyer's confirmation letter. When this did not arrive, the seller withheld dispatch of the goods and urged for a written confirmation. In response, the buyer sent a message stating 'you may send the goods'. In reliance on this, the goods were sent to the buyer. Shortly thereafter, the buyer reneged on the contract and sent a message stating 'do not send the goods'. The reason for the buyer's change of mind was because the fertilizer could be obtained at a cheaper price elsewhere. When sued, the buyer argued that there was no contract between the parties as there was no formal written confirmation letter signed by the buyer. The court held that there was clearly a contract between the parties and the lack of formality could not be used in bad faith in avoiding proper contractual obligations.

Good faith in discharging/terminating the contract

5-523 Article 92 states that after the rights and obligations of the parties under the contract have been discharged, the parties shall perform their post-contractual obligations such as giving notice, rendering assistance and maintaining confidentiality, etc in accordance with the usage of trade and adhering to the principle of good faith.

5-524 Under Chinese law and practice, a contract is viewed as a long-term commitment even if the contract is terminated or discharged by one of the parties. In mediating contractual disputes, the Chinese courts have often stressed the need for consensual resolution of the dispute and the preservation of contractual relationships. The courts will have little sympathy for parties who stand on their rights and take unilateral actions and then look to the breaching party to make up their losses. In China, the innocent party must involve the other party in solving the dispute. For instance, a buyer who receives defective goods, disposes of them and substitutes conforming goods without the consent of the seller appears unlikely to be able to claim the difference in price and losses suffered from the breaching party.

Broadcast Television Service Co v Industrial and Commercial Trade Centre
(Source: Duncan Webb: 'Towards a Contract Law of China: Some Salient Features' (1996) *Lloyd's Maritime and Commercial Law Quarterly* 245.)

The case involved a simple contract for the sale of 300 television sets by the defendant to the plaintiff. The television sets turned out to be defective, and the plaintiff attempted to negotiate with the defendant, the manufacturer and a wholesaler, for a settlment. The negotiations were not successful, and the plaintiff then sent the television sets to an official inspection authority for appraisal. The authorities confirmed that the television sets were below standard. The plaintiff then disposed of the television sets at a significantly lower price and sued the defendant for damages. One of the defendant's arguments was that the plaintiff should not have unilaterally disposed of the goods without consulting the defendant. The court agreed with the defendant and held that the plaintiff's action must fail. It laid emphasis on the fact that the plaintiff did not act in consultation with the defendant, and that the plaintiff was in breach of strict regulations as to the manner of disposal of the defective goods.

Duty to negotiate an amicable settlement

5-525   The duty to negotiate an amicable settlement of the dispute with the breaching party appears also to extend to a contract with a foreign party.

Singapore Co v Ceramics Co
(Source: Duncan Webb, 'Towards a Contract Law of China: Some Salient Features' (1996) *Lloyd's Maritime and Commercial Law Quarterly* 245.)

The plaintiff entered into a contract with the defendant for the purchase of ceramic tiles. Upon arrival, it was found that the goods did not conform to the contract in that the colour and luster were inconsistent and many of its designs were crooked. Some of the tiles were sent to the People's Insurance Company and an independent assessor for appraisal. After negotiations, the defendant agreed to make up the deficiencies in a second shipment. The second shipment never arrived and the defendant stalled the negotiations. After about six months, the plaintiff unilaterally disposed of the goods and sued the defendant. The court held that the damage appraisal was carried out unilaterally and could not bind the defendant, even though the appraisal was carried out by a Chinese representative and an independent assessor. The buyer's action therefore failed.

Good faith in contract interpretation

5-526   Article 125 provides that if a dispute arises between the parties concerning the interpretation of a clause of the contract, the court shall determine the true intention of that clause by making reference to the words and sentences used in the contract, the relevant clauses of the contract, the objective of the contract, usage of trade and the principle of good faith.

A contract case
(Source: Wang Liming, 'China's Proposed Uniform Contract Code' (1999) 31 *St Mary's Law Journal* 7. Reprinted by permission of the copyright owner, St Mary's Law Journal.)

In one case, a seller agreed to sell 30 'vehicles' loaded with sand to the buyer for construction purposes. Prior to the date of delivery, the price of sand increased dramatically and it appeared that the price increase would continue. The seller proposed to increase the price which was turned down by the buyer. The seller then delivered 30 small truckloads of sand to the buyer. The buyer refused to accept delivery arguing that they were entitled to 30 large truckloads of sand. The main issue was how to interpret the term 'vehicles' in the contract.

5-527   It is quite clear that the principle of good faith would sway the court to hold that the term 'vehicle' meant large truckloads as this was the original and true intention of the parties at the time of the contract.

Fostering transactions

Oral contracts are valid

5-528   Unlike the ECL and FECL, a contract under the UCL does not have to be in writing.[4] Oral contracts are allowed. To suit the fast pace

---

4   Under the ECL, a contract could be orally formed if it was performed immediately after formation.

of modern commercial transactions where a contract may be concluded within minutes of a telephone call or electronic message, the UCL defines 'writing' to mean 'any form which is capable of tangibly representing its contents ... and includes electronically transmitted documents'. This has the effect of fostering transactions which is in stark contrast to the previous law that invalidated oral contracts.

Acceptance of performance validates contract

5-529   In addition, where a law or administrative regulation provides that the contract shall be in writing or if the parties have agreed that their contract shall be in writing, but the parties did not do so, a contract is, nevertheless, formed if one of the parties has already performed his main obligations and the other party accepts the performance (article 36). Again, this has the effect of fostering transactions.

5-530   Similarly, if a contract is to be concluded in the form of a written instrument but one of the parties has already performed his main obligations before the signing and sealing of the instrument, a contract is formed if the other party accepts the performance (article 37).

Default clauses

5-531   Article 61 provides that after a contract is made, the parties may make further supplementary agreements on the quality, price or remuneration, place of performance, etc if such provisions are not explicitly stipulated in the original contract. Failing agreement on such supplementary provisions, the provisions shall be determined in accordance with the usage of trade. Article 62 then enumerates a list of 'default' provisions that will apply in the event that the parties cannot agree on the supplementary provisions. These 'default' provisions are as follows:

(a)   If the contract is not explicit as to the quality requirements, the quality shall accord with state or industry standards; or failing that, the customary standards or such specific standards as are consistent with the objective of the contract.

(b)   If no price or remuneration is stated in the contract, then the market price prevailing in the place of performance at the time the contract was made shall be used.

(c)   If the contract is silent as to the place of performance, and the performance is the payment of a sum of money, then payment shall be made at the place where the recipient is located. If immovable property is to be delivered, then performance shall occur at the place where the immovable property is located. For other subject matters, performance shall occur at the place where the party performing the obligation is located.

(d) If the contract is not explicit as to the time limit for performance, performance may be carried out by the obligor at any time. The obligee may also demand performance at any time provided he gave the obligor necessary preparation time to perform the obligation.

(e) If the contract did not state the method of performance, performance shall be made by a method that is conducive to attaining the objective of the contract.

(f) If the contract did not state which party shall bear the costs of performance, the costs shall be borne by the party performing the obligation.

CONTRACT FORMATION

Offer

What is an offer

5-601   The UCL for the first time lays down a set of rules on offer and acceptance. The provisions on offer and acceptance appear to draw heavily from the common law and civil law traditions. The CISG also had significant influence on the UCL with respect to the offer and acceptance provisions.

5-602   Article 14 of the UCL defines an offer as 'a party's declaration of his intent to conclude a contract with another party'. Its content must be specific and definite and it shall indicate that the offeror will be bound by it upon its acceptance by the offeree. Article 15 makes a distinction between an offer and an invitation to treat. It states that an invitation to treat is 'a party's declaration of his intent to have another party make him an offer'. Delivered price lists, auction announcements, tenders, share prospectuses and commercial advertisements are invitations to treat. However, commercial advertisements may also be offers depending on the contents (article 15). Unilateral offers are not explicitly dealt with in the UCL although the drafters of the UCL may have had unilateral offers in mind when they drafted article 15 which provides that commercial advertisements may also be offers.

Offer must be communicated

5-603   An offer becomes effective (ie communicated) when it reaches the offeree. As regards offers made by electronic means, the UCL follows the UNCITRAL Model Law on electronic commerce. Article 16 provides that an electronic offer is communicated when it enters the recipient's designated system, or if no system is designated, the offer is deemed communicated when it first enters the recipient's systems regardless of whether the recipient has seen it or not.

Termination of an offer

5-604   An offer can be terminated by a withdrawal or revocation. A distinction is made between a withdrawal and a revocation of an offer. A withdrawal of offer takes place when the letter of withdrawal reaches the offeree before or at the same time as the offer. A revocation of offer takes place when the notice of revocation reaches the offeree before he has dispatched his acceptance. An offer may not be revoked if the offeror has indicated that he will keep his offer open for a fixed time, or that the offer is irrevocable or where the offeree has reasonable grounds to believe that the offer is irrevocable and has made preparations to perform the contract. These rules are similar to German law where an offer must remain open for acceptance for a considerable time and cannot be revoked within that period unless it is made subject to express reservations. This is unlike the common law system where an offer can be revoked at any time before acceptance unless the offeror's promise to keep his offer open is supported by consideration.

When offer becomes invalid

5-605   An offer becomes invalid in the following circumstances:

(a)   if it is rejected by the offeree;

(b)   if the offeror revokes the offer;

(c)   if the time fixed for acceptance expires without acceptance by the offeree; or

(d)   the offeree materially alters the particulars of the offer.[5]

Acceptance

What constitutes an acceptance

5-606   Article 21 defines an acceptance as 'the offeree's declaration to assent to an offer'. Acceptance may be manifested by word or deed according to the intention of the parties or by usage of trade. An acceptance shall be communicated to the offeror within the time stated in the offer. If no time is stipulated in the offer for acceptance, then if the parties are present in person, the acceptance must be communicated promptly unless otherwise agreed. In other cases where the parties are not present, the acceptance shall be communicated within a reasonable time.

Acceptance must be communicated

5-607   An acceptance is effective when it reaches the offeror. A contract is then formed at that moment. If communication of the

---

5   This reflects the common law 'mirror image' rule and article 19 of the CISG.

acceptance is not required, then a contract is formed at the moment of performance of the act signifying acceptance as required by the offeror or according to usage of trade. An acceptance by electronic form must accord with article 16 stated above.

Withdrawal of acceptance

5-608 Like the CISG, an acceptance may be withdrawn if the withdrawal notice reaches the offeror before or at the same time as the acceptance (article 27). If the offeree's acceptance is dispatched after the period of time fixed for acceptance, it constitutes a new offer unless the offeror notifies the offeree in a timely manner that he accepts the notice of acceptance. If the offeree's acceptance is dispatched within the time fixed for acceptance but is delayed due to other factors, the acceptance is effective unless the offeror notifies the offeree in a timely manner that he does not accept the acceptance due to its late arrival.

Modification of offer

5-609 An acceptance may contain non-material modifications of the offer. It is effective and the terms of the acceptance shall be taken to be the terms of the contract unless the offeror raises objections to the modifications in a timely manner. But if the offer states that an acceptance may not modify the offer, then the *'mirror image'* rule[6] applies and the acceptance may not make modifications to the offer.

Consideration

5-610 The rule on exchange of equivalent value under the previous contract laws has been abolished under the UCL. There is no requirement for consideration under the UCL.

Terms of the contract

Major terms

5-611 Article 12 provides that the particulars of the contract shall include the following terms: name, domicile of the parties; the subject-matter; the quantities; quality; price; time limit for and place and method of performance; liability for breach of contract; and method of dispute settlement. It is unclear if the absence of any of these major terms would render the contract invalid. It is submitted that in the interests of promoting and encouraging transactions as well as according freedom to contract to contracting parties, the Chinese

---

6   The 'mirror image' rule is a common law concept that means that the terms of the acceptance must correspond exactly with those stated in the offer.

courts are unlikely to invalidate a contract that is merely lacking in certain regard. This contention is supported by articles 61 and 62 which contain the gap-filling clauses that permit the parties the right to make supplemental agreements on particulars that are lacking in the original contract.

Standard form contracts, exemption and limitation clauses

5-612   Articles 39 to 41 of the UCL govern the use of standard form contracts. Article 39 defines standard form contracts as 'contracts that are formulated by one party in advance for repeated use, and which he did not negotiate with the other party when concluding the contract'. When a standard form contract is made, the party who provides the standard form contract shall abide by the principles of fairness when determining the rights and obligations of the parties, and shall, in a reasonable manner, draw the attention of the other party to the presence of any exemption or limitation clause in the contract, and if so requested, explain such clauses to the other party.

5-613   Unlike the UK Unfair Contracts Terms Act 1977 (UCTA), the UCL makes no distinction between a consumer contract and a commercial contract. It, however, incorporates the common law requirements on 'notice'. Instead of 'reasonableness', the UCL brings in the notion of 'fairness' when using standard form contracts. The UCL goes further than the UCTA in requiring the other party relying on the exemption or limitation clause to explain the meaning of such terms to the other party if requested to do so.

Contra proferentum rule

5-614   Article 41 incorporates the *contra proferentum* rule and states that in case of any ambiguity as to the meaning of a standard clause, the clause shall be interpreted against the party who drafted the clause. If there is an inconsistency between a standard clause and a non-standard clause, the non-standard clause shall prevail. Furthermore, standard clauses are to be interpreted according to the usual meaning of such a clause. As such, court decisions and usage of trade and custom would be relevant.

Invalid exemption clauses

5-615   Article 53 specifically provides that exemption clauses are void if they exempt a party from liability from bodily harm caused to the other party; or if they exempt a party from liability for property losses caused to the other party either wilfully or as a result of gross negligence. In this respect, the UCL is wider than the UCTA as it disallows the exemption of liability for property losses caused by negligence. In the UCTA, losses arising from property damage may be exempted if the exemption clause is reasonable. Like the UCL, the

UCTA also disallows exemption of liability for death and personal injuries.

5-616   An important point to note is that the UCL only governs exemption and limitation clauses found in a contract. It does not extend to the use of exemption and limitation clauses in a tortious or other context.

Privity of contract

Adoption of the doctrine in UCL

5-617   According to Professor Wang Liming who was a member of the NPC that drafted the UCL, a third party who is not a party to the contract cannot enforce the contract. This is in line with the doctrine of privity of contract that existed previously under English law.[7] Wang explained that under the Chinese civil law concept of 'contract relativity', contracts are viewed as only effective between the parties which have effected them.

5-618   Articles 64 and 65 clearly state the doctrine of privity of contract. Article 64 states that if the parties have agreed that the obligor's obligations shall be performed for the benefit of a third party and the obligor fails to do so or performs in a non-conforming way, it is the obligor who is liable to the obligee, not the third party. Similarly, if the parties agree that the obligation towards the obligee shall be performed by a third party, and the third party fails to do so or performs in a non-conforming way, it is the obligor who is liable to the obligee for breach of contract.

Exceptions to the doctrine

5-619   However, it is to be noted that in the past, Chinese judicial practice has held parties who are not privy to the contract liable for damages to a contracting party. This was demonstrated by the case of *Broadcast Television Service Co v Industrial and Commercial Trade Centre* stated above. It will be recalled that the case involved the sale of 300 television sets to the plaintiff. Before the case was heard, the defendant closed down. The supervisory body of the defendant, the local Economic Planning Commission, was ordered to attend the trial. What is noteworthy was that the wholesalers of the television sets were also joined as defendants, and had actively defended themselves at the trial, even though they were not a party to the contract between the plaintiff and defendant.

---

7   In recent years, the UK has enacted legislation to confer enforceable rights under a contract to third party beneficiaries. Singapore has followed suit and enacted the Contracts (Rights of Third Parties) Act 2001 on 17 October 2001.

Hong Kong Hing Fat Trading Co v Shenyang Pharmaceutical and Health Import and Export Co
(Source: Duncan Webb, 'Towards a Contract Law of China: Some Salient Features' (1996) *Lloyd's Maritime and Commercial Law Quarterly* 245.)

This case involved a contract for the sale of two million latex surgical gloves to be delivered in instalments. There was a delay in the shipment of the first instalment of the goods and the shipping documents did not conform with the terms of the letter of credit. The parties negotiated for a reduction in price and the non-conformance was waived. A complaint then arose that the gloves were defective due to inconsistent thickness. The buyer sought to reject the goods but the seller insisted that the manufacturer was the responsible party. The court ordered that both the manufacturer and seller should compensate the buyer. The manufacturer was ordered to pay 60% of the price while the seller was only liable for incidental costs.

The two cases illustrate the fact that under Chinese law, the web of contractual relations may well spread beyond the parties to the contract. It is, however, unclear whether the past practice of holding third parties liable on a contract to which they are not parties will continue in the light of articles 64 and 65 of the UCL.

Validity of certain contracts

Contracts subject to government approval

5-620 Despite the general spirit of fostering transactions instead of invalidating contracts, the UCL still provides that contracts that are subject to government approvals will be valid only upon such approval (article 44). In addition, where the state imposes a mandatory plan, the contract shall be concluded in accordance with that plan (article 38).

5-621 During the era of the planned economy, contracts were made by the state administrative organs as part of their administrative duties. Thus, state interference in contracts tended to be excessive. Therefore many contracts were rendered void or invalid under the previous contract laws on the grounds that they violated the laws and administrative regulations. In addition, contracts that were concluded by fraud or duress, or were signed by agents without authority, were void. The scope of void contracts was too large under the previous contract laws.[8] The UCL thus attempts to limit the grounds upon which a contract can be rendered void or invalid.

Contracts made by agents without authority

5-622 The UCL also creates a category of contracts known as contracts whose validity is pending (*xiaoli daiding*). A contract pending validity means that although the contract is formed, because it does not fully comply with the relevant provisions on validity, whether it is valid will hinge on the right-holder's manifest ratification. Thus, article 47 provides that if a contract is concluded by a person with limited capacity for civil acts, the contract will be valid if it is ratified. Similarly, article 48 provides that if a contract is concluded by an agent who has no authority, or who exceeds his authority or whose authority has expired, the contract will be valid if the principal ratifies. In all cases, the other party to the contract has a right to demand ratification by the principal within one month. If the principal refuses to ratify, the contract becomes invalid, and the *bona fide* opposite party may rescind the contract by notice.

Ultra vires contracts

5-623 Article 50 provides that if a legal representative or a responsible person of a legal person or organization acts *ultra vires* when concluding the contract, the act of the legal representative is valid unless the other party knew or ought to have known that the contract was concluded *ultra vires*. At first glance, it appears that article 50 represents the abolition of the *ultra vires* rule in China. But further examination reveals that article 50 is actually concerned with 'Turquand's rule'.[9] Incidentally, article 49 incorporates the doctrine of ostensible authority.

---

8   Under the ECL, contracts that were entered into by persons that were ineligible to enter into contracts were void. These included persons who entered into a contract before obtaining a business licence, units or departments of a legal person who concluded contracts in their own name, persons who signed contracts by using another person's name without authorization, and persons who entered into contracts to conduct business beyond what was approved and registered. Under the FECL, contracts could be declared void in the following circumstances: (a) the contractual parties were not legally qualified; (b) a party in a foreign trade contract that was not granted the right to engage in foreign trade; (c) the Chinese party exceeded his registered scope of business; (d) approval of contract was not obtained when required including approval for the variation of contract; (e) contracts that were not in writing; and (f) contracts entered into by agents who had no authority or who exceeded their authority and their principals did not ratify the contract.

9   Under 'Turquand's rule', a person who deals in good faith with a company in a manner consistent with the company's public documents is entitled to rely on a presumption that all matters of internal management will comply with the said documents; see *Royal British Bank v Turquand* (1856) 6 E & B 327.

5-624   *Ultra vires* contracts were all treated as invalid under the previous contract laws. The previous laws did not consider that it would be entirely proper to validate a contract upon the principal's voluntary ratification. Neither would this violate any laws or public interest, or even state interest. On the contrary, allowing for voluntary ratification would promote more transactions that are in the contracting parties' interests and accords more free will to the parties.

PERFORMANCE OF CONTRACT

Full performance

5-701   Chinese contract law emphasizes full and actual performance of contracts (article 60). This is in line with the view held during the planned era where contracts were nothing more than administrative orders, and hence a contracting party must 'perform specifically what he had agreed' to do, no matter how impractical or costly.

Fulfilment plea

5-702   Fulfilment plea is a contractual right commonly recognized in continental law countries to be applied to bilateral contracts. The basic notion of the right is that since the contracting parties were mutually responsible to each other for the performance of the contract, any non-performance or non-conforming performance by one party shall constitute a ground for the other party to refuse to perform.

5-703   Thus, article 66 provides that if there is no sequence for the performance of the contractual obligations, the obligations shall be performed concurrently. But if one party fails to perform the contract or performs in a non-conforming way, the other party has a right to refuse a corresponding performance. Similarly, article 67 provides that where the parties have mutual obligations and the performance of the obligations takes an order of priority, and the party who had to perform his obligations first fails to perform the obligations or performs the obligations in a non-conforming way, the other party has the right to refuse performance of his corresponding obligations.

Suspended performance

5-704   Like the FECL, the UCL grants a party a right to suspend the performance of the contract in certain circumstances. The ECL and TCL did not give such rights to a contracting party. Article 68 provides that one party may suspend performance of his obligations if he has conclusive evidence that:

(a)   the other party's business circumstances have significantly deteriorated;

(b)   the other party has transferred assets and/or surreptitiously withdrawn funds in order to evade his obligations;

(c)   the other party has lost his goodwill; or

(d)   the other party has lost his ability to perform his obligations.

5-705   The party seeking to suspend performance shall notify the other party of his intention to do so in a timely manner (article 69). If, however, the other party provides adequate security, performance must be resumed. On the other hand, if the other party does not recover his ability to perform his obligations or fails to provide adequate security within a reasonable time, the first party may terminate the contract.

5-706   It is, however, unclear from the UCL as to what would constitute 'conclusive evidence' or 'adequate security' under articles 68 and 69.

DISCHARGE OF CONTRACT

Grounds for discharge

5-801   Article 91 provides that the contractual rights and obligations under a contract are discharged when:

(a)   the obligations have been performed as agreed;

(b)   the contract is terminated by one party;

(c)   the obligations are mutually offset;

(d)   the obligor lodges the subject-matter in accordance with the law;

(e)   the obligee releases the obligor from his obligations;

(f)   the claim and the obligation become vested in the same person; or

(g)   other grounds stipulated by law or agreed between the parties.

The discharge of a contract shall not affect the dispute settlement clause in the contract, nor does it affect one party's rights to claim damages from the breaching party.

Termination of contract

5-802   Article 93 provides that the parties may terminate the contract by agreement. In addition, the parties may also agree upon conditions under which one party is entitled to terminate the contract. Article 94 sets out the circumstances under which a party may terminate the contract. They are as follows:

(a)   an event of *force majeure* has occurred which makes the objective of the contract unattainable;

(b)   one party expressly indicates by word or conduct that he will not perform his main obligation;

(c)   one party has delayed performance of his main obligations, and still fails to render performance within a reasonable time after the other party's request to do so; and

(d)   one party delays performance of an obligation or has committed a breach of contract which makes the objective of the contract unattainable; or other circumstances stipulated by law.

5-803   If a party wishes to terminate the contract under article 93 or 94 of the UCL, he shall notify the other party of his intention to do so. The contract is terminated when the notice of termination reaches the other party. If the other party objects to the termination, he may bring a suit to the People's Court or arbitration agency to determine the validity of the termination (article 96).

5-804   After a contract has been terminated, any executory portion is discharged. As regards obligations that have been performed, the innocent party may demand a return to the *status quo ante* or resort to other remedies or claim damages from the other party (article 97).

Contractual set-off

5-805   Where both parties owe contractual duties toward the other, and such contractual duties have the same type of subject-matter and quality, either party shall have the right to set off his contractual duties against the other party's contractual duties unless the law or the nature of the contract does not permit such set-off (article 99). A party wishing to set off must notify the other party of his intention of doing so.

5-806   On the other hand, if the subject matter of their obligations are not of the same type and quality, they may nevertheless still effect a set-off after reaching a consensus through consultation.

VITIATING FACTORS

Voidable contracts

5-901   Under article 52 of the UCL, a contract is void on account of fraud or duress only if it harms the interests of the state. Where there is merely fraud or duress on the part of one party without concomitant harm to the state interests, the contract is only voidable. Other incidences that will render a contract void include the malicious collusion to harm the state interests, a collective or third party;

illegality; the harming of public interests and the violation of mandatory provisions of the laws or administrative regulations. This latter provision is crucial as it signifies that not just any regulatory document (*guifanxing wenjian*) will invalidate a contract; only the violation of a national law (*falü*) or administrative regulation (*xingzheng fagui*) will render a contract void.

5-902   Article 54 states the grounds upon which a contract may be rendered voidable. They are: (a) if the contract was concluded as a result of a major mistake; (b) if the contract was clearly unconscionable at the time of conclusion; or (c) if a party uses fraud or duress or took advantage of the other party's vulnerability to cause him to conclude a contract that is against his true intentions. In these circumstances, the injured party may petition the People's Court or arbitration agency to have the contract modified or rescinded. The right to cancel these contracts must be exercised within one year of the date on which he learned or ought to have learned of the cause for rescission (article 55).

Enlarging scope of voidable contracts

5-903   It is important to note that restricting the scope of void contracts and enlarging the scope of voidable contracts has the effect of fostering transactions as it depends on the free will of the injured party whether he decides to avoid the contract or not. In addition, it does away with state paternalism that was prevalent in the previous contract laws. It also creates more certainty and party autonomy in concluding contracts. Lastly, it minimizes jeopardizing innocent third parties' rights where the rights in the contracts have been transferred to the third party.

Effect of a void or voidable contract

5-904   Under the UCL, void contracts or voidable contracts that are rescinded have no legal effect *ab initio*. If only parts of a contract are void and the void parts do not affect the other parts of the contract, the other parts shall remain valid. Article 57 explicitly states that the invalidity, rescission or termination of a contract will not affect the validity of the dispute settlement clauses of the contract.

5-905   Void contracts have certain legal consequences. Any property received under the void contract shall be returned to the owner. If restoration is impossible, the equivalent money value should be paid. In addition, the guilty party shall compensate the other party for any loss sustained by him. If, however, both parties are at fault, each shall bear his corresponding liability.

MODIFICATION AND ASSIGNMENT OF CONTRACTS

Modification and variation

5-1001   Under article 77 of the UCL, the parties to a contract may modify or vary their contract by agreement. Unlike the common law position which requires a variation of a contract to be supported by consideration, Chinese contract law does not have such a requirement. A variation of a contract shall be clear and precisely stated by the parties (article 78).

Assignment

5-1002   A contracting party may assign all or part of his *rights* under a contract to a third party unless: (a) the nature of the contract does not permit their assignment; (b) the parties have agreed that they may not assign their rights; or (c) the law provides that the rights may not be assigned. It is important to note that the assignment of rights to a third party does not require the consent of the other party. All that is needed is that the party assigning the rights notifies the other party.

5-1003   An assignment of rights cannot be revoked without the consent of the other party. Upon assignment of the rights, the assignee obtains all the incidental rights concomitant with the claim unless such incidental rights are personal to the party assigning the rights. On the other hand, the other party may set off a claim or raise against the assignee all the defences which he had against the assignor.

5-1004   In contrast, an assignment of *obligations* to a third party requires the consent of the other party to the contract. In the same manner, the assignee of the obligations is subject to all the defences that are available against the assignor, and bears all the incidental obligations that come with the principal obligation, unless the incidental obligations are personal to the assignor.

5-1005   Article 88 provides that a party may assign *all his contractual rights and obligations* to a third party with the consent of the other party to the contract.

REMEDIES FOR BREACH OF CONTRACT

Specific performance

5-1101   The previous contract laws favoured specific performance as the primary form of remedy available to the injured party upon a breach of contract. This view was adopted because a contract was seen as an administrative order from the government hierarchy. Only continuing and actual performance could let the injured party realize his expected interests under the contract.

5-1102 The UCL has shifted from this position. It provides that specific performance is only available as a remedy in respect of a non-monetary obligation (article 110). Specifically, specific performance will not be granted if: (a) performance is impossible in law or in fact; (b) the subject matter of the obligation is not suitable for specific performance or the cost of performance is too high; or (c) the injured party fails to demand specific performance within a reasonable time.

Damages

Remoteness

5-1103 Article 107 provides that if one party fails to perform his contractual obligations or performs in a non-conforming way, he shall bear liability for a breach of contract. The injured party shall be entitled to seek specific performance of the contract, or remedial measures, or damages from the breaching party.

5-1104 Article 112 provides that damages may be sought for losses suffered in addition to specific performance or other remedial measures. Article 113 provides that the measure of damages shall be equal to the loss incurred as a result of the breach including expectation losses. However, the damages awarded to an injured party shall not exceed the loss foreseeable by the breaching party at the time the contract was made. This is similar to the common law position as laid down in *Hadley v Baxendale*.[10]

Liquidated damages

5-1105 Article 114 provides that the parties to the contract may agree to a pre-determined amount of money as damages, ie liquidated damages, or may agree to a method of calculating the measure of damages in the contract.

5-1106 If the liquidated damages stipulated are lower than the loss suffered, the injured party may petition the People's Court or arbitration agency to increase the amount. Conversely, if the liquidated damages are higher than the actual loss suffered, the breaching party may petition the People's Court or arbitration agency to reduce the amount appropriately. This notion of increasing or reducing liquidated damages is entirely Chinese in origin. It has no parallel in the common law tradition.

Other remedies

5-1107 Remedial measures may be employed when the quality of performance does not conform with the contractual standard.

---

10   (1854) 9 Exch 341.

According to article 111, the injured party may reasonably elect to demand that the breaching party bear liability for breach of contract by carrying out remedial measures such as repairs, replacement of goods, reworking or returning the goods or reducing the price or remuneration.

Anticipatory breach

5-1108   Article 108 incorporates the common law doctrine of anticipatory breach. It provides that if a party expressly states or through his conduct indicates that he will not perform his contractual obligations, the other party may hold him liable for breach of contract before the time limit for performance has expired.

MITIGATION

5-1201   Article 119 provides that where a party has breached the contract, the injured party shall take appropriate measures to mitigate his losses. If the loss is aggravated as a result of the injured party's failure to mitigate his loss, the injured party may not demand compensation for the aggravated loss. The reasonable expense paid by a party in mitigating his loss shall be borne by the breaching party.

REBUS SIC STANTIBUS

Meaning

5-1301   *Rebus sic stantibus* is a doctrine found in the continental legal systems. According to this doctrine, 'contracts providing for successive acts of performance over a future period of time must be understood as subject to the condition that the circumstances will remain the same'. In other words, one party may be excused from performance when a change in circumstances occurs beyond the parties' expectation and control and frustrates the original basis of the contract, making continued performance by that party unfair.

5-1302   *Rebus sic stantibus* should not be confused with frustration of contract or *force majeure*. *Force majeure* excuses performance only if there is an unforeseeable event that happens that makes it impossible for the contract to be performed. On the other hand, *rebus sic stantibus* excuses performance in the event of economic hardship.

5-1303   Although *rebus sic stantibus* was not expressly mentioned in the previous contract laws, it has been accepted in judicial practice.

Wu Han Gas Co v Chongqin Testing Instruments Factory
(Source: Mo Zhang, 'Freedom of Contract with Chinese Characteristics: A Closer Look at the New Chinese Contract Law' (2000) 14 *Temple International and Comparative Law Journal* 237.)

The case involved a contract for the sale of 70,000 sets of J2.5 gas meters at Rmb 57.30 per set. The sets were made of aluminium. Some time after the contract was made, the state adjusted the price of aluminium from Rmb 4,400–4,600 per ton to Rmb 16,000 a ton, thereby inflating the costs of producing the gas meters to Rmb 79.22 a set. The seller sought to modify the price but the buyer refused. To prevent heavy losses, the seller did not deliver the meters and was sued by the buyer. On appeal to the High Court of Hubei Province, it was held that there was a material change in the circumstances which the parties could not have foreseen at the time the contract was made, and the continued performance would have been manifestly unfair to the seller. The doctrine of *rebus sic stantibus* was applied.

5-1304 The Supreme People's Court also upheld the Hubei's High Court opinion. The issue that arises is whether the doctrine still applies in the light of the UCL which did not incorporate the doctrine in its provisions. Professor Wang Liming has clarified that the doctrine was ultimately excluded from the final draft of the UCL as it was strongly opposed by some legislators. They viewed that the doctrine may be abused as there is no commonly accepted definition of the doctrine, and it is very difficult to draw a line between the doctrine and normal commercial risks.

CONCLUSION

5-1401 The UCL has made remarkable achievements in consolidating the law of contract in China. But several thorny questions remain. Firstly, does the UCL apply to a contract between the government and a company or individual? The legislators of the UCL held opposing views on this question. It is unfortunate that the UCL did not clarify this point. Secondly, the UCL does not apply to many important contracts such as employment contracts, partnership contracts, deposit and settlement contracts and tourism contracts. These categories of contracts had been successfully lobbied out of the UCL. The result of such lobbying is that the UCL has failed to fulfil its purpose of being a uniform law on contract issues in China. Lastly, the success of the UCL will very much depend on whether the Chinese bench and bar will enforce the legal framework laid down in the UCL instead of relying on *guanxi* and good offices to resolve contractual disputes as they had done in the past.

REFERENCES AND FURTHER READING

Books

Pitman B Potter, *The Chinese Legal System: Globalization and Local Legal Culture* (Routeledge, 2001).

Wang Guiguo and John Mo, *Chinese Law* (Kluwer Law International, 1999).

Yu Guanghua and Gu Minkang, *Laws Affecting Business Transactions in the PRC* (Kluwer Law International, 2001).

Articles

Feng Chen, 'The New Era of Chinese Contract Law: History, Development and a Comparative Analysis' (2001) 27:1 *Brooklyn Journal of International Law* 153.

John Gregory, 'Uniform Contract Law of the People's Republic of China: First Comparative Look' (1998-2000) 12 *Florida Journal of International Law* 467.

Wing Wo Lam, 'A Big Step Forward: The New PRC Contract Law' (1999) *ICCLR* 229.

Clement Shum, 'Chinese Contract Law' (1998) 13 *Journal of Contract Law* 214.

Wang Liming and Xu Chuanxi, 'Fundamental Principles of China's Contract Law' (1999) 13 *Columbia Journal of Asian Law* 1.

Wang Liming, 'China's Proposed Uniform Contract Code' (1999) 31 *St Mary's Law Journal* 7.

Duncan Webb, 'Towards a Contract Law of China: Some Salient Features' (1996) *Lloyd's Maritime and Commercial Law Quarterly* 245.

Mark Williams, 'An Introduction to General Principles and Formation of Contracts in the New Chinese Contract Law' (2001) 17 *Journal of Contract Law* 13.

Mo Zhang, 'Freedom of Contract With Chinese Legal Characteristics: A Closer Look At China's New Contract Law' (2000) 14 *Temple International and Comparative Law Journal* 237.

Zhong Jianhua and Yu Guanghua, 'China's Uniform Contract Law: Progress and Problems' (1999) 17 *UCLA Pacific Basin Law Journal* 1.

CHAPTER 6

Intellectual Property Rights

Samtani Anil

INTRODUCTION

6-101   In this chapter, the reader will be introduced to the salient principles of intellectual property law in China. It should be noted at the outset that this area of the law encompasses many different topics that contain detailed and complex rules and regulations. What we will attempt to do in this chapter is to look at the general principles applicable in the field and not concern ourselves too much with the minutiae surrounding the subject (except in those cases where the specific rules are unclear or create particular difficulties for businessmen wishing to do business in China). Readers who are interested in a detailed and current description of the law of intellectual property in China should refer to *Chinese Intellectual Property Law in the 21st Century* by Xue Hong and Zheng Chengsi (Sweet & Maxwell Asia, 2002) or the relevant chapters dealing with intellectual property rights in *Doing Business in China: Volume 2* edited by Freshfields Bruckhaus Deringer (Juris Publishing, 2002).

6-102   The reader should also note that this area of the law is extremely dynamic in nature and is susceptible to frequent changes. Readers desiring to keep abreast of the latest changes in the field may wish to subscribe to online services such as those offered by the Isinolaw Research Centre (at http://www.isinolaw.com) or refer to sites such as Chinalaw Web (at http://www.qis.net/chinalaw/) or specialist magazines such as *IP Asia*. Other sources of relevant information pertaining to the intellectual property laws in China can be found in the references and further readings section of this chapter.

6-103   The author would also like to acknowledge the fact that in the writing of this chapter, reference has been made to the English translation of the relevant laws as provided in Isinolaw Research Centre's site and the listing and reproduction of relevant legislation provided in Xue Hong and Zheng Chengsi's text on *Chinese Intellectual Property Law in the 21st Century.*

BRIEF HISTORY OF INTELLECTUAL PROPERTY PROTECTION IN CHINA

6-201   The redrafting of intellectual property laws in China began in earnest sometime during the late 1970s. These changes were motivated by several factors. It was felt that changes to the existing state of the law were needed to ensure that foreigners felt comfortable investing in China. There was also a perceived need to enhance the position of intellectuals in China, after the stigma brought on by the Cultural Revolution.

6-202   When China announced its policy of utilizing direct foreign investment in 1979, there was an inadequate legal regime in relation to the protection of intellectual property rights. A flurry of legislative activities has taken place since then to make up for this deficit. The Trademark Law was enacted in 1982 followed by the Patent Law in 1985. The Copyright Law and the Regulations for the Protection of Computer Software were enacted in 1991. The Anti-Unfair Competition Law was promulgated in 1993 followed by the Regulations for Customs Protection of Intellectual Property Rights of the PRC in 1995. The Regulations on the Protection of New Varieties of Plants was passed in 1997. China's Criminal Law was revised in 1997 through the addition of a special chapter dealing with crimes relating to intellectual property infringement.

6-203   China has also been relatively active on the international scene and has acceded to various international treaties since 1979. China became a member of the World Intellectual Property Organization (WIPO) in 1980. In 1985, China became a party to the Paris Convention for the Protection of Industrial Property. In 1989, China acceded to the Madrid Agreement Concerning the International Registration of Marks. In 1992, China acceded to the Berne Convention for the Protection of Literary and Artistic Works and the Universal Copyright Convention. These were followed by ratification of various other conventions such as the Patent Co-operation Treaty, the Budapest Treaty on the International Recognition of the Deposit of Micro-organisms for the Purposes of Patent Procedure, the Locarno Agreement Establishing an International Classification for Industrial Designs and the Strasbourg Agreement Concerning the International Patent Classification. By virtue of its World Trade Organisation (WTO) entry on 11 December 2001, China is obliged to modify its intellectual property laws to conform to the Agreement on Trade Related Aspects of Intellectual Property Rights (the TRIPS Agreement). It is noteworthy that during the negotiations leading to its entry into the WTO, China had conducted a major overhaul of its existing intellectual property laws and this had led to a revision of several major laws. These revisions will be discussed in subsequent sections of this chapter.

6-204 A discussion of the development of China's intellectual property laws is incomplete without a brief mention of the role of the US in the modernization and stricter enforcement of these laws. Relations between the two countries have been characterized by numerous disputes pertaining to the perceived lackluster efforts on the part of the Chinese government to combat its piracy problems. In its efforts to develop pro-active solutions to, amongst other things, compel China to improve its record of protecting the intellectual property rights of US businesses, section 301 of the Trade Act of 1974 was devised. This was developed as a result of the US Congress's frustration with the then outdated General Agreement on Tariffs and Trade and its impotency in protecting the interests of US businesses. Section 301 enables the US President to investigate and impose sanctions on countries that engage in unfair trade practices that threaten American economic interests. The passing of the Omnibus Trade and Competitiveness Act in 1988 amended section 301 via its inclusion of two new provisions – Super 301 and Special 301.

6-205 Super 301 provides a list of priority country trade practices that significantly impact US trade. The list of priority countries comes from the 'National Trade Estimate Report on Foreign Trade' (NTE), which is an annual report by the United States Trade Representative (USTR) that reviews foreign trade barriers. Within 21 days, the USTR must initiate an investigation on every priority country named in the report. Special 301, by contrast, requires the USTR to identify countries that deny protection of intellectual property rights or deny fair and equitable market access for persons who rely on intellectual property rights. After the issuance of the NTE (which is typically made on 31 March annually), the USTR has 30 days to identify countries whose policies adversely impact the US (referred to as a 'priority foreign country'). If a country is identified as a 'priority foreign country', the USTR has another 30 days to decide if an investigation should be initiated. Countries with trade practices that have less of an impact, but that are serious, are placed on either a 'priority watch list' or 'watch list'. Both of these tools have been used repeatedly by the American government to pressure foreign countries, including China, to reform their intellectual property regimes.

6-206 In line with the aims of this chapter, the discussion pertaining to the development of intellectual property law in China has been intentionally kept brief. Readers who are interested in a detailed analysis of the historical development of intellectual property laws in China should refer to the specialist texts and articles listed in the reference section of this chapter.

INTERNATIONAL TREATIES

6-301   China has acceded to the following international treaties:

(a)   the Agreement on Trade-Related Aspects of Intellectual Property Rights (the TRIPS Agreement);

(b)   the Berne Convention for the Protection of Literary and Artistic Works (the 1971 Paris Version);

(c)   the Universal Copyright Convention;

(d)   the Convention for the Protection of Producers of Phonograms Against Unauthorized Duplication of their Phonograms;

(e)   the Paris Convention for the Protection of Industrial Property (the 1967 Stockholm Version);

(f)   the Patent Co-operation Treaty;

(g)   the Budapest Treaty on the International Recognition of the Deposit of Micro-organisms for the Purposes Patent Procedure;

(h)   the Locarno Agreement Establishing an International Classification for Industrial Design;

(i)   the Strasbourg Agreement Concerning the International Patent Classification;

(j)   the Patent Law Treaty;

(k)   the Madrid Agreement Concerning the International Registration of Marks and Protocol Relating to the Madrid Agreement Concerning the International Registration of Marks;

(l)   the Nice Agreement Concerning the International Classification of Goods and Services for the Purposes of the Registration of Marks; and

(m)   the Trademark Law Treaty.

6-302   The obligations imposed by these treaties will not be discussed separately in this chapter. An examination of the relevant laws in China in the course of our discussion will, however, reveal that there has been an attempt on the part of the lawmakers in China to update the laws to incorporate these obligations. Readers who are interested in examining the provisions in these treaties may wish to visit the WIPO website (at http://www.wipo.org). This site contains an excellent repository of international conventions, treaties and related legislation in the field of international intellectual property law but it should be observed that this site contains the full text of only those treaties that are administered by the WIPO.

COPYRIGHT LAW

Introduction

6-401 Beginning from the 1980s, China has been fairly active in enacting various laws, administrative regulations and rules on copyright protection and acceding to several international copyright treaties. The key law of copyright protection adopted by the National People's Congress (NPC) is the Copyright Law. The Copyright Law, which was adopted on 7 September 1990 and came into effect on 1 June 1991, was subsequently revised. The revisions came into effect on 27 October 2001. All subsequent references to the Copyright Law in this chapter shall refer to this latest modified and revised version of the Copyright Law.

6-402 In addition, the NPC has also adopted the following laws that have some bearing on certain aspects of copyright protection:

(a) General Principles of the Civil Law, adopted on 12 April 1986 and which came into effect on 1 January 1987;

(b) Criminal Law, adopted on 1 July 1979, revised on 14 March 1997 and which came into effect on 1 October 1997; and

(c) Decisions on Safeguard of Security on the Internet, adopted on 28 December 2000.

6-403 The reader should note that these laws impinge on the other intellectual property rights discussed in the course of this chapter as well. These laws will not be repeated during the course of our discussion of the other intellectual property rights but the reader should take note of their continued relevance in these other fields.

6-404 The State Council has also adopted the following regulations:

(a) Implementing Regulations of the Copyright Law, adopted on 24 May 1991 and which came into effect on 1 June 1991 (these regulations are currently being amended);

(b) International Copyright Treaties Implementing Rules, adopted on 25 September 1992 and which came into effect on 30 September 1992;

(c) Regulations on Computer Software Protection, adopted on 4 June 1991, amended on 20 December 2001 and which came into effect on 1 January 2002;

(d) Regulations of the Customs Protection of Intellectual Property, adopted on 5 July 1995 and which came into effect on 1 October 1995;

(e) Regulations on Publications, adopted on 25 December 2001 and which came into effect on 1 February 2002;

(f) Regulations on Motion Pictures, adopted on 25 December 2001 and which came into effect on 1 February 2002; and

(g)   Regulations on Sound Recordings and Video Recordings, adopted on 25 December 2001 and which came into effect on 1 February 2002.

6-405   The National Copyright Administration of China has also made several administrative stipulations in the field of copyright but it is not necessary for us to list them here for the purposes of our discussion in this section.

Salient aspects of China's copyright laws

6-406   We will now turn our attention to several key principles underlying copyright in China. Once again, our focus will not be on the technical or detailed aspects of copyright. We will, instead, look at several general and key principles that will enable us to appreciate the role and importance of copyright in China.

Nature and scope of copyright

6-407   Under the Copyright Law, any form of works, which is original and can be reproduced in a given form may be protected. Registration is not a prerequisite for copyright to vest in a work.

6-408   A copyright is essentially a set of exclusive legal rights authors have over their works for a limited period of time. Article 10 of the Copyright Law sets out these rights:

(a)   the right of publication (ie the right to decide whether to make a work available to the public);

(b)   the right of authorship (ie the right to claim authorship and to have the author's name mentioned in connection with the work);

(c)   the right of alteration (ie the right to alter or authorize others to alter one's work);

(d)   the right of integrity (ie the right to protect one's work against distortion or mutilation);

(e)   the right of reproduction (ie the right to produce one or more copies of a work by printing, photocopying, lithographing, making a sound recording or video recording, duplicating a recording, or duplicating a photographic work or by any other means);

(f)   the right of distribution (ie the right to make available to the public the original or reproductions of a work through sale or other transfer of ownership);

(g)   the right of rental (ie the right to authorize, with payment, others to temporarily use cinematographic works, works created by virtue of an analogous method of film production, and computer software, except any computer software that is not the main subject matter of rental);

(h)   the right of exhibition (ie the right to publicly display the original or reproduction of a work of fine art and photography);

(i)   the right of performance (ie the right to publicly perform a work and publicly broadcast the performance of a work by various means);

(j)   the right of showing (ie the right to show to the public a work of fine art, photography, cinematography and any work created by virtue of an analogous method of film production through film projectors, overhead projectors or any other technical devices);

(k)   the right of broadcast (ie the right to broadcast or communicate to the public a work by wireless means, to communicate to the public a broadcast work by wire or relay means, and to communicate to the public a broadcast work by a loud speaker or by any other analogous tool used to transmit symbols, sounds or pictures);

(l)   the right of communication on information networks (ie the right to communicate to the public a work, by wire or wireless means in such a way that members of the public may access these works from a place and at a time individually chosen by them);

(m)   the right of making a cinematographic work (ie, the right to fix a work on a carrier by way of film production or by virtue of an analogous method of film production);

(n)   the right of adaptation (ie the right to change a work to create a new work of originality);

(o)   the right of translation (ie the right to translate a work in one language into one in another language);

(p)   the right of compilation (ie the right to compile works or parts of works into a new work by reason of the selection or arrangement); and

(q)   any other rights a copyright owner is entitled to enjoy.

6-409 Copyright and its related rights are viewed as being essential to human creativity, by giving creators incentives in the form of recognition and fair economic rewards. Within the context of this system of rights, creators are assured that their works can be disseminated without fear of unauthorized copying or piracy. The benefit to society that this system provides is that it helps increase access to and enhances the enjoyment of culture, knowledge, and entertainment all over the world.

6-410 For copyright to subsist, the work must be protected under article 3 of the Copyright Law. Copyright protection can be claimed in the following categories of works or materials:

(a)   written works;

(b)   oral works;

(c)   musical, dramatic, *quyi* (defined to refer to traditional art forms such as ballad singing, story telling, comic dialogues, clapper talks and cross talks) and choreographic works;

(d)   works of fine art and architecture;

(e)   photographic works;

(f)   cinematographic works and works created by virtue of an analogous method of film production;

(g)   drawings of engineering designs, and product designs;

(h)   maps, sketches and other graphic works and model works;

(i)   computer software; and

(j)   other works as provided for in laws and administrative regulations.

6-411   Copyright protection arises automatically and, unlike patent and trademark protection, is not subject to any formalities.

6-412   There is copyright in any original expression. It is also essential to note that copyright protects the form of expression of an idea and not the underlying idea itself.

Who can claim copyright in China?

6-413   Article 2 of the Copyright Law provides the framework pertaining to who is entitled to copyright protection in China:

> Chinese citizens, legal persons and other organizations shall enjoy the copyright in their works, whether published or not, in accordance with this Law.
>
> The copyright enjoyed by foreigners and stateless persons in their works according to agreements signed with China by countries where their permanent residences are registered or where they reside regularly or international treaties acceded to by the PRC and the aforesaid countries jointly shall be protected by this Law.
>
> Foreigners and stateless persons shall enjoy the copyright in their works first published within the territory of the PRC in accordance with this Law.
>
> Any works of an author from a country which neither enters into any agreement with nor accedes to any international treaty jointly with the PRC and of a stateless person, which is first published in any member country to an international treaty to which the PRC accedes, or published in member countries and non-member countries simultaneously shall be protected by this Law.

Length of protection

6-414   Pursuant to the Copyright Law, the rights of authorship, alteration and integrity is permanently enjoyed by the author without being restricted by the copyright protection period. As for the other rights, article 21 provides as follows:

> For a citizen's work, the duration of protection for the right of publication and the right as provided in from Item (5) to Item (17) of Paragraph I of Article 10 herein shall be the lifetime of the author and 50 years more after his decease, expiring on 31st December of the 50th year after this decease. In the case of a work of joint authorship, the duration shall expire on 31st December of the 50th year after the decease of the last survivors among the authors.

> For a work of a legal person or any other organization, or an occupational work in which the copyright (except the right of authorship) is enjoyed by a legal person or any other organization, the duration of protection for the right of publication and rights as provided in from Item (5) to Item (17) of Paragraph I of Article 10 herein shall be 50 years, expiring on 31st December of the 50th year after the first publication of the work; however, any such work which has remained unpublished for 50 years since the completion of this creation shall no longer be protected by this Law.

> For cinematographic works, works created with similar cinematographing means, and photographic works, the duration of protection for the right of publication and rights as provided in from Item (5) to Item (17) of Paragraph I of Article 10 herein shall be 50 years, expiring on 31st December of the 50th year after the first publication of the work; however, any such work which has remained unpublished for 50 years since the completion of this creation shall no longer be protected by this Law.

Permissible uses of works

6-415   Article 22 of the Copyright Law states that the following acts may be made in relation to copyrighted works without the need to seek the permission of the copyright owner or make any payment to the copyright owner:

(a) the use of another person's published work for purposes of personal study, research, or amusement;

(b) appropriate quotation in one's work from another person's published work for the purpose of introducing, commenting on a certain work or explaining a certain point;

(c) inevitable reappearance or quotation of published works in newspapers, periodicals, broadcasts, television programmes, etc, for the purpose of making news reports;

(d) reprinting by newspapers or periodicals or rebroadcasting by radio or television stations topical articles in politics, economy, and religion having been published by other newspapers, periodicals, and radio or television stations, except where the authors have announced that the printing or broadcasting of such articles are not allowed;

(e)   putting into print in newspapers or periodicals, or into broadcasts of radio or television stations, a speech having been delivered at a public gathering, except where the author has announced that the printing or broadcasting of the speech is not allowed;

(f)   translation or reproduction in a small quantity of copies of a published work for use by teaching and scientific research personnel in classrooms or in researches, provided that the translation or reproduction shall not be published for distribution;

(g)   the use of published works by governmental agencies for the purpose of carrying out official duties within a reasonable scope;

(h)   reproduction of works in their collections by libraries, archives, memorial halls, museums, art galleries, etc, for the purposes of exhibition or the preservation of facsimiles of such works;

(i)   gratuitous performances of published works, for which no charges are collected from the public, and no remuneration is paid to performers;

(j)   copying, drawing, photographing, or video-recording of works of arts being sited or displayed outdoors and in public places;

(k)   translation of works published in the Chinese language by Chinese citizens, legal persons, and other organizations into other ethnic minority languages for domestic publication and distribution; and

(l)   transliteration of published works into Braille for publication.

6-416   The caveat in invoking article 22 is that the name of the author and the title of the work must be mentioned in the course of any of the above uses and the other rights enjoyed by the copyright owner pursuant to the Copyright Law are not prejudiced.

6-417   Article 23 then goes on to state that in compiling and publishing textbooks for implementing the nine-year compulsory education and the national educational programmes, parts of published works, short written works, music works or single copies of works of painting or photographic works may be compiled into textbooks without the authorization of the authors (except where the authors have declared in advance that such use of their works is not permitted) with remuneration paid in accordance to the regulations.

Infringement

6-418   Article 46 of the Copyright Law provides that anyone who commits any of the following acts shall, depending on the circumstances, bear civil liability for remedies such as ceasing the infringement, eliminating its ill effects, making an apology, and compensating for damages:

(a) publishing a work without the permission of the copyright owner;

(b) publishing a work of joint authorship as his very own without the consent of his co-authors;

(c) affixing his name to a work created by another person, for fame or for gain, without having participated in its creation;

(d) misrepresenting or distorting a work created by another person;

(e) plagiarizing a work created by another person;

(f) making use of a work either by means of exhibition, cinematographing, similar cinematographing means, or through means of adaptation, translation, or annotation, without permission of its copyright owner, unless otherwise provided in the Copyright Law;

(g) not paying remuneration that should be paid to the copyright owner when using a work;

(h) leasing cinematographic works, works created by similar cinematographing means, computer software, sound and video recordings without permission from the corresponding copyright owners or right owners related to the copyrights, unless otherwise provided in the Copyright Law;

(i) without permission of the publisher, using the publishing style and design of his published books, and periodicals;

(j) without permission of a performer, making live broadcasts and publicly transmitting his or her live performances, or recording his or her performances; or

(k) other acts of infringement upon the copyright and rights and interests related to the copyright.

6-419 Article 47 of the Copyright Law then goes on to state that anyone who commits any of the acts stated below shall, depending on the circumstances, bear civil liability for such remedies as ceasing the infringement, eliminating its ill effects, making an apology, or compensating for damages:

(a) reproducing, distributing, performing, televising, broadcasting, compiling, spreading to the public via information networks a work without permission of the copyright owner, unless otherwise provided by the Copyright Law;

(b) publishing a book of which the exclusive right of publication is enjoyed by another person;

(c) reproducing and publishing a sound or video recording, or spreading a performance via information networks to the public without permission of the performer, unless otherwise provided by the Copyright Law;

(d) reproducing, publishing, spreading via information networks to the public sound and video recordings without permission of producers of such works, unless otherwise provided in the Copyright Law;

(e) broadcasting or reproducing a radio or television programme without the permission of the radio or television station, unless otherwise provided in the Copyright Law;

(f) intentionally avoiding or damaging technical measures adopted by another person for protecting his copyright or rights related to the copyright without the permission of the copyright owner or right owners related to the copyright, unless otherwise provided in the Copyright Law;

(g) intentionally expurgating or altering electronic information for management of rights of a work, a sound or video recording without the permission of the copyright owner or right owners related to the copyright, unless otherwise provided by laws or administrative regulations; or

(h) producing or selling a work with the forged signature of another author.

6-420   If in committing the acts stipulated in article 47, the infringer simultaneously damages the public interest, he shall be ordered to cease such infringement, have his illegal gains confiscated, have infringing reproductions confiscated and destroyed, and may be imposed a fine by the administrative department in charge of copyright. If the circumstances are serious, the administrative department in charge of copyright may also confiscate material, instruments, and equipment used to produce the infringing reproductions. In addition, if the act constitutes a crime, the infringer shall be prosecuted for the crime.

6-421   In cases where the plaintiff's damage or the infringer's profits cannot be determined, article 48 states that statutory damages up to Rmb 500,000 may be awarded.

New Copyright Law Implementing Regulations

6-422   The Implementing Regulations for the Copyright Law of the PRC were promulgated by the State Council on 2 August 2002 and came into force on 15 September 2002. The Implementing Regulations repeal the earlier regulations issued by the National Copyright Administration on 30 May 1991. The Implementing Regulations were introduced to bring the Copyright Law's subsidiary legislation into line with the amended Copyright Law and to meet China's WTO obligations.

6-423 The Implementing Regulations provide definitions for numerous terms used in the Copyright Law. In addition, they also provide rules addressing fines for infringement, protection of certain rights of foreigners and stateless persons, the time when copyright comes into existence, the exercise of copyright in works of joint authorship, alterations when a movie is made from a work, rules concerning works done in the course of employment, rules that apply when the author is unknown, the status of the copyright after an author dies, remuneration for use of a work when a licence is not required, licence contracts, recordal of licence contracts and assignment contracts, neighbouring rights, copyright rules in book publishing and declarations prohibiting certain uses. A detailed discussion of the Implementing Regulations lies outside the scope of this chapter.

Software regulations

6-424 Article 58 of the Copyright Law provides that regulations for the protection of computer software and the right of communication on an information network shall be established separately by the State Council. The Regulations on Computer Software Protection were first enacted in 1991. These regulations were subsequently modified: the amended regulations were published on 20 December 2001 and entered into force on 1 January 2002. A discussion of the content of these regulations is outside the scope of this chapter.

Copyright Cases Involving the Internet

(The following discussion is based on information provided in *Doing Business in China: Volume 2* edited by Freshfields Bruckhaus Deringer.)

Read Online v Yibin City Cuiping District Dongfang Information Service Co

In this case, the defendant (without obtaining the plaintiff's permission) had used the plaintiff's web page as its own. The Beijing Haidian held that this amounted to copyright infringement of the plaintiff's copyright in its web page design.

Daxuesheng v Li Xiang

Without obtaining prior permission from the plaintiff, acknowledgment of the source or payment to the authors, the defendant posted on his personal web site articles from the magazine compiled and published by the plaintiff. The Beijing

Haidian People's Court held that the defendant had infringed the plaintiff's copyright. The decision was also significant in that the court held that 263.net, the Internet service provider that hosted the defendant's web site, was not liable for copyright infringement. The court held that Internet service providers can be held liable only for content that is strictly prohibited by law from being posted on local web sites.

PATENT LAW

Introduction

6-501   Inventions are critical to the success of many businesses, particularly those that are dependent on technological products or processes. If a person or a business has developed a new and better product or process that satisfies the requirements of patentability, steps may be taken to protect the competitive advantage that this product or process gives by obtaining a patent.

6-502   The development of China's patent laws can probably be traced back to the Qing Dynasty. This arose as a consequence of China entering into several international treaties in her quest towards modernization. In 1903, for example, the US and China entered into a treaty on navigation and commerce which provided for a reciprocal patent-granting arrangement in which citizens of one contracting party could apply for and secure patent rights for their inventions in the other contracting party. The first law pertaining to patents, titled Charter of Rewards on Invigoration of Industry and Art, was adopted on 12 July 1889, although oddly enough, the first patent in China was granted earlier in 1882.

6-503   Several interesting developments in the interim (arising from the overthrow of the Qing Dynasty, measures adopted by the Nationalist government, the founding of the People's Republic in 1949, China's open-door policies and pressure from the West, particularly from the US) culminated in the adoption of the Patent Law in 1984 and its subsequent amendment in 1992.

6-504   Motivated by the aims and principles of 'accommodation' of the socialist market economy, strengthening the protection of patent rights, simplification and acceleration of patent approval and harmonizing China's patent law with international standards and treaties, China undertook a major overhaul of its Patent Law in 2000 which took effect on 1 July 2001.

6-505 The State Council has adopted the following administrative regulations:

(a) Implementing Regulations of the Patent Law, amended for the second time on 15 June 2001 and which came into effect on 1 July 2001; and

(b) Regulations on Patent Commissioning, published on 4 March 1991 and which came into effect on 1 April 1991.

6-506 The State Intellectual Property Office has several administrative stipulations on patent protection but for the purposes of our discussion in this chapter, it is not necessary to list or examine those stipulations.

Patentability requirements in China

Types of Inventions

6-507 Article 2 of the Patent Law permits the granting of a patent for three types of 'inventions-creations': namely 'inventions', 'utility models' and 'designs'. Readers familiar with American patent law should note that inventions, as referred to in the Patent Law, correspond to American utility patents. Utility models would correspond to American improvement patents. Design patents are essentially equivalent in China and the US.

Term

6-508 The term of invention patents is 20 years from the date of filing of the patent application. The term of utility model and design patents is ten years from the date of filing of the patent application.

'Service' and 'non-service' inventions

6-509 The Patent Law makes a distinction between 'service' and 'non-service' inventions. Article 6 of the Patent Law defines a 'service' invention as an invention that is made by an inventor in execution of the tasks of the entity to which he belongs, or made by the inventor mainly using the material and technical means of the entity. The patentee for patented service inventions is the entity whilst the patentee for non-service inventions is the inventor.

Requirements for patentability

6-510 Article 22 of the Patent Law provides that an invention must satisfy the requirements of novelty, inventiveness and practical applicability for it to be patentable. It then goes on to define what each of these terms mean.

6-511   'Novelty' means that, before the filing date of the application, no identical invention or utility model has been publicly disclosed in domestic or foreign publications or has been publicly used or made known to the public by any other means in the country, nor has any other person previously filed with the Patent Administrative Department an application describing an identical invention or utility model which was recorded in patent application documents published after the said date of filing.

6-512   'Inventiveness' means that, compared with the technology existing before the filing date of the application, the invention has prominent and substantive distinguishing features and represents a marked improvement, or the utility model possesses substantive distinguishing features and represents an improvement.

6-513   'Usefulness' means that the invention or utility model is manufacturable or usable and can produce positive results.

6-514   In the case of design patents, article 22 stipulates that the design must not be identical or similar to any other design which, prior to the date of filing, has been publicly disclosed anywhere in the world or publicly used in China. In addition, the design must not 'conflict with the prior lawful right and interest of others'. Louis Sorell has observed that this phrase was probably included to prevent conflicts with prior copyright and trademark rights, which are intended to pre-empt subsequent design patent protection.

6-515   Article 24 provides that an invention for which a patent application has been made does not lose its novelty where, within six months before the filing date, any of the following events occur:

(a)   it was first exhibited at an international exhibition sponsored or recognized by the Chinese government;

(b)   it was first made public at a prescribed academic or technological meeting; or

(c)   it was disclosed by any person without the consent of the applicant.

6-516   Article 25 lists the products for which no patent right will be granted. These are:

(a)   scientific discoveries;

(b)   rules and methods for mental activities;

(c)   methods for the diagnosis or for the treatment of diseases;

(d)   animal and plant varieties; and

(e)   substances obtained by means of nuclear transformation.

6-517   Article 26 clarifies that the bar on patentability for animal and plant varieties (ie item (d) above) does not extend to the processes used in producing such animal or plant varieties.

Enforcement

Infringement

6-518 Pursuant to article 57 of the Patent Law, a person who exploits a patent, without the patentee's authorization, is infringing the latter's patent right. The provision then goes on to provide that aggrieved parties may institute legal proceedings in the People's Court or request the authorities for patent work to handle the matter.

6-519 As explained by Louis Sorell, if 'the administrative route is chosen, the request is made to the patent administrative office having jurisdiction over the matter. An administrative authority for patent affairs is established in every province, autonomous region, and municipality. The patent administrative office has the power to enjoin acts of infringement and may mediate the damages issued upon the request of the parties. If mediation is unsuccessful, a lawsuit may be initiated in the People's Court in accordance with China's Civil Procedure Law. There are tactical advantages in using the administrative route to establish infringement: namely, the administrative procedure is faster and the administrative decision of infringement may be used as evidence of infringement in a subsequent judicial proceeding. However, as a practical matter, the issue of damages may be difficult to resolve using the administrative route.'

6-520 Article 63 goes on to provide that none of the following will be deemed an infringement of the patent right:

(a) the use, an agreement to sell or sale of a patented product after the sale of that patented product which has been manufactured, imported by the patentee or has been manufactured or imported with the authorization of the patentee or obtained directly according to the patented process;

(b) the continued manufacture of an identical product, use of identical process only within its original scope, by a party that, prior to the date of application for the patent in question, had already manufactured that identical product, used that identical process or made the necessary preparations for such manufacture or use;

(c) the use of the patent by a foreign means of transport which temporarily passes through the territorial land, water or airspace of China for its own needs, in its devises and installations, in accordance with any agreement concluded between China and the country to which the foreign means of transport belongs, or any international treaty to which both countries are parties, or on the basis of the principle of reciprocity; or

(d) the use of the patent in question solely for the purposes of scientific research and experimentation.

6-521 The provision also stipulates that any person who uses for commercial purpose or sells a patented product or a product obtained directly by a patented process, not knowing that it was made and sold without the authorization of the patent owner, is not liable for compensation, provided that the person is able to prove the legitimate source of the product. It is instructive to note that this provision, which has been narrowed considerably from an extremely broad and unreasonable exception in the old law, does not restrict all legal remedies in the case of innocent infringements. For instance, remedies such as permanent injunctions or return of illegal profits may be awarded to a patentee in a situation involving innocent infringement.

Injunctive relief

6-522 Pursuant to article 61 of the Patent Law, patentees or interested parties are entitled to, in situations where there is evidence to prove that their patent rights are being infringed, or that such infringement is imminent, and that their legitimate rights and interests will suffer irrecoverable damage if the infringing act is not stopped immediately, apply to the courts for adoption of measures to reprimand and order the ceasing of the infringing activity and property preservation. Article 57 extends to an administrative patent authority, in situations where an administrative patent action is brought, the power to immediately enjoin acts of patent infringement.

Damages

6-523 The quantum of the compensation for infringing a patent right shall be ascertained in accordance with the loss suffered by the patentee arising from the infringement or the benefit gained by the infringer from the infringement (article 60 of the Patent Law). If such loss or gain is difficult to ascertain, the quantum shall be reasonably ascertained with reference to appropriate multipliers of the royalties for licenses for the patent.

Passing off patented products or processes

6-524 China's patent law imposes civil liability, administrative penalties and/or penal penalties for acts of passing off patented products or processes (articles 58 and 59 of the Patent Law). Such passing off can arise in two ways. The first is where a person passes off another person's patent (ie where the former makes a false representation as to the ownership or authority to use another person's patent rights). The second is where a non-patented product or process is passed off as a patented product or process.

Compulsory licences

6-525 The patent regime in China permits compulsory licensing of patents under certain circumstances notwithstanding the patentee's refusal to grant a licence. These situations are described in articles 48 (read together with article 72 of the Implementing Regulations), 49 and 50 of the Patent Law:

(a) where any entity which is qualified to exploit the invention or utility model has made requests for authorization from the patentee of an invention or utility model to exploit its or his patent on reasonable terms and such efforts have not been successful within a reasonable period of time, the patent administrative organ under the State Council may, upon the application of that entity, grant a compulsory licence to exploit the patent for invention or utility model;

(b) where a national emergency or any extraordinary state of affairs occurs, or where the public interest so requires, the patent administrative organ under the State Council may grant a compulsory licence to exploit the patent for invention or utility model; and

(c) where the invention or utility model for which the patent right was granted is of important technical advance of considerable economic significance compared with another invention or utility model for which a patent right has been granted earlier and the exploitation of the later invention or utility model depends on the exploitation of the earlier invention or utility model, the patent administrative organ under the State Council may, upon the request of the later patentee, grant a compulsory licence to exploit the earlier invention or utility model.

6-526 Article 52 of the Patent Law goes on to state that the grant of the compulsory licence must be limited in duration and scope on the basis of reasons that justify the grant. In addition, if and when the circumstances that led to the compulsory licence cease to exist, the compulsory licence may, upon the request of the patentee, be terminated. There are restrictions on the licensee and these include the following:

(a) the licensee does not have an exclusive licence and it cannot sub-licence the compulsory licence to others (article 53 of the Patent Law); and

(b) the licensee must pay the patentee a reasonable exploitation fee – if such fee cannot be agreed upon between the parties, the patent administrative organ will determine the fee (article 54 of the Patent Law).

6-527 Where the patentee is dissatisfied with either the decision pertaining to the granting of a compulsory licence or the adjudicated fee, the patentee may, within three months of receipt of the notification pertaining to the decision, institute proceedings in the People's Court (article 55 of the Patent Law).

A Patent Case

Glaxo Group Ltd v South-West Hecheng Pharmaceutical Factory (Source: Louis S Sorell, 'A Comparative Analysis of Selected Aspects of Patent Law in China and the United States' (2002) 11 *Pacific Rim Law & Policy Journal* 319.)

China's patent law expressly shifts the burden of proof when the infringement action involves a process patent for the manufacture of a new product: 'When any infringement dispute relates to a process patent for the manufacture of a new product, any entity or individual manufacturing the identical product shall furnish proof to the effect that a different process is used in the manufacture of its or his product.'

It is believed that this 'burden shifting' provision for process patents is intended to overcome the disadvantages a patentee has in proving infringing use of a patented process, in view of the lack of pre-trial discovery in patent litigation in China.

This provision was decisive in *Glaxo Group Ltd v South-West Hecheng Pharmaceutical Factory.* The multi-national pharmaceutical company Glaxo owned a Chinese invention patent for a process of manufacturing the drug Ondansetron, which is used to prevent nausea and vomiting caused by cancer chemotherapy. Glaxo learned of defendant South-West's unauthorized manufacture of the drug and initially filed a complaint with the local administrative authority for patent affairs, requesting an investigation and handling of the matter. Subsequently, Glaxo withdrew the administrative complaint and instituted a patent infringement lawsuit in the Chongqing Municipal First Intermediate People's Court, seeking a cessation of infringement, a public apology, and damages of Rmb 320,000.

Upon court order, the defendant submitted details of the processes it used to manufacture the drug to the court, and suggested that the court conduct an on-site inspection and technical appraisal if deemed necessary. The defendant also asserted that it did not infringe Glaxo's patent because the defendant's processes were essentially different than Glaxo's patented process. However, Glaxo contended that the information submitted by the defendant to the court failed to establish that the submitted processes were actually used by the defendant to manufacture its drug. Accordingly, Glaxo requested the defendant to produce its regulatory documents previously furnished to China's Ministry of Health to obtain approval for the defendant's manufacture of the drug, and to testify that the approved processes were the methods of manufacture actually being used by the defendant.

The defendant refused to produce the requested regulatory documents. The court eventually ruled that the defendant's drug was identical to the drug obtained from Glaxo's patented process. In addition, the court held that the defendant had failed to meet its statutory burden of proving that the process it submitted to the court was the process actually used by the defendant to make its drug product. The court also ordered the defendant to immediately cease its manufacture and sale of the drug, and to make a public apology to the plaintiff. The plaintiff was awarded Rmb 320,000 in compensatory damages, and the defendant was also ordered to pay the litigation fee of Rmb 15,363. This was the first case involving a foreign patentee in which the defendant lost due to its failure to meet the statutory burden of proof.

TRADEMARKS

Introduction

6-601 The key law of trademark protection adopted by the NPC is the Trademark Law. The Trademark Law, which was adopted on 23 August 1982 and came into effect on 1 March 1983, was subsequently revised. The second and latest revisions came into effect on 1 December 2001. All subsequent references to the Trademark Law in this chapter shall refer to this latest modified and revised version of the Trademark Law.

6-602 The State Council has also adopted the following regulations:

(a) Implementing Regulations of the Trademark Law, the latest version of which was issued on 3 August 2002 and came into force on 15 September 2002; and

(b) Regulations on Special Signs, which were issued and came into effect on 13 July 1996.

6-603 The State Administration of Industry and Commerce (SAIC) has also made several administrative stipulations on trademark protection but it is not necessary for us to list them here for the purposes of our ensuing discussion.

6-604 A person who desires to obtain exclusive rights to the use of a trademark in China must first register the mark (article 4 of the Trademark Law). There is, however, an exception to this rule: unregistered famous marks are recognized in China and these marks may have the effect of blocking the registration of similar marks if they meet certain conditions specified in the Trademark Law (see discussion below).

6-605   Unlike the position under the old Trademark Law, individuals are now allowed to own trademarks as private property (article 4 of the Trademark Law). Two or more individuals, juristic persons or organizations may jointly apply for registration of a mark, and jointly own and exercise trademark rights (article 5 of the Trademark Law).

China's trademark system and requirements

What marks may be registered?

6-606   Article 8 of the Trademark Law stipulates that any visually perceptible sign capable of distinguishing the goods of any natural or legal person or any other organization from those of others is eligible for registration. The sign may include words, devices, letters, numbers, three-dimensional signs and combinations of colours or any combination of the foregoing.

Marks that may not be used or registered

6-607   Article 10 of the Trademark Law states that the following symbols shall not be used as trademarks:

(a)   those identical with or similar to the state name, national flag, national emblem, military flag, or military decorations, of the PRC, and those identical to names of specific places where central government agencies are located, or names and drawings of symbol buildings;

(b)   those identical with or similar to the state names, national flags, national emblems, or military flags of foreign countries, unless these countries allow the use of those as trademarks;

(c)   those identical with or similar to the flags, emblems, or names, of international intergovernmental organizations, unless these organizations allow the use of those symbols as trademarks and they shall not misguide the public;

(d)   those identical with or similar to official symbols and checkup impressions that are subject to control and are guaranteed, unless the use is authorized otherwise;

(e)   those identical with or similar to the symbols, or names, of the Red Cross or the Red Crescent;

(f)   those that discriminate against any nationality;

(g)   those having the nature of exaggeration and fraud in advertising goods; and

(h)   those detrimental to socialist morals or customs, or having other unhealthy influence.

6-608 Article 10 also goes on to state that the geographical names of the administrative divisions at or above the county level and the foreign geographical names well known to the public shall not be used as trademarks, unless they have other meanings or are the components of collective marks or certificate marks. Where a trademark using any of the abovementioned geographical names has been approved and registered, it continues to be valid.

6-609 Pursuant to article 11 of the Trademark Law, the following symbols shall not be registered as trademarks:

(a) symbols containing general name, graphics, and model of a certain commodity;

(b) symbols only directly indicating quality, raw material, functions, purposes, weight, quantity, and other characters of commodities; or

(c) symbols lacking distinct characters.

6-610 The symbols referred to above may be registered as trademarks if they have acquired distinctiveness through use and are distinguishable.

Trademark Decisions

(The following discussion is based on information provided in *Doing Business in China: Volume 2* edited by Freshfields Bruckhaus Deringer.)

CONFLICT WITH REGISTERED TRADEMARKS OR PENDING APPLICATIONS

Similarity in Meaning

The meaning of a trademark is not necessarily understood literally and may include similar variations. The Trademark Review and Adjudication Board (TRAB) refused registration for the mark 'nautica' because there was a prior registration of a Chinese character trademark 'Hang Hai'. The following extract from the board's decision gives the reasons for its decision:

'Although, literally, "nautica" may have no meaning, it will very likely be understood by the consumers as "nautical" because these two words are almost identical both in pronunciation and in spelling except for a one-letter difference. Since "nautical" and "Hang Hai" (meaning "nautical") have the same meaning, the two trademarks cannot be distinguished by the consumers and, as a result, will very likely cause confusion and misrecognition.'

Similarity in Appearance or in Pronunciation

The TRAB denied registration for the word 'TANGO' on account of the prior registration of the word 'TANG' for similar goods. The TRAB reasoned as follows:

> '"TANG" and "TANGO" are similar trademarks, because they are similar in appearance and in pronunciation and the difference in their respective meanings is not obvious since they are not common words and not familiar to the consumers. If they are used concurrently on similar goods, they can hardly be distinguished by the consumers and, therefore, "TANGO" cannot be allowed for registration.'

DISTINCTIVENESS REQUIREMENT

The following marks were successfully registered with the Trademark Office on account of possessing sufficient distinctiveness:

(a)   a Chinese character trademark meaning 'Good Night' circled in an oval for bedding;

(b)   a Chinese character trademark meaning 'the last supper' for pesticides;

(c)   'EUROCLEAN' for vacuum cleaners;

(d)   'DRINK IN THE SUN' for fruit juice;

(e)   'EASY TONE' for telephone sets; and

(f)   a Chinese character trademark meaning 'beautiful lady' for leather bags.

Examples of trademarks rejected on the grounds that they lacked distinctiveness include the following:

(a)   'EASY CALL' for pagers;

(b)   'AMERICAN OPTICAL' for spectacles; and

(c)   'China No. 1' and 'U.S. No. 1' (these were also rejected on the grounds that they referred to names of countries and exaggerated the quality of the products).

Protection of collective marks and certification marks

6-611   With a view to complying with TRIPS requirements, article 3 of the Trademark Law states that a registered trademark means a trademark that has been approved and registered by the Trademark Office, including goods trademarks, service marks, collective marks, and certification marks. The trademark registrant shall enjoy an exclusive right to use the trademark, which is protected by law.

6-612   Collective marks are defined in the Trademark Law to mean signs which are registered in the name of bodies, associations or other organizations to be used by their members in their commercial activities to indicate their membership of the organizations (article 3). Certification marks are defined to mean signs which are controlled by organizations capable of supervising some goods or services and used by entities or individual persons outside the organization for their goods or services to certify the origin, material, mode of manufacture, quality or other characteristics of the goods or services (article 3).

Protection for geographical indications

6-613 Geographical indications are defined in article 16 of the Trademark Law as indications that signify the place of origin of the goods in respect of which the signs are used, their specific quality, reputation or other features as mainly decided by the natural or cultural factors of the regions.

6-614 There are provisions in the Trademark Law that enable geographical indications to be registered as trademarks and permit aggrieved parties to apply for the cancellation of trademarks containing geographical indications that have been registered in bad faith (articles 3, 10, 16 and 41). It is apt to note that China's unfair competition laws may also provide appropriate remedies to interested parties who wish to take actions against activities that infringe on their rights over their geographical indications.

Protection of well known trademarks

6-615 In the past, there was concern amongst foreign investors that China's laws did not provide adequate protection for well known trademarks. The Paris Convention and TRIPS contain specific provisions requiring well known trademarks to be protected. The old Trademark Law did not contain provisions conferring any such rights although it should be noted that pursuant to the Interim Provisions Concerning the Recognition and Management of Well-Known Trademarks promulgated by the SAIC, some degree of protection was accorded to well known trademarks. The amended Law seeks to remedy this deficiency in the law by formally establishing a legal system for the protection of well known marks.

6-616 The Trademark Law now provides that a mark copying, imitating or translating an unregistered foreign famous mark on identical or similar goods or services with likelihood to cause confusion will not be granted registration or will be prohibited from being used (article 13(1)). A mark copying, imitating or translating a registered foreign famous mark on goods or services not identical or similar to those covered by the registered famous mark, causing confusion to the public and possibly causing damage to the trademark holder, will not be granted registration or will be prohibited from being used (article 13(2)).

6-617   Pursuant to article 14 of the Trademark Law, the following elements will be taken into account in determining whether a mark is well known:

(a)   reputation of the mark to relevant sectors of the public;

(b)   time of continued use of the mark;

(c)   consecutive time, extent and geographical area of advertisement of the mark;

(d)   records of protection of the mark as a well known mark; and

(e)   any other factors relevant to the reputation of the mark.

Protection of existing prior rights

6-618   The Trademark Law contains several key provisions to deal with conflicts that arise between the registrants of trademarks and the owners of legal prior rights. In order to prevent bad faith registration and uses, article 9 stipulates that any trademark for which registration is filed must not conflict with any prior right acquired by another person. Article 31 then goes on to impose the requirement that an application for the registration of a trademark must not create any prejudice to the prior right of another person. In addition, no unfair means must be used to pre-emptively register the trademark used by another person that has acquired some degree of reputation.

6-619   Xue Hong and Zheng Chengsi have explained that in view of the framework adopted in the Trademark Law, it is presumed that the Trademark Office will not *ex officio* examine the legal prior rights of each trademark application. Instead it is only when interested parties file an opposition to a trademark registration that has been preliminarily approved will the Trademark Office look into the matter and determine whether the opposition is justified. The two commentators further bolster their view by highlighting the fact that the provision on legal prior rights (article 31) appears just after the provision on oppositions (article 30).

6-620   In situations involving a breach of article 31, a trademark owner or any interested party may, within five years from the date of registration of the trademark, file a request with the TRAB for adjudication to cancel the mark (article 41). In cases involving the bad faith registration of a well known mark, the genuine owner of the mark shall not be bound by the five-year limitation.

Claims for priority

6-621 The provisions on claims for priority are contained in articles 24 and 25 of the Trademark Law. Article 24 provides that any applicant for the registration of a trademark who files an application for registration of the same trademark for identical goods in China within six months from the date of filing the first application for the trademark registration overseas may enjoy the right of priority. This will be in accordance with any agreement concluded between China and the country to which the applicant belongs, or according to the international treaty to which both countries are parties, or on the basis of the principle where each country acknowledges the right of priority of the other.

6-622 Article 25 provides that where a trademark is first used for goods in an international exhibition sponsored or recognized by the Chinese government, the applicant for the registration of the trademark may enjoy the right of priority within six months from the date of exhibition of the goods.

6-623 There are some formalities that must be adhered to in order to claim priority under both articles 24 and 25.

Judicial review

6-624 With a view to adhering to the requirement listed in article 62 of the TRIPS Agreement, articles 32, 33, 43, 49 and 50 of the Trademark Law remove the power of final adjudication of the TRAB and allow aggrieved parties to commence legal proceedings in the People's Court. In the light of these changes, decisions of administrative departments on the establishment of trademark rights are now subject to judicial review.

Infringing acts

6-625 Article 52 of the Trademark Law provides that the following acts amount to an infringement of the exclusive right to use a registered trademark:

(a) using a trademark that is identical with or similar to a registered trademark in respect of the identical or similar goods without the authorization of the trademark registrant;

(b) selling goods that a seller knows bears a counterfeited registered trademark;

(c) counterfeiting or making, without authorization, representations of a registered trademark of another person, or selling such representations of a registered trademark that are counterfeited or made without authorization;

(d)   replacing a registered trademark and putting onto the market the goods in respect of which the trademark has been replaced without the authorization of the proprietor of the registered mark; and

(e)   causing, in other respects, prejudice to the exclusive right of another person to use a registered trademark.

Administration

6-626   The changes introduced by the amendments to the Trademark Law include increases in the penalties for acts of infringement (article 56) and authorization to administrative law-enforcement organs to exercise certain powers. These include the power to impose fines as well as the power to seal up, impound, confiscate or destroy the infringing goods and instruments specifically used to manufacture the infringing goods (article 53).

Domain name disputes

6-627   The original aim for domain names was for them to perform the technical function of facilitating connectivity between computers through the Internet. As businesses caught on to the potential of the Internet, domain names started to be used in advertising and other commercial activities as business identifiers. Domain names raise attendant trademark issues due to the lack of connection between the system for registering trademarks and the system for registering domain names. The key difficulties derive from the fact that the system of trademark registration is territorial and limited to specific categories of goods or services whilst the system of domain name registration is global and operates essentially on a first come, first served basis. The differences in the two systems have given rise to situations where people have deliberately registered as domain names for themselves, the trademarks, signs and/or business identifiers belonging to other persons or businesses.

6-628   The flurry of domain name disputes that have arisen as a result has triggered various responses in China (as they have elsewhere) to address the unique issues brought up by such cases. These have involved the issuance of judicial explanations to deal with such cases and resort to alternative dispute resolution mechanisms.

6-629   The Supreme Court, in July 2001, issued the following document: Interpretations of the Supreme People's Court on Some Issues Concerning Application of Laws When Trying Civil Dispute Cases Related to Network Domain Names (Domain Names Interpretations). This document sought to summarize the experience of the courts in dealing with such disputes and absorbed an earlier document issued by the Beijing High Court to deal with domain name related disputes.

6-630 Article 4 of the Domain Names Interpretations states that a court, when trying a domain name dispute case, shall determine that the defendant's act of registration or use of domain name constitutes infringement or unfair competition if the following conditions are satisfied:

(a) the civil rights and interests for which the plaintiff seeks protection are legitimate and valid;

(b) the defendant's domain name or the main part thereof constitutes the reproduction, imitation, translation or transliteration of the plaintiff's well known mark, or is so identical with or so similar to the plaintiff's registered mark or domain name that it creates confusion on the part of the relevant public;

(c) the defendant does not enjoy any right or interest in the domain name or the main part thereof nor does the defendant have any justifiable reasons for registration or use of the domain name; and

(d) the defendant registers and uses the domain name in bad faith.

6-631 Article 5 goes on to state that in the following circumstances, the defendant shall be held as having acted in bad faith:

(a) registering a famous trademark of another as a domain name for commercial purposes;

(b) registering or using a domain name that is the same as or similar to a registered trademark or domain name of the plaintiff for commercial purposes, intentionally causing confusion in products or services provided by the plaintiff or the website of the plaintiff, and misguiding network users to visit its website or other online websites;

(c) selling, leasing or transferring by other means the domain name at a high price to seek unjust benefits;

(d) not using or not preparing to use the registered domain name by itself, and preventing the rightful owner to register the domain name intentionally; or

(e) acting in any other manner in bad faith.

6-632 Where the defendant is able to show that its domain name had acquired a reputation and may be differentiated from the registered trademark or domain name of the plaintiff, or that it did not act in bad faith, the court may hold that there is an absence of bad faith.

6-633 There has also been considerable work to provide a framework for the resolution of domain name disputes through non-governmental alternative dispute resolution processes. These include the Dispute Resolution Policy issued and subsequently revised by the China Internet Network Information Centre (CNNIC), the manager of the Chinese top-level domain, 'CN'. This is for the purposes of the domain name dispute resolution service to be provided by the Domain Name

Dispute Settlement Centre of the China International Economic and Trade Arbitration Centre (CIETAC). In November 2001, CNNIC formally started keyword registration services and this was preceded by the publication of the Interim Policy of Keyword Dispute Resolution three months earlier. This field is too complex to be dealt with in detail in an introductory chapter of this nature. Interested readers should refer to the relevant listings provided in the references section of this chapter for recommended readings on the subject. CNNIC's Domain Name Dispute Resolution Policy and Rules can be accessed at CNNIC's homepage at http://www.cnnic.net.cn.

A domain name decision (June 2000)

Ikea v Beijing Internet Information Responsibility Co Ltd

In a case brought by Ikea, a Swedish company, against Beijing Internet Information Responsibility Co Ltd (BIIRC), alleging that the registration of the domain name 'ikea.com.cn' by the latter was unfair, it was held that the use of the domain name was not valid. The judge held that the 'ikea' trademark was a well known trademark and that BIIRC's actions constituted infringement of the trademark and unfair competition. BIIRC was accordingly ordered to cease its use of the domain name within ten days of the hearing. The decision is also noteworthy for being the first decision in China involving the recognition of the rights of a well known trademark.

LEGAL PROTECTION FOR INTEGRATED CIRCUITS

6-701   The issue of the type of protection that should be given to the layout-design of integrated circuits is one that has cropped up fairly recently. The Layout-Designs of Integrated Circuits Protection Regulations (IC Regulations) were published by the State Council on 19 April 2001 and entered into force on 1 October 2001. The Implementing Rules of Layout-Designs of Integrated Circuits Protection Regulations were published by the State Intellectual Property Office on 18 September 2001 and entered into force on 1 October 2001. These regulations were passed for the purposes of ensuring that China complies with her obligations under the TRIPS Agreement.

6-702   Article 3 of the IC Regulations provides that any layout-design created by a Chinese natural person, legal person or organization, and any layout-design created by foreigners but first commercially exploited in China, shall enjoy exclusive rights pursuant to the Regulations. Any other layout-design created by foreigners shall be accorded the rights pursuant to the Regulations if the country to which the foreigner belongs has concluded an agreement with China to protect layout-designs or the country to which the foreigner belongs and China are both parties to an international treaty concerning the protection of layout-designs.

6-703 To enjoy protection under the IC Regulations, a layout-design must be 'original'. 'Original' has been defined in article 4 to mean that the layout-design is the intellectual achievement of the creator himself and is not commonplace among creators of layout-designs and manufacturers of integrated circuits at the time of its creation. Article 7 provides that the right-holder of a layout-design shall enjoy the following exclusive rights:

(a) reproducing the layout-design under protection in its entirety or for any creative part thereof; and

(b) commercially exploiting a layout-design under protection, an integrated circuit in which the layout-design is incorporated, or an article incorporating such an integrated circuit.

6-704 For protection to accrue, the layout-design must first be registered with the Intellectual Property Administration Department of the State Council (article 8). Article 12 stipulates that the length of protection shall be ten years beginning from the date of filing of the application for registration or from the date on which the layout-design was first commercially exploited anywhere in the world, whichever expires earlier. In any event, a layout-design will not be protected at the expiration of 15 years from the date of completion of its creation.

LEGAL PROTECTION FOR PLANT VARIETIES

6-801 Article 27 of the TRIPS Agreement imposes a requirement on member states to provide for the protection of plant varieties. This protection may be accorded either via the patent route or through an effective *sui generis* system (or a combination of the two). Article 25 of the Patent Law specifically excludes patent protection for plant varieties and China has, in this respect, elected to opt for a *sui generis* system of protection for plant varieties, via the enactment of the Regulations on the Protection of New Varieties of Plants.

6-802 In order to qualify for rights under the Regulations on the Protection of New Varieties of Plants, the plant variety must have the requisite characteristic of novelty, distinctiveness, uniformity and stability and an adequate denomination. A detailed discussion of these requirements and other aspects of plant variety protection falls outside the scope of this chapter.

CONCLUSION

6-901   The enforcement of intellectual property rights is typically commenced with an investigation to ascertain the scope and level of infringement. An investigation will also be useful in extracting the evidence required for filing a complaint. An investigation would also usually assist in determining whether the infringer manufactures and/or sells the goods, the volume of infringing goods produced or sold and the possible location of these goods. The outcome of these investigations would then enable the rights holder to make an educated determination of whether to proceed with issuing a cease and desist letter, raid actions or filing a lawsuit. The details and mechanics pertaining to each of these courses of action are outside the scope of this chapter. The interested reader desiring additional information on these actions may benefit from the information provided at the following site: http://wangandwangcom/china_enforcement.htm.

6-902   A rights holder who wishes to enforce his intellectual property rights in China should note that enforcing these rights is sometimes a tricky hit-and-miss affair. Scott Palmer, in his incisive article 'An Identity Crisis: Regime Legitimacy and the Politics of Intellectual Property Rights in China', highlights the anomalies that sometimes take place in the topsy-turvy world of intellectual property enforcement in China:

> The Kellogg's Corn Flakes case is perhaps a good example of the complexities of enforcement in light of China's unique political and legal landscape. In 1994, Kellogg sued a Chinese company selling cereal in packaging that was essentially identical to the packaging used by Kellogg – from a transliteration of the Kellogg name written in its distinctive script, to famous Kellogg copyrighted slogans replicated on the box. In a lower Chinese court, Kellogg lost its case for trademark infringement. The lower court, relying on a 'tendentious line of reasoning and reading of the evidence,' not only found for the Chinese party, but ordered Kellogg to pay court costs and damages.
>
> Kellogg then appealed to the Provincial High Court, which, just after the United States and China signed the 1995 Memorandum of Understanding, overturned the initial decision. Although the High Court provided sound legal reasons, critics suggest that the Court acted with instruction from political authorities. If the critics are correct in their evaluation, this case may be illustrative of several of the points discussed above. First, it exemplifies the tendency of lower level courts to favor local interests, even if the court lacks sufficient evidence to support its decision. Second, the outcome at the court of first instance may be further justified by a jurisprudential emphasis on the centrality of legal formalism and procedural compliance over the substantive consequences or equitable nature of the outcome. And third, the ultimate outcome illustrates the absence of judicial independence, regardless of whether, as in this case, it actually proved favorable for US businesses.

6-903 It should, however, be noted that the legal landscape pertaining to intellectual property law and enforcement is gradually changing in China. There is a marked difference in the quality of some of the recent judgments delivered by the Chinese courts when compared to judgments rendered in the past. This serves to give many rights holders a certain degree of optimism that the authorities and judiciary in China are starting to take a firm and a less tolerant attitude towards intellectual property infringement.

REFERENCES AND FURTHER READING

Books

Chow D K, *A Primer on Foreign Investment Enterprises and Protection of Intellectual Property in China* (Kluwer Law International, 2002).

M Cohen, Bang E and S Mitchell, *Chinese Intellectual Property Law and Practice* (Kluwer Law International, 1999).

Freshfields, Bruckhaus Deringer (ed), *Doing Business in China: Volume 2* (Juris Publishing, 2002).

Wang Guiguo and John Mo (eds), *Chinese Law* (Kluwer Law International, 1999).

C Heath and A K Sanders (eds), *Intellectual Property in the Digital Age: Challenges for Asia* (Kluwer Law International, 2001).

Hong Xue and Chengsi Zheng, *Chinese Intellectual Property Law in the 21st Century* (Sweet & Maxwell Asia, 2002).

Hong Xue, *Software Protection in China: A Complete Guide* (Sweet & Maxwell Asia, 1999).

T Kourdi, *Strategies and Techniques for Doing Business in China* (Thorogood, 2000).

Clarisa Long, *Intellectual Property Rights in Emerging Markets* (AEI Press, 2000).

M L Riley, *Protecting Intellectual Property Rights in China* (Sweet & Maxwell Asia, 2001).

Tan L K and C Borg-Marks, *Trade Mark Law in the People's Republic of China* (Oxford University Press, 1998).

Wang K H, *Chinese Commercial Law* (Oxford University Press, 2000).

Yu G and Gu M, *Laws Affecting Business Transactions in the PRC* (Kluwer Law International, 2001).

Articles

O M Baratta and D L Hanaman, 'A Global Update on the Domain Name System and the Law: Alternative Dispute Resolution for Increasing Internet Competition – Oh, the Times They Are a-Changin'!' (2000) 8 *Tulane Journal of International and Comparative Law* 325.

Chen J, 'Better Patent Law for International Commitment – The Amendment of Chinese Patent Law' (2001) 2 *Richmond Journal of Global Law and Business* 61.

J Litman, 'The DNS Wars: Trademarks and the Internet Domain Name System' (2000) 4 *The Journal of Small and Emerging Business Law* 149.

S A McKenzie, 'Global Protection of Trademark Intellectual Property Rights: A Comparison of Infringement and Remedies Available in China Versus the European Union' (1998–1999) 34 *Gonzaga Law Review* 529.

S J Palmer, 'An Identity Crisis: Regime Legitimacy and the Politics of Intellectual Property Rights in China' (2001) 8 *Indiana Journal of Global Legal Studies* 449.

A Samtani, 'Electronic Commerce Law in Asia: A Case for Convergence' (2000) 30 *Asia Business Law Review* 50.

Louis S Sorell, 'A Comparative Analysis of Selected Aspects of Patent Law in China and the United States' (2002) 11 *Pacific Rim Law & Policy Journal* 319.

R L Taylor, 'Tearing Down the Great Wall: China's Road to WTO Accession' (2001) 41 *IDEA: The Journal of Law and Technology* 151.

J P L Teoh and C Smith, 'New Chinese Language Domain Name Resolution Procedures: ICANN Can't, But Can China?' (March 2001) 15(2) *China Law & Practice*.

B Williams, 'Global Trade Issues in the New Millennium: The Influence and Lack of Influence of Principles in the Negotiation for China's Accession to the World Trade Organization' (2001) 33 *George Washington International Law Review* 791.

Wu R, 'New Rules for Resolving Chinese Domain Name Disputes – A Comparative Analysis' (2001) *The Journal of Information, Law and Technology*.

Xiang J Y, 'How Wide Should the Gate of "Technology" Be? Patentability of Business Methods in China' (2002) 11 *Pacific Rim Law & Policy Journal* 795.

B T Yonehara, 'Enter the Dragon: China's WTO Accession, Film Piracy and Prospects for Enforcement of Copyright Laws' (2002) 12 *DePaul-LCA Journal of Art and Entertainment Law* 63.

Yu P, 'From Pirates to Partners: Protecting Intellectual Property in China in the Twenty-First Century' (2000) 50 *The American Law Review* 131.

Zhou J J, 'Trademark Law & Enforcement in China: A Transnational Perspective' (2002) 20 *Wisconsin International Law Journal* 415.

Chapter 7

Due Diligence

Tan Chong Huat, Chew Boon Kheng and Terence Lin

INTRODUCTION

7-101　The main objective of conducting due diligence is to obtain full disclosure in relation to the investment target thereby permitting a fair evaluation of the transaction. Although the lack of transparency and the relative lack of maturity of the legal system in China poses significant obstacles to the due diligence process in China, these factors do not render the process any less vital to commercial transactions. Undisclosed liabilities and non-compliance with legal and regulatory requirements remain very real risks and although due diligence may not completely expose or detect certain potential pitfalls, the due diligence process should not be taken lightly or dispensed with.

7-102　Part of the reason why due diligence exercises carried out in China may be less vigorous compared to those in other countries could be due to the fact that many new investors to China simply rely uncritically on the representations of the Chinese party without proper investigation. This is particularly so where the Chinese party is a state-owned enterprise (SOE). Foreign investors may then be under the mistaken impression that the Chinese party speaks as a representative of the government and that its pronouncements and statements on ownership issues and licensing requirements accurately represent the law and policy of China. Proper due diligence in the PRC can also be complicated and time consuming, and many investors may be willing to settle for a less thorough investigation due to lack of time, business competition or market volatility.

7-103　The quality of the information obtained in the course of due diligence is becoming increasingly important with the growing maturity of the Chinese market and increasing pressure created by international underwriters with the growing number of Chinese companies attempting to list on stock exchanges outside China.

DUE DILIGENCE PROCESS

7-201　The nature of foreign investment in China has changed significantly since the launch of the 'open door' policy in 1979. During the 1980s, most of the projects involving foreign investment were 'greenfield' projects in which the foreign investor and Chinese partner agreed to build on or develop a parcel of undeveloped land. Since the only significant asset was the land itself, due diligence on these projects was relatively uncomplicated and required relatively less investigation.

7-202   During the 1990s, activities such as merger and acquisition transactions and overseas listings became more prevalent, subjecting Chinese companies to a more rigorous standard of due diligence in line with international practice. At that time, due diligence exercises were not well received by the Chinese parties. Prior to the 'open door' policy, permitting access to the financial and operating records and other sensitive documents of a SOE could amount to an illegal act, risking the invocation of state secrets laws and policies. Offenders and anyone assisting them could expect to be severely punished if found guilty.

7-203   Many of the senior managers and decision makers in Chinese companies today may remember the days before the 'open door' policy and as such, cling to old mindsets and business practices and be resistant to making full disclosure. It is therefore good practice for foreign investors to clarify any doubts and issues that the senior management of the Chinese party may have prior to the due diligence exercise to ensure full co-operation.

Letter of intent

7-204   It is a common practice in China for the foreign and Chinese business partners to execute a non-binding letter of intent prior to the due diligence examination. The letter of intent will usually set out the amount invested and the main 'conditions' agreed to by both parties. It is also increasingly common to sign mutual confidentiality agreements or non-disclosure agreements prior to commencing due diligence. This will often help to overcome the reluctance of the China party to turn over sensitive commercial information.

7-205   The due diligence process will typically consist of several avenues and means of investigation, often carried out concurrently by various professionals and advisers.

Due diligence checklist

7-206   Usually, the first step in due diligence involves the lawyers of the foreign investor preparing and sending to the Chinese party a written due diligence checklist requesting various relevant documents, licences and approvals. Although it may be more convenient to use the standard template used in other countries, the checklist should be customized to suit the transaction and requirements of the Chinese legal system. In particular, the lawyers preparing the checklist should pay attention to the queries relating to the problem areas peculiar to the Chinese system.

Chinese translation

7-207 The due diligence checklist should be translated into Chinese, preferably by the investor's own lawyers. This is because Mandarin is the official language in China and proficiency in the English language cannot be taken for granted. Chinese parties who are not proficient in English may delay their response, give meaningless or irrelevant responses or even ignore a checklist in the English language. If the checklist is translated by the Chinese party, the translation may not be of sufficiently high quality for the purposes of due diligence. The poor quality of the translation, especially if carried out by inexperienced or non-legally trained translators, may result in miscommunication and delayed responses as clarification is sought. As a result, the speed and quality of the information obtained in the course of due diligence may be compromised.

Customization

7-208 Like the due diligence checklists meant for use in other countries, the checklist should be tailored to take into account the nature of the transaction. If the nature of the proposed transaction has already been determined by the parties, the due diligence checklist should be prepared with that transaction in mind. For example, it may be inappropriate in a simple asset acquisition for the investor to be granted full access to the financial and operating records of the Chinese party.

7-209 A sample due diligence checklist is found in the Appendix to this chapter. The second half of this chapter will deal with the issues raised in each section of the sample checklist in greater detail.

On-site inspections and management interviews

7-210 The due diligence checklist itself is merely a starting point and is insufficient to give a complete picture of the Chinese party. On-site visits, interviews with management and extensive follow up are *de rigeur* for thorough due diligence.

7-211 In a case where the Chinese party's response to the checklist is insufficient or inadequate, the manager and relevant department heads may be interviewed to obtain the desired information. In this respect, the lawyers and other advisers of the investor are advised to work closely with the manager or department heads in charge of the administration or records of the Chinese party to ensure that the objectives of due diligence are met.

Personnel involved

7-212   On-site inspections are usually essential for environmental auditors, accountants, appraisers and other professionals and advisers. Lawyers are also advised to conduct an on-site review of the Chinese party's documents to ensure comprehensive replies to the checklist. Sometimes on-site inspection by lawyers is the only way to obtain the necessary information as the Chinese party may reject the idea of making copies of the relevant documents.

Public searches

7-213   The importance of on-site inspections is further emphasized by the lack of publicly available information. Most of the information databases in China are kept by the various authorities with limited access to the public, making it difficult, if not impossible, to obtain a comprehensive and integrated picture of the Chinese party.

Professionals and advisers

7-214   A due diligence team should comprise lawyers, accountants, bankers, appraisers, environmental assessors, and any other professionals or advisers as determined by the nature of the transaction and the needs of the parties.

Lawyers

7-215   Lawyers play perhaps the most crucial role in due diligence and often form the nexus co-ordinating the other elements of the due diligence team. Lawyers will usually prepare the due diligence checklist and examine the documents produced in response thereto. Lawyers may also be involved in conducting interviews with the Chinese party's management and other follow-up action.

7-216   The findings are usually compiled into a written report listing the documents examined and the contents thereof and will usually include an analysis of, amongst other things, potential and actual pitfalls, problems, and reflect the lack of legal compliance, and any information relevant to the transaction.

7-217   Depending on the transaction, the lawyers and accountants on the team may work hand in hand in the evaluation of the financial risks and potential legal liabilities of the Chinese party.

Accountants, bankers and other financial consultants

7-218   The amount of investigation carried out by accountants and the depth and detail of the accountant's report may vary depending on the size and significance of the acquisition, the availability of financial information, and the degree of risk and time allowed. Typically, the examination of the Chinese party by accountants may involve anything from a simple review of financial statements and records to a full audit. Depending on the concerns of the investor and the transaction, the accountants may also render advice on tax efficiency and foreign exchange issues.

7-219 In cases where the accounting standards of the Chinese party depart from international standards, it is not uncommon, especially in transactions in contemplation of an overseas public offering, for international accounting firms to convert existing financial statements into financial statements consistent with international accounting practices.

7-220 If the transaction contemplates a public offering, the investment banker plays a critical role in the due diligence process, particularly when it will act as the underwriter in the proposed offering. In order to ensure both a market for the Chinese party's shares and to avoid liability, investment bankers usually work hand in hand with lawyers and accountants in examining the financial condition of the Chinese company, its ownership of assets and potential legal and financial liabilities.

Appraisers

7-221 Professional appraisers are also often employed or contracted to assist in the valuation of assets of the Chinese party.

Environmental assessors

7-222 China's push for modernization and industrialization has resulted in heavy pollution and considerable environmental damage. The Chinese government is tightening its laws to control environmental damage, curb pollution and punish polluters. New rules and regulations have been promulgated to reduce effluent discharges and impose fines and liabilities on offenders. Depending on the nature of the investor's operations, the investor may wish to engage an environmental assessor to conduct a thorough environmental audit.

7-223 If the transaction contemplates the formation of a joint venture company, the impact on the environment by the operations of the company is taken into consideration in the feasibility study report. An environmental audit report can form the basis for this part of the feasibility study to be submitted to the government.

DUE DILIGENCE CHECKLIST

7-301   The main objective of the due diligence checklist is to facilitate the disclosure of actual and potential liabilities in relation to the Chinese party. The remainder of this chapter will examine the issues and potential risks peculiar to the Chinese legal system which may arise in the course of a transaction. This checklist has been drafted on the basis of an investor transacting with a Sino-foreign equity joint venture.

Group structure and summary on the development history of the company

7-302   This section serves as an introduction to the Chinese party and may contain valuable information about the context in which the transaction will take place. The investor may wish to pay special attention to the other companies or entities related to the Chinese party. This will help to establish the legitimacy and substance of the Chinese party. For example, if the Chinese party is part of an established group with a sound reputation and enters into the transaction with the backing of that group, there may be less risk exposure to the investor. The opposite is also true. If the Chinese party has not been in existence for very long and does not appear to have any relationships, links or contacts with any other established entities, the investor would be advised to exercise extra caution in the due diligence exercise as the business entity may be a front set up by unscrupulous individuals to fleece gullible investors.

7-303   The information contained in this section may also serve as a springboard for further investigation by the investor. For example, what is the nature of the relationship of the Chinese party with the group? Is the Chinese party or its group known for giving trouble to their business partners and for backing out of deals? How does this transaction factor into the business direction or strategy of the group?

Incorporation documents of the company

7-304   The reason for examining the constitutional documents of the company is to confirm that the Chinese party is a duly established legal person and that its constitutional documents do not restrict it from engaging in the transaction.

Capacity

7-305   Generally, the Chinese party is duly established if it has obtained the requisite approvals from the various authorities. Care must be taken to ensure that the approvals are obtained not only from all the necessary authorities, but also from the correct level of the authority as well. For example, all projects above US$30 million involving foreign investment must be approved by the central government. For joint ventures, approval must be obtained from the local government authorities as well as the Ministry of Foreign Trade and Economic Co-operation (MOFTEC).[1]

Authorization

7-306 The investor should take care that the transaction to be undertaken by the Chinese party is within its business scope. The business scope of the Chinese party can be found in its business licence, articles of association and/or joint venture contract, if it is a joint venture. The documents will also allow the investor to ensure that the procedures taken to authorize the transaction are adequate and in compliance with the company's constitutional documents.

7-307 The exact form of the constitutional documents will differ according to the type of entity in question.

State-owned enterprise

7-308 Usually SOEs do not have articles of association or by-laws and the only constitutional document available would be its business licence. The business licence, which should be issued by the State Administration of Industry and Commerce (SAIC) will indicate the following:

(a) whether the entity is a legal person with the capacity to contract;

(b) the nature of the enterprise, whether state-owned, collectively-owned, limited liability company, equity or co-operative joint venture or other;

(c) the business scope of the enterprise;

(d) the name of the enterprise's legal representative.

7-309 Important contracts and documents will usually require the signature of the legal representative together with the official seal. If the company has a board of directors, it is also advisable to require a board resolution authorizing such execution.

Limited liability companies

7-310 Also known as 'limited liability stock companies' under the PRC Company Law. If a state enterprise has been converted into a limited liability company, it should have constitutional documents and a board of directors. As stated above, the constitutional documents, including the business licence and articles of association, should be

---

1 MOFTEC has now merged with the State Economic and Trade Commission (SETC) to form the Ministry of Commerce.

reviewed to verify that the proposed transaction is within the company's authorized business scope and that the procedures taken to authorize the transaction are adequate and in compliance with the company's constitutional documents. Unlike foreign jurisdictions, a Chinese company's charter documents are usually not available to the public for inspection, and must be produced by the company. The documents should also be certified as having been duly filed with the proper authorities.

Foreign joint ventures and enterprises

7-311   Entities involving foreign investment or foreign invested enterprises (FIEs) may take the form of equity joint ventures, contractual joint ventures, co-operative joint ventures or wholly foreign-owned enterprises (WFOE). In such a case, a whole range of documents must be obtained.

Application form

7-312   This is an initial document submitted in the process of establishing a FIE and contains basic information about the FIE.

Project proposal

7-313   The project proposal (*lixiang*) is one of the initial documents submitted by the Chinese party to the approval authorities as part of the process of establishing a FIE. Based on the project proposal, if the Chinese party is granted official approval by the relevant approval authority to proceed with establishing the FIE, the foreign investor will then proceed to prepare the feasibility study report. The project proposal will provide fairly basic information about the FIE, but more than the application form.

Feasibility study report

7-314   This is a formal business plan demonstrating the commercial viability of a project. The feasibility study is fairly detailed and will include particulars of how the FIE proposes to balance its foreign exchange receipts and payments and how its resources will be used.

7-315   The feasibility study must not be taken at face value, however, as it also serves a promotional function. The information contained therein has been carefully organized to elicit the approval of the Chinese approval authorities. Although this study should contain a fair amount of detail, however, the foreign investor will usually temper disclosure with discretion in order to maintain a degree of flexibility in the future. In the case of a WFOE, the foreign investor will prepare the feasibility study, although a local agent will usually be appointed to assist with this task.

Approvals from the various authorities

7-316   The various approvals should be reviewed to ensure that all the necessary approvals have been obtained and that the Chinese party has been validly established. The scope of the approvals should also be carefully scrutinized in order to ensure that the Chinese party is allowed to do what it is purporting to do.

Joint venture contract and articles of association

7-317   The joint venture contract and articles of association of a joint venture are the key documents of the joint venture. If the investor is executing a joint venture contract with a Chinese party, the investor may wish to prepare the contract itself to ensure that its interests are fully protected. One of the more important functions of due diligence at this point is to establish that the Chinese party has the authority and capacity to negotiate and enter into the transaction with the foreign investor. The joint venture contract and articles of association will provide fairly intimate details about the joint venture in question, including provisions reflecting the business scope of the joint venture, the type, amount and timing of capital contributions, responsibilities of the parties, grounds for early termination of the joint venture contract, a mechanism for liquidation and provisions for dispute resolution.

Shareholders' agreement

7-318   Where a WFOE has two or more investors, a shareholders' agreement may be executed by the shareholders to define the rights of one shareholder against another, although such is not necessary for approval purposes. Such agreements may be governed by foreign law and the investor may wish to ensure that *vis-a-vis* the WFOE, the procedures taken to authorize the transaction are adequate and in compliance with the shareholders' agreement.

Other types of entity

7-319   The Chinese partner may also be a collective enterprise, an 'institutional legal person' (a form of quasi-governmental or non-profit entity), or a private enterprise. Each of them must be investigated by the lawyers on a case by case basis, notwithstanding that many such entities have received approvals from certain authorities. It is possible that these entities may be barred from carrying out certain acts or from entering into the transaction with the investor because of some irregularity in its formation or the failure to obtain the approval of some authority.

6-320   Also, the documents referred to under each category of entities (SOEs, FIEs, etc) above apply only generally. In specific cases, the entity may be validly established notwithstanding that a relevant constitutional document may not be present as Chinese government approval authorities generally have broad discretion and latitude to interpret or waive published restrictions or to impose unpublished requirements in a particular instance.

Capital structure

7-321   The information referred to in this section can be ascertained from the financial records and other reports kept by the Chinese party. This is usually done via on-site inspection by accountants. In a share or asset acquisition, one objective of reviewing the financial records is to verify the Chinese party's valuation of its contributions to the joint venture. If the investor is entering into a joint venture with the Chinese party, the balance sheet can assist in determining which of the Chinese party's assets and liabilities should be transferred into the joint venture. The profit and loss statement may reveal important information about how well (or how badly) the Chinese partner is performing, and its main sources of income, revenue or profits or the main causes of its losses. The capital verification report issued by PRC registered accountants will assist the investor by certifying the amount of capital that has been paid-up to the company or joint venture by the Chinese party. Chinese accounting practices may appear alien and difficult for foreign accountants to comprehend, and sometimes a close examination of the Chinese party's financial records, perhaps even a full audit, may be necessary for effective due diligence.

7-322   The appraisers may wish to examine the asset valuation reports of the Chinese party and may then verify the reports independently in order to ascertain the true value (as opposed to book value) of the assets. This step is crucial in an asset acquisition exercise as unscrupulous parties may try to sell off obsolete assets or attempt to pass off inventory as being of higher quality to the unwary investor.

Real properties

7-323   Real properties and the rights attached to them usually pose the greatest potential for mischief in a transaction, with any neglect or mistake in due diligence resulting in unanticipated liabilities at best, and cessation of operations at worst. The investor is well advised to pay close attention to the land use rights of the Chinese party as it may have serious implications in the future.

7-324   The purpose of due diligence is to ensure that the land use rights in question allow uninterrupted use of the land for the required duration without any undisclosed or unanticipated liabilities in the form of land use premiums or compulsory acquisition by the government without compensation.

7-325 There are two types of land use rights in China, namely, allocated land use rights and granted land use rights.

Allocated land use rights

7-326 Prior to April 1988, the state allocated land use rights without consideration. Although allocated land use rights are transferred to the user for free, an annual land use tax is usually payable. The most important characteristic of allocated land use rights is that the user has no right to transfer it and that the state may recover the land at any time without paying compensation. In other words, these allocated land use rights cannot be transferred, mortgaged or leased unless and until they have been converted into granted land use rights. Buildings constructed on state-owned land where the land users only have allocated land use rights may be mortgaged or leased, but the land users are required to turn over a portion of the rental to the state.

7-327 To effect a conversion from allocated rights to granted land use rights, the holder of the allocated land use rights must submit an application to the local land bureau. Upon approval by the land bureau, the holder of the allocated land use rights must execute a land grant contract with the local land bureau and pay a land premium to the local land bureau. Upon payment and receipt of the land premium, a state-owned land use certificate will be issued by the local land bureau to the new granted land use rights holder. Thereafter, the land use right may be transferred, mortgaged or leased to other parties.

Granted land use rights

7-328 In a nutshell, when land use rights are 'granted', the user pays the state a land grant premium for the right to use the land for a specified period. The granted land use right is transferable (including by mortgage and lease) by the grantee.

7-329 The PRC Land Administration Law was adopted in 1987 to permit the assignment of land rights for value. Although ownership remains with the state, legal entities were permitted to lease the land under the concept of land use rights.

7-330 The state may grant land use rights to a land user under a grant agreement for the purposes stated in the grant agreement for a definite period of time and against payment of a grant premium. In general, the state may not resume possession prior to the expiration of the term of grant without compensation. Subject to annual 'land use fees' and compliance with covenants in the grant agreement, a holder of granted land use rights may exercise practically all the rights of ownership during the term of grant, including the right to transfer or assign the property to another party.

Risks in acquiring allocated land use rights

7-331   A substantial land premium is required for conversion of allocated land use rights into granted land use rights. As a result, with the exception of property development projects, allocated land use rights held by cash-strapped Chinese parties are rarely converted into granted land use rights prior to any transfer or assignment. Notwithstanding that allocated land use rights are technically non-transferable, Chinese parties have been known to persuade sympathetic local land bureaux to register the allocated land right in the name of the another party, thereby effecting a 'transfer' of sorts.

7-332   A foreign investor that does not insist on conversion from allocated land use rights to granted land use rights prior to the transfer faces several risks. The government authority that permitted the transfer of allocated land use rights is empowered to recover the allocated land use rights without compensation as the development of urban construction and urban planning may require or where the land user to whom the land was allocated ceases to use the land due to removal, dissolution, cancellation, bankruptcy or other reasons. Proper compensation will only be given for the structures on and other attachments to the land in light of the actual circumstances. If the Chinese party has transferred its allocated land use rights to the joint venture in contravention of the applicable law and regulation, it is uncertain whether such compensation will be paid by the government.

7-333   During due diligence, this issue of recovery or acquisition by the government authority must be identified, the risk carefully assessed and, if assumed, allocated to the Chinese party with a suitable indemnity in the acquisition documents if the conversion to granted land use rights is not workable.

Acquiring granted land use rights from the state

7-334   Certain transactions, for example, establishing a joint venture with a Chinese partner, may involve the acquisition of granted land use rights. In general, there are two methods of acquiring granted land use rights. The first is to obtain a grant directly from the state, and the second is to obtain an assignment from a current land user.

7-335   Newly granted land use rights can only be obtained by entering into a land grant contract with the relevant land bureau. In the case of a joint venture, either the joint venture can enter into the land use contract directly, in which case the joint venture will be liable to pay the land grant premium, or the Chinese party can contract for the land, and then transfer the land use right to the joint venture. A deposit on the land premium is usually paid and an instalment schedule will be implemented for the payment of the balance of the land premium. Upon payment of the land premium in full and subject to the other requirements of the local land bureau, a state-owned land use certificate will be issued to the land use rights holder. Where the Chinese party contracts for the land, the land grant premium should be paid in one lump sum rather than in instalments, since under Chinese law a default on payment of the land grant premium empowers the land bureau to recover the land.

7-336 The grant of land use rights by the government will be in accordance with the land use master plans and land use annual plans approved by the central and provincial governments.

Transfer of granted land use rights from the Chinese party

7-337 Where the land use rights are transferred by the Chinese party to the joint venture or investment vehicle, the investor should ensure that the transfer is in strict accordance with the prescribed procedure and that the land use rights are in order and properly acquired.

7-338 In the case of granted land use rights being transferred from the Chinese party, the Chinese party must enter into a land transfer contract with the investor and register the same with the local land bureau. A new state-owned land use certificate would then be issued by the local land bureau, evidencing the transfer of the granted land use rights for the remaining term under the original land grant contract. During due diligence, the investor should ensure that any conditions precedent to alienation in the land grant contract have been complied with.

7-339 In summary, the prudent investor contemplating a transaction involving land use rights in China must pay special attention to the nature of the rights it is acquiring. The land use rights certificate, the land grant contract or land transfer contract must be requested from the Chinese party and carefully examined. Where there is some question over title, the investor is well advised to retain local Chinese counsel to issue a legal opinion on this issue. Typically only local counsel can access local land bureau records to confirm the chain of title.

7-340 Generally, the investor is advised to demand granted land use rights, except in fairly limited circumstances: when the land is intended to be used for only a limited period of time, when the investment is small; or when the use rights relate to a portion of a larger allocated facility where it would be impractical to subdivide and create granted land use rights.

Other fixed assets

7-341 In addition to land use rights, the investor should also try to ascertain whether the Chinese party's other fixed and intangible assets are owned by it. Whereas a land use rights certificate is usually good evidence of the right to use land, documents of title do not exist for most other assets, such as machinery and equipment. Developments on the land (ie buildings, factories, warehouses, etc) are one notable exception. Building ownership certificates or real estate certificates are usually issued to owners once construction is completed. These should be requested from the Chinese party during the course of the due diligence examination and examined to confirm that the Chinese party is the owner on record.

7-342 A foreign investor should prepare a comprehensive list of assets to be acquired, incorporate the list as a schedule to the acquisition documents and include proper representations and warranties as to title and fitness for the intended purposes.

Intellectual property rights and other intangible assets of the company

Intellectual property

7-343 Ownership of intangible property rights like trademarks and patents can be confirmed through patent and trademark searches. These must be conducted through authorized PRC patent and trademark agents. The foreign investor should also ensure that intellectual property and technology acquired are not subject to restrictions on export.

Company's business

7-344 The queries in this section are especially relevant if the transaction contemplates a purchase of shares in the Chinese party as these may amount to contractual representations by the Chinese party. However, the Chinese party may be understandably reluctant to disclose sensitive information relating to its distribution channels, future product launches, customer base, suppliers, competitors and creditors. In this regard, the mutual confidentiality agreements or non-disclosure agreements signed prior to due diligence may help to overcome the reluctance of the Chinese party to turn over sensitive commercial information.

Creditors and debtors

7-345 In 1995, China adopted a national legal framework for registering security interests, including encumbrances on land use rights and buildings for the first time. Although compliance has been slow, eventually when the framework is fully effective, it should be easier to determine the existence of any mortgage, lien or other encumbrance on the property of the Chinese party.

7-346 Meanwhile, until registration becomes more widespread, another method of verification is to examine the Chinese party's loan and guarantee agreements. Most Chinese bank loan documents, although usually quite simple, almost always contain a provision creating a lien on all the borrower's assets.

7-347 In the event that due diligence examination reveals the existence of mortgages or other liens on the Chinese party's assets, the appropriate provisions should be drafted into the acquisition documents. Such provisions may require the release of any mortgage or lien or a waiver from the third party as conditions precedent to closing, and/or include a comprehensive indemnity protecting the investor. Alternatively, the purchaser may seek to adjust the price to balance the risks created by such competing interests.

Material contracts and business documents of the company

7-348 Although written contracts may not be as extensively used in China or as sophisticated as that found in the West, existing contracts which the Chinese party is party to should be investigated. This not only provides the foreign investor insight into the business operations of the Chinese party, but existing contractual obligations may also conflict with the Chinese party's dealings with the investor, necessitating waivers or consents from the third party.

Financing, loan, guarantee and mortgage agreements

7-349 These agreements should be examined closely as default under any of them may result in severe financial repercussions on the Chinese party.

Technology transfer and assistance agreements

7-350 Technology licence agreements with third parties, especially agreements of this type entered into within the last ten years, should be examined to determine whether they contain provisions that would affect any proposed acquisition by the investor.

7-351 As an example, the Chinese party may have previously entered into a licence agreement to use a third party's technology which contained a covenant not to compete that extended for several years beyond the end of the licence. An issue may then arise as to whether, by entering into the proposed transaction with the foreign investor, the Chinese party would be in breach of the covenant not to compete.

7-352 As can be seen from the above example, an examination of significant contracts entered into by the Chinese party can often reveal the existence of undisclosed and unduly burdensome obligations the investor may not wish to assume.

Tax

7-353   The return on investment of the foreign investor is dependent on the applicable tax liabilities to which the Chinese party is subject. It is important to confirm that the Chinese party has no undisclosed tax liabilities in order to arrive at a fair evaluation of the investment. As it is not currently possible to obtain tax clearance certificates from the authorities, the appropriate representations and warranties should be incorporated into the transaction documents.

7-354   The corporate income tax rates in China vary according to a myriad of factors such as the location of the enterprise, the industry involved and whether the enterprise comprises domestic investment or foreign investment. Frequently, local governments, eager to compete for desirable foreign investment funds, will offer lower tax rates than those prescribed by national legislation.

7-355   During due diligence, the foreign investor should confirm the applicable income tax rates and, if preferential rates are extended, confirm whether the rates are consistent with national law. If not, there can be no assurance that the business entity in question will be able to continue to enjoy such favourable treatment over the life of the venture.

7-356   Tax holidays are available in connection with some forms of foreign investment and the foreign investor should consider the availability of such holidays during the due diligence evaluation process.

7-357   If the investor uncovers any questionable tax avoidance structures employed by the Chinese party, they should require the tax structure to be 'cleaned up' as a condition precedent to the completion of the transaction.

Board of directors and senior management personnel

7-358   The directors and management personnel of the Chinese party will usually command remuneration and benefits far exceeding that of the ordinary worker. The benefits package offered to all senior personnel should be monitored closely to ensure that remuneration is commensurate with performance. The severance benefits of the senior personnel should also be examined closely as these may prove to be significant burdens should the senior management personnel leave the Chinese party. In any event, as the following cautionary example will show, the track record of the Chinese party's management should be closely scrutinized for its integrity as well as ability.

7-359 Recently, a world leader in domestic white ware terminated its joint venture investment in China within three years after investing US$70 million in the Chinese joint venture. The foreign investor built a state-of-the-art plant and left its operation to the local partner with the foreign partner providing only technical support and financial supervision. The plant never reached more than 8% of capacity, supposedly because the local partner could not operate it.

7-360 Only in the third year of operation did they appoint a foreign manager. By that stage, the local partner had effective control over the operation and was utilizing the facilities for its own business plans. After a great deal of frustration and irreconcilable differences in business objectives and motives, the foreign firm finally decided to write-off a loss of US$42 million rather than pursue the lucrative China market in their current form.

Employees of the company

Pressure to retain

7-361 Another key objective of due diligence is to investigate the current staffing and compensation structure of any business unit to be transferred. In asset acquisitions, the foreign investor is not legally obligated to take on the seller's employees, but as a practical matter, it may come under pressure to hire most, if not all, of its employees from the Chinese party. When taking over an existing plant from a Chinese party, who then becomes the partner to a newly established joint venture company, local government policy strongly encourages the hiring of the Chinese party's existing workers. An internal directive from the municipal government in Shanghai requires Chinese parties to try to seek a firm commitment in the acquisition documents to hire all or a large part of the existing employees. Existing national labour laws, however, give foreign invested enterprises autonomy in relation to employment of workers and investors should resist pressure to take on unnecessary or unqualified workers from the Chinese party.

Practicalities of laying off employees

7-362 Given Chinese employment practices, it is very likely that the existing factory will be burdened with excess workers, and laying off redundant employees may not be simple or cheap. In China, an employer who lays off a worker is often responsible to support such a person and his or her family, and may be required to find that worker acceptable alternative employment. Foreign investors are usually advised to accept into the joint venture only those workers that it can actually sustain, so that the joint venture entity will not be responsible for lay-offs.

Welfare obligations

7-363 A foreign investor also needs to ascertain the nature of the employee welfare obligations it will inherit. Chinese businesses often provide benefits, such as housing, clinics and schools, at no cost or nominal cost to their employees. Building new housing and social welfare facilities for joint venture workers is an expensive option. Many investors have been able to arrive at an arrangement whereby the Chinese party continues to provide some or all of the benefits; but this may not be realistic where the Chinese partner's entire operation will become part of the joint venture. An investor also should be aware that workers' hourly wages may not represent the majority of their cash compensation. Sino-foreign joint ventures are required to pay mandatory labour benefits, in the form of insurance, welfare funds, incentive funds and various subsidies, that may double direct labour cost. The Chinese employer may also have paid its workers non-mandatory subsidies, for example food and clothing allowances, or other bonuses and incentives, which the joint venture may be expected to maintain. In share purchase acquisitions, the foreign investor buys into the company as it exists and may be subject to pension liability.

Advantages to retaining employees

7-364 There may be certain advantages to retaining the employees of the Chinese party. The Chinese party's employees will be well trained, experienced and may be familiar with the nature of the work and their fellow colleagues. They will also have housing and a household registration near their area of work. Foreign investors should be aware that hiring from outside the locality of the plant can be problematic in some cities because of the difficulty in obtaining a transfer of household registration and because of a general unwillingness on the part of the Chinese party to displace its own local workers.

Litigation/arbitration

7-365 Although litigation and arbitration in China is much less prevalent than in the West, it is increasingly common for Chinese business entities to bring its debtors and competitors to court. It is difficult to ascertain the existence of pending litigation because court records are not typically made public.

7-366 However, these questions should be raised during interviews with the Chinese party's management and in the due diligence checklist to determine whether the Chinese party is the subject of litigation or claims or is pursuing any claims in the People's Courts (or foreign courts) or before any arbitration tribunal and to gauge the materiality of any such proceeding.

CONCLUSION

7-401   The foregoing sketches a bird's eye view of the due diligence process in China. The singular difficulty facing the due diligence process in China is the lack of public access to documents and legal instruments that are filed with the various registries, if any. The success of any due diligence process in China depends on how much the Chinese party may be persuaded to divulge their records and information. Verification with third parties such as bankers and trade creditors or debtors may be possible although it comes with a price. The whole process is also complicated by the language barrier as well as the fact that financial statements and legal documents often do not conform with international norms and standards.

REFERENCES AND FURTHER READING

Books

Cole R Capener, 'Due Diligence' in *Doing Business in China: Volume 2*, Freshfields Bruckhaus Deringer (ed) (Juris Publishing, 2002).

Articles

Howard Chao, Lawrence Tu and Fiona Connell, 'Negotiating Joint Ventures in China: Updated Guidelines for the Practitioner' January 1996. Available at http://www.omm.com/webcode/navigate.asp?nodeHandle=817.

APPENDIX

LEGAL DUE DILIGENCE CHECKLIST FOR COMPANIES INCORPORATED IN THE PEOPLE' S REPUBLIC OF CHINA
在中华人民共和国成立的公司之法律审查清单

The following sets out a list of documents, materials and information to be provided by the relevant entity (the 'Company') for the purpose of conducting a legal due diligence exercise. This list is not comprehensive and may be updated, supplemented or modified from time to time.
以下是为进行法律审查工作而要由相关公司提供的文件，材料和信息的清单。此清单并不详尽，并可能不时地作出修改，补充和修正。

1.   GROUP STRUCTURE AND SUMMARY OF THE DEVELOP-MENT HISTORY OF THE COMPANY
集团公司的结构及其公司前身的发展历史简介

   1.1   Existing shareholding structure of the Group

集团公司目前股权结构关系图

1.2 Shareholding structure of the Group after proposed restructuring
重组计划下集团公司股权结构关系图

1.3 Documents relating to all previous changes to the departments in charge of the Company
公司隶属和主管机关历次变更的文件

1.4 List and shareholding structure of the Company's subsidiaries, related companies and affiliates (if any), and all the documents required in this checklist in relation to the above subsidiaries, related companies and affiliates
公司之子公司, 关联公司和分支机构的名单 (若有) 和股权结构关系图, 以及有关该等子公司, 关联公司和分支机构的本核查清单中所列的所有文件

2. INCORPORATION DOCUMENTS OF THE COMPANY
公司建立情况

2.1 Application Form
成立公司的申请表格

2.2 Project Proposal
成立公司的项目建议书

2.3 Feasibility Study Report
成立公司的可行性研究报告

2.4 Opinion of the competent authorities in relation to the project proposal and the feasibility study report, including, but not limited to:
各主管部门对可行性研究报告的意见书。包括但不限于:

(a) Approval from the Ministry of Foreign Trade and Economic Co-operation;
对外经济贸易合作部的批复

(b) Approval from State Planning Commission;
国家计委的批复

(c) Approval from Pricing Authorities;
物价部门的批复

(d) Approval from Construction Authorities;
建设规划部门的批复

(e) Approval from Land Authorities; and
土地管理部门的批复

(f) Approval from Chinese authorities and/or the local government agency
中方的主管部委和 / 或地区政府的批复

2.5 Approval of Equity/Co-operative Joint Venture Contract and the Articles of Association from the Ministry of Foreign Trade and Economic Co-operation or its local representatives

对外经济贸易合作部或其地方代表批准合资／合作公司合同及其章程的批复

2.6 Business Licence of the Company, including but not limited to the existing Business Licence of the Company and all previous business licences that have been amended and registered

公司的营业执照，包括现行有效的执照及历次变更登记的营业执照

2.7 Equity/Co-operative Joint Venture Contract and the Articles of Association, including any previous revisions and amendments

合资／合作公司合同及其章程，包括历次修改和修订

2.8 Approval of any amendments to the Equity/Co-operative Joint Venture Contract and Articles of Association from the original examination and approval authority,

原审批机构对和资／合作公司合同及其章程的修改的批文

2.9 Minutes of all Board meetings, meetings of any committees of Directors/Shareholders/Members and written resolutions passed by the Board of Directors and Shareholders/Members of the Company since incorporation

所有自公司成立以来召开的董事会，股东／成员的委员会的会议记录，以及由董事会，股东／成员通过的书面决议

2.10 Copies of all returns, receipts, forms and documents filed with any government departments/authorities.

所有任何其他政府部门备案的回执，表格和文件

2.11 All government permits, approvals, consents, authorizations and other licences required for the operation of the Company, including but not limited to:

公司所有为开展业务必需的政府许可，批准，同意，授权和其他证照（包括但不限于）

   (a) Foreign Currency Registration Certificate;
       外汇签记证

   (b) Loan Certificate;
       贷款证

   (c) Approval of Bank Account Opening;
       银行开户许可

(d) Tax Registration Certification;
税务簦记证

(e) Customs Registration Certificate (if any);
海关簦记证

(f) Import and Export Permits (if any);
进、出口许可证

(g) Permits and other licences required for specific types if business (if any); and
从事其特定行业之业务所需的许可证或其他类似准证

(h) Planning Permit for Land Use and Construction, Planning Permit for Construction Project, Building Licence and other relevant permits and licences
公司用地和建设用地规划许可证，建设工程规划许可证，施工许可证及其它有关批文和准证

3. CAPITAL STRUCTURE
资本结构

3.1 Total investment / Registered Capital / Paid-up Capital / Outstanding CapitalI Location of Share Certificates (if any) / Unissued Capital / Reserves / Convertible Securities
投资总额 / 注册资本 / 缴足资本 / 未付清资本 / 股份证书收放地 / 未发放资本 / 储备 / 可转换资本

3.2 Outstanding rights and options under employee benefit plans or shareholders' agreements or any other documents
未决的处于雇员收益计划项下应享有的权利和期权或股东们的协议或其他相关文件

3.3 Capital Verification Report issued by accountant registered in the PRC
中国注册会计师事务所签发的验资报告，证明公司的注册资本已到位

3.4 Investment Certificate issued by the Company based on the Capital Verification Report
由公司出具的出资证明，以验资报告为依据

3.5 Asset Valuation Report of the Company and all reports issued by the State Assets Bureau for state-owned assets
公司的资产评估报告，及由国管局签发的涉及国有资产的资产评估报告

3.6 Documents authorizing the increase/decrease of the capital of the Company, including board resolutions
公司增资 / 减资的文件，包括董事会决议

3.7 Approval for the increase/decrease of the Company's capital
对公司增资 / 减资的批复

3.8 Documents and approvals for any previous amalgamation and division between the Company and other companies or organizations
公司和其他公司或机构历次合并，分立的文件和批复

3.9 Limitations on Dividend (if any)
红利限制

3.10 The rights of each class of shares (dividend policy, capital, redemption, any priority or *pari passu*)
各级别股份的权利（分红政策，资本，赎回，任何优先权或同等权利）

4. PROPERTIES
公司的房地产

4.1 Granted Land Use Right Agreement
土地使用权出让合同

4.2 Agreement to Transfer Land Use Right
土地使用权转让合同

4.3 Documents approving the allocation of Land Use Right
土地使用权划拨批文

4.4 Land Use Right Leasing Agreement
土地使用权租赁合同

4.5 Evidence of approval by the collectively-owned enterprises to any transfer and conversion to granted Land Use Right
证明联合拥有企业同意转让或转换为出让土地使用权的许可

4.6 Other documents evidencing the Company's Land Use Right
证明公司用地权利的其他文件

4.7 Receipt for Payment of Land Grant Premium
地价款支付凭证

4.8 Land Use Right Certificate
土地使用证

4.9 Building Ownership Certificate or Property Title Deed
房屋所有权证及房地产证

4.10 Certificate of other right of the Company's Land Use Right and Ownership Right to Properties and the Documents evidencing the change of registration for the said Land Use Right and Ownership Right

公司的土地使用权和房屋所有权的它项权利证明以及土地使用权和房屋所有权的变更签记

4.11 Agreements or arrangements relating to the properties leased by the Company and the documents evidencing the registration of such leases

公司租赁房地产的合同，协议或安排及其签记证明

4.12 Approval of Construction of Buildings

公司兴建建筑物的批文

5. OTHER FIXED ASSETS

其他固定资产

5.1 List of machinery, equipment and fixed assets of the Company and the documents of title relating thereto

公司的机器设备／固定资产清单及所有权证明

5.2 List of Insurance Policies, documentary proof of insurance and the relevant documents (renewal dates, premiums, amount of cover, nature of risk, etc)

公司的保险清单，保险凭证及有关文件

6. INTELLECTUAL PROPERTY RIGHTS AND OTHER INTANGIBLE ASSETS OF THE COMPANY

公司的知识产权和其他无形资产

6.1 List of intellectual property rights owned or utilized by the Company

公司拥有或使用的知识产权清单

(a) Patents

专利权

(b) Trademarks

商标权

(c) Copyright

著作权

6.2 Documents and registration documents relating to the intellectual property rights

公司的知识产权文件和注册文件

(a) Agreement to transfer intellectual property rights entered into by the Company

公司签订的知识产权转让合同

(b) Licence Agreement of the intellectual property rights entered into by the Company
公司签订的知识产权使用许可合同

(c) Agreements for (non-patent) Technological Transfer, Licensing, Service or assistance
公司签订的（非专利）技术转让，许可，服务或协助合同

(d) Examination, approval, filing and registration of the above documents relating to intellectual property and technology (if required by law)
有关公司上述知识产权和技术合同的审批，备案和登记文件

6.3 Any complaints, objections or claims for alleged infringement notified in relation to the above
针对山述文件的侵权行为存在的任何指控，反对或诉求

6.4 List of other intangible assets of the Company and the relevant documents
公司的其他无形资产的清单和有关文件

6.5 Valuation documents of the intangible assets of the Company (if any)
公司的无形资产评估文件（若有）

7. COMPANY'S BUSINESS
公司业务

7.1 Business Scope (according to its Business Licence)
营业范围（根据其营业执照）

7.2 General competitive conditions in the industry in which the group is engaged.
集团公司所处行业的克争情况

7.3 Details of the major products, domestic and export market share of the Company and geographical analysis of the business operations of the Company
公司的主要产品，公司占国内和出口市场份额及公司经营运作的区域分析

7.4 The details of importation of materials arrangements, inventory control
进口原料的安排，库存保管

7.5 Company's production capacity and the percentage of capacity utilized for each of the last five years
公司的生产规模及过去五年的利用率

7.6   Method of manufacturing, quality control, marketing and distributing products, inclusive of production process involved for each main product or service, rejection rates, distribution channels and credit terms
产品的制造方法，质量管理，市场营销，包括产品的制造过程，废弃率，分销渠道和信用条款

7.7   Annul output for the preceding five years and the projected output for the current and next financial year. Reasons for any substantial increase or decline in annual output should be provided
过去五年的产量及目前和以后一个财政年度的产量。对大幅度的增加及减少作出的解释

7.8   Description of any significant product to be launched, including the type and stage of development, target markets and customer base and expected date of launch
是否有重要产品将要投产，包括型号，进度阶段，目标市场，客户群及预期投产日期

7.9   List of major customers of the Company
公司的主要客户清单

7.10 List of major suppliers of the Company
公司的主要供应商的清单

7.11 List of major competitors of the Company
公司的主要竞争者的清单

7.12 List of main creditors and debtors of the Company
公司的主要借款人及贷款人

7.13 Any PRC regulations relating to the Company's Business
公司业务相关的国家有关规定

8.   MATERIAL CONTRACTS AND BUSINESS DOCUMENTS OF THE COMPANY
公司重要的合同及业务文件

8.1   Contracts for material acquisitions and disposals of assets and services entered into by the Company and its subsidiaries in the last three years, whereby the consideration represents 5% or more of the Net Tangible Assets of the Company
在最近三年内，公司和其子公司签订的关于购置及出售资产／服务的重大交易合同。'重大交易合同'指所涉及的对价相当于或超过公司净有形资产的百分之五的合同

8.2   List and Summary of material contracts which are entered into by the Company and its subsidiaries in the ordinary course of business within the last two years, including without limitation:

在最近两年，公司和其子公司已签订的重大日常业务合同清单

Date 日期	Party 和约方	Brief Description 主要内容	Present Status 目前状况

8.3 Material contracts which are entered into by the Company not in the ordinary course of business and its subsidiaries within the last two years, including without limitation:

在最近两年内，公司和其子公司签订的其日常业务以外的重大合同

(a) Joint Venture Agreement
合资合同

(b) Contracts For Contract Management or Business Operation Under Lease
承包 / 租赁经营合同

(c) Franchise Agreement
特许经营合同

(d) Distribution Agency Agreement
分销或代理合同

(e) Management Agreement
管理合同

(f) Agency Agreement
代理合同

(g) Financing/Loan Agreement
融资贷款合同

(h) Guarantee/Mortgage Agreement
担保 / 抵押合同

(i) Technology Transfer and Assistance Agreements
技术转让和协助合同

(j) Lease Agreement
租赁合同

(k) Purchase and Sales of Option Rights
收购 / 出售选择权 / 期权合同

(l) Agreement to Assign Rights and Benefits
权益转让合同

8.4 Approval, confirmation or registration of documents and permits for the abovesaid Agreements as required by law (if any)

法律要求的对上术合同的批准，确认或登记注册文件和准证

8.5 Contracts and documents relating to transactions entered into within the last three years by the Company with its parent company, subsidiary and related company
在最近三年内，公司和其母公司，子公司，关联公司之间签订的所有交易合同及文件

8.6 List of outstanding borrowings of the Company and other long-/short-term banking and credit facilities
公司未清偿的资款及其他长期/短期的银行贷款或信贷的清单

8.7 List of Banks (domestic and overseas) with which the Company has dealings and bank accounts
公司有业务往来的银行及其帐号清单

8.8 All contracts, agreements and proof of registration of mortgages and instruments of hypothecation created by the Company over its own properties or assets (including cash)
公司在其拥有的或占有的房地产或资产之上所设定的抵押和质押的所有合同，协议及登记证明

8.9 List of other debts and liability of the Company (including without limitation, contingent liabilities)
公司承担之其他债务和责任的清单（包括或然债务和责任）

8.10 List and summaries of material contracts which are being contemplated or negotiated by the Company
公司目前正在筹划或正在洽谈的合同清单

9. TAX
税 务

9.1 Information in relation to the following taxes paid at present to the Government or other relevant departments:

Enterprise Income Tax, VAT, Business Tax, Consumption Tax, Construction/Real Estate Tax, Land Use Tax/Fee, Customs Duties, Transportation Tax, Vehicle and Vessel Licence Tax, Individual Income Tax, City Construction Tax/Fees, Fees/Fund for Transportation Construction, Surcharges for Education and Hygiene, and other taxes /fees
公司目前向政府或有关部门缴交税收的情况（包括但不限于）：企业所得税，增值税，营业税，消费税，建设/房产税，海关税，交通税，车船使用税，个人所得得税，城市建设费，交通建设基金，教育及卫生保健附加税和其他税收

9.2 List of all preferential tax treatments and the relevant government approval
税收优惠待遇清单及相关政府批文

9.3 List of all current, pending or threatened disputes with or claims by any tax authority which may affect the Company

目前所有待决的或对公司业务有影响的税务争议

10. BOARD OF DIRECTORS AND SENIOR MANAGEMENT PERSONNEL

公司董事会和高级管理人员

10.1 Name list of the Board of Directors and other management personnel of the Company, including name, nationality, address and duration of appointment

公司董事会和其他管理层人员名单，包括姓名，国籍，住址和任期

10.2 Documents appointing the directors of the Company

委任以上董事的文件

10.3 Appointment and Service Contracts and other related documents between the Company and the key management personnel (eg the General Manager and the Deputy General Manager, the Factory Manager, the Assistant Factory Manager)

公司与主要管理人员（如正副经理，正副厂长）的聘任／服务合同及其他相关文件

11. EMPLOYEES OF THE COMPANY

公司职工

11.1 Documents relating to the formation of the Congress of Employees of the Company and its power

公司职工代表大会的组成及其权利的文件

11.2 Resolution of the Congress of Employees approving the restructuring and listing of the Company

公司职工代表大会关于同意公司重组和上市的决议

11.3 Collective Agreement between the Company and the union and the Labour Agreements of the Employees (sample)

公司的工会集体合同和职工的劳动合同样本

(a) Benefits, rewards, insurance schemes (such as basic old age insurance premiums, basic medical insurance premiums and unemployment insurance premiums), arrangements and other related contracts pertaining to the Employees of the company

公司的雇员的福利，奖励，保险（三项基本基金：养老保险费，基本医疗保险费和失业保险费）计划，安排和有关合同

(b)   Documents relating to the internal issue and distribution of Employee Shares (if any) and the latest update on the shareholding spread and transactions relating to these shares

公司分配发行内部职工股的文件，最新的内部职工股股权分布及交易状况

(c)   All other special agreements or arrangements entered into between the Company and the employees (including without limitation such as non-competition confidentiality agreements or arrangements)

公司与职工签订的所有其他特别协议或安排（包括但不限于有关不竞争和／或保密的协议或安排）

12   LITIGATION/ARBITRATION
诉松或仲裁

List of litigation, arbitration, claims, judicial and administrative investigations and other similar procedures in which the Company is involved or expects to be involved and other relevant documents

公司已涉及的或预计将会涉及的诉松，仲裁，素偿，司法调查，行政调查或其他类似程序的清单及有关文件

13   OTHERS
其他

13.1   Other agreements entered into by the Company that are especially long or possess onerous terms

公司签订的其他特别长期的或条件特别苛刻的合同

13.2   List of agreements or arrangements that may be terminated, altered or are likely to be terminated, altered due to the proposed transaction and the detailed explanation

可能因本项协议中的交易而终止，变更或可以终止，变更的合同安排的清单和情况说明

13.3   Any expected effect, if any on the PRC's entering the WTO

如果中国加入世贸组织，对公司是否有影响

CHAPTER 8

Arbitration

Tan Chong Huat, Fu Rong and Terence Lin

INTRODUCTION

Background

8-101 The influx of foreign investments into the PRC began in the early 1970s with the advent of the 'Open Door Policy'. The volume of foreign investments has increased steadily with the introduction of ambitious economic development programmes by the PRC government. To date, partially and wholly foreign-owned businesses account for a significant proportion of the economic growth of the PRC and with the accession of the PRC to the World Trade Organization (WTO) in December 2001, the flow of foreign investments into the PRC will increase even further. One of the problems created by the PRC's fast growing economy is the increase in the number of disputes.

8-102 Unfortunately, due to political and historical reasons, the legal system of the PRC is underdeveloped and woefully inadequate to deal with the complex nature of modern commercial transactions. In addition, since the Chinese judicial officials are remunerated by the state, there is a justified fear that any litigation proceedings involving a foreign party and a Chinese party would be biased in favour of the Chinese party. As a result, in the event of a dispute, many foreign investors have found themselves without effective recourse.

8-103 The PRC government acknowledged that the injection of foreign investment would be adversely affected by the lack of a fair, efficient and effective means of dispute resolution. Culturally and historically, the Chinese have preferred mediation to litigation as a means of dispute resolution. However, mediation is of limited utility given the need for the parties to negotiate in good faith and to eventually come to an agreement. Since these elements are not a given in commercial disputes, commercial parties have come to rely on arbitration as a more reliable means of dispute resolution.

Arbitration agencies

8-104 Arbitration is one of the primary means of dispute resolution in the legal system of the PRC. The PRC operates on a dual arbitration regime, with separate systems for dealing with domestic arbitration and international arbitration. The PRC's domestic arbitration system handles disputes between Chinese parties. This means that foreign invested enterprises (FIEs), including sino-foreign equity joint ventures, sino-foreign co-operative joint ventures and wholly foreign-owned enterprises, may fall within the domestic arbitration regime if they are involved in a dispute with another Chinese legal person.

8-105   International arbitrations are conducted mainly under the auspices of the Chinese International Economic and Trade Arbitration Commission (CIETAC), which deals with commercial disputes, and the China Maritime Arbitration Commission (CMAC), which, as the name suggests, deals with maritime disputes.

8-106   The CIETAC and the CMAC are both agencies of the China Council for the Promotion of International Trade (CCPIT). The CCPIT was founded in 1952 with ties to the Ministry of Foreign Trade and Economic Co-operation (MOFTEC). The Beijing based CCPIT was founded with the objective of promoting foreign trade.

8-107   The CIETAC, formerly known as the Foreign Trade Arbitration Commission, was established in April 1956 within the CCPIT in accordance with the Central People's Government of the PRC. Its role is to provide a forum for the resolution of foreign trade disputes between foreigners and the Chinese.

8-108   The role of the CMAC is to promote the development of the domestic and international shipping industry, economy and trade.

Legal framework

8-109   International arbitrations conducted by the CIETAC and CMAC are subject to the legal framework as follows:

(a)   international treaties and conventions;

(b)   laws, statutes or legislation issued with the authority of the government or the Supreme People's Court; and

(c)   the CIETAC Arbitration Rules and CMAC Arbitration Rules.

International treaties and conventions

8-110   The PRC is party to a number of international economic and trade-related treaties and conventions. The provisions of the treaties and conventions, where applicable, will usually take precedence over the provisions of the legislation of the PRC unless specifically excluded by the parties to the contract.

8-111   The PRC is a party to the New York Convention on the Recognition and Enforcement of Foreign Arbitral Awards 1958, which provides for the reciprocal recognition and enforcement of arbitral awards between parties to it.

Chinese law

8-112   There is no single exhaustive source of Chinese arbitration law. However, arbitration in the PRC is mainly governed by the Arbitration Law of the People's Republic of China (Arbitration Law), which was adopted at the Ninth Session of the Standing Committee of the Eighth National People's Congress on 31 August 1994 and came into effect on 1 September 1995.

Arbitration rules

8-113   CIETAC arbitrations are generally governed by the CIETAC Arbitration Rules (CIETAC Rules) which were first unveiled by the CIETAC on 1 June 1994. After revision, the CIETAC Rules were adopted by the Chinese Chamber of International Commerce (CCIC) on 4 September 1995 and became effective on 1 October 1995. The version of the CIETAC Rules referred to in this chapter was adopted by the CCPIT and CCIC on 5 September 2000 and came into effect on 1 October 2000.

8-114   Arbitrations conducted before the CMAC are likewise governed by the CMAC Arbitration Rules (CMAC Rules), which also came into effect on 1 October 1995. At the time of writing, the current version of the CMAC Rules was adopted by the CCIC on 22 November 2000 and came into effect on 1 January 2001.

8-115   Although neither set of rules carries the force of law, each is binding on the parties and arbitrators before the respective arbitration commissions. As the CIETAC Rules and CMAC Rules are quite similar, for ease of discussion, the remainder of this chapter shall, unless otherwise specified, deal only with the CIETAC Rules.

APPLICATION FOR ARBITRATION

Request for arbitration

8-201   The parties requesting arbitration by the CIETAC must meet the following requirements:[1]

(a)   there must be an existing arbitration agreement;

(b)   there must be a specific request, facts and reasons for the request; and

(c)   the dispute shall be within the CIETAC's jurisdiction.

---

1   Article 21 of the Arbitration Law.

8-202   Under the CIETAC Rules, the CIETAC takes cognizance of a dispute only upon the submission of a written application by one of the parties to the dispute and if there is a concluded arbitration agreement between the parties to refer the dispute to the CIETAC.[2] Sufficient copies of the application and arbitration agreement must also be provided.[3]

Written application

8-203   The application for arbitration shall disclose the following:[4]

(a)   in the case of natural persons, the names, gender, age, profession, work units and addresses of the parties; or in the case of non-natural persons, the names and addresses of the entity or other organization concerned; and the names and professions of the legal representative and other principal persons in charge of the entity or organization;

(b)   the request for arbitration, the facts on which the request is based and the reasons for the request; and

(c)   any relevant evidence and its sources and the names and addresses of the witnesses, if any.

Arbitration agreement

8-204   The arbitration agreement may be concluded before or after the dispute has arisen and may take the form of an arbitration clause in the contract in dispute or any other written form.

8-205   A valid arbitration agreement must specify the following:[5]

(a)   an expressed intent to request for arbitration;

(b)   items for arbitration; and

(c)   the chosen arbitration commission.

8-206   After the CIETAC has received and examined the application and attached documents, it will notify the parties within five days whether the application meets the CIETAC's requirements. In the event that the application does not meet the CIETAC's requirements, the CIETAC shall notify the parties in writing that their case will not be accepted and provide reasons for the non-acceptance.[6]

8-207   Where an arbitration agreement does not clearly specify the items for arbitration or an arbitration commission, the parties may

---

2   Article 3 of the CIETAC Rules and article 4 of the Arbitration Law.
3   Article 22 of the Arbitration Law.
4   Article 23 of the Arbitration Law.
5   Article 16 of the Arbitration Law.
6   Article 24 of the Arbitration Law.

enter into a supplementary agreement to remedy the defect. If the parties fail to enter into a supplementary agreement, the arbitration agreement shall be deemed invalid.[7]

8-208   An arbitration agreement is invalid under any of the following circumstances:[8]

(a)   the items for arbitration agreed upon by the parties are beyond the scope of arbitration as prescribed by law;

(b)   a party to the arbitration agreement is a person who lacks the capacity or has limited capacity for civil conduct; or

(c)   the arbitration agreement is imposed by one party on the other party by means of coercion.

Applicable rules

8-209   Although the CIETAC Rules will be applicable by default if the parties agree to submit their dispute to the CIETAC, the parties are free to agree otherwise, and the parties' agreement will prevail subject to the CIETAC's consent.[9]

Severability

8-210   An arbitration clause contained in a contract or an arbitration agreement attached to a contract is treated as independent from the rest of the agreement. The validity of an arbitration clause or an arbitration agreement shall not be affected by any modification, rescission, termination, expiry, invalidity, or non-existence of the agreement.[10]

JURISDICTION

CIETAC jurisdiction

8-301   The jurisdiction of the CIETAC is limited to contractual and non-contractual disputes arising from economic and trade transactions, including the following:

(a)   international or foreign related disputes;

(b)   disputes related to the Hong Kong Special Administrative Region (SAR), Macao SAR or Taiwan;

(c)   disputes between FIEs and other FIEs, Chinese legal persons, natural persons and/or other economic organizations;

---

7   Article 18 of the Arbitration Law.
8   Article 17 of the Arbitration Law.
9   Article 7 of the CIETAC Rules.
10   Article 5 of the CIETAC Rules and article 19 of the Arbitration Law.

(d)   disputes arising from project financing, invitation for tender, bidding, construction and other activities conducted by Chinese legal persons, natural persons and/or other economic organizations involving the use of capital, technology or services from foreign countries, international organizations or from the Hong Kong SAR, Macao SAR and Taiwan;

(e)   disputes that may be recognized by the CIETAC in accordance with special provisions of, or upon special authorization from, the laws or administrative regulations of the PRC; and

(f)   any other domestic disputes that the parties have agreed to submit for arbitration before the CIETAC.

8-302   There is some academic opinion[11] to support the view that limb (d) is superfluous as any dispute arising from 'project financing, invitation for tender, bidding, construction' or otherwise involving foreign countries, international organizations, Hong Kong SAR, Macao or Taiwan would presumably fall within limb (a) or limb (b). It is clear from the above, however, that domestic disputes from domestic enterprises do not fall within the jurisdiction of the CIETAC unless the parties have agreed to submit the matter for arbitration by the CIETAC.

8-303   Disputes over the following matters are not subject to arbitration:

(a)   marital, adoption, guardianship, maintenance and succession/inheritance disputes;

(b)   administrative disputes that the law requires to be handled by the administrative authorities; and

(c)   labour disputes and disputes within agricultural collectives in relation to management contracts.[12]

CMAC jurisdiction

8-304   The jurisdiction of the CMAC is limited to the following:[13]

(a)   disputes arising from salvage and general average;

(b)   disputes arising from collision between ships and/or other offshore mobile units, or from contact of ships or other offshore mobile structures or any installation on the sea, navigable waters adjacent thereto and in the harbours, as well as with a submarine or underwater installation;

---

11   Page 9217 at para 9~0736, *People's Republic of China Corporate Secretarial Practice Manual* (Sweet & Maxwell Asia, 1998).

12   Cf with article 3 of the Arbitration Law, which is similar, except there is no mention of (c).

13   Article 2 of the CMAC Rules.

(c) disputes arising from carriage of goods at sea or on coastal water or on navigable waters adjacent to the sea under a bill of lading, waybill, voyage charter party or a contract of multi-model transport containing a mode of transport by sea or any other transport documents, as well as from carriage of passengers at sea or on waters referred to above;

(d) disputes arising from time and bareboat-chartering of ships, or from leasing of other offshore mobile units and containers or other transport articles, and from management, operation, agency, towage, raising and demolition of ships or other offshore mobile units;

(e) disputes arising from ownership of ships or other offshore mobile units and maritime liens;

(f) disputes arising from insurance on ships on sea, coastal waters or navigable waters adjacent to sea and on other offshore mobile units, or from insurance on carriage of goods, or from insurance on carriage of passengers, or from insurance on offshore exploitation of resources, and from their reinsurance, as well as from ship's protection and indemnity;

(g) disputes arising from sale, construction and repair of ships or other offshore movable units and containers or other transport articles;

(h) disputes arising from mortgage for loan on ships or other offshore mobile units;

(i) disputes arising from contracts of freight forwarding, supply of ship's stores, seamen's labour service, fishery production or fishing and so on;

(j) disputes arising from exploitation and utilization of marine resources, or pollution damage to marine environment;

(k) disputes arising from maritime security; and

(l) other maritime disputes or disputes relating to maritime events submitted for arbitration by agreement between the parties.

Existence and validity of arbitration agreement

8-305 Although the CIETAC has the power to decide on the existence and validity of an arbitration agreement and on jurisdiction over an arbitration case, where a party takes exception to the validity of the arbitration agreement, he may request that the CIETAC make a decision or that the People's Court make a judgment. Where one party is requesting the CIETAC to make a decision and the other party is requesting the People's Court to make a ruling, the issue in relation to the validity of an arbitration agreement will be decided by the People's Court.[14]

Time frame for objecting to jurisdiction issues

8-306   Any objection in relation to an arbitration agreement and/or jurisdiction over an arbitration case must be raised before the first hearing conducted by the arbitration tribunal. Where a dispute is to be examined on the basis of documents only, an objection relating to jurisdiction must be raised before the 'submission of the first substantive defence'.[15] Thereafter, the hearing of the dispute shall not be affected by any objections relating to the validity of the arbitration agreement and/or jurisdiction.

ARBITRATION PROCEEDINGS

Application for arbitration, defence and counterclaim

8-401   Arbitration proceedings will be deemed to have commenced from the date on which the Notice of Arbitration is issued by the CIETAC or its Sub-Commissions.[16]

8-402   The arbitration process is initiated by the claimant submitting a written application to the CIETAC. The claimant submitting an Application for Arbitration must fulfil the following conditions:[17]

(a)   Submit an Application for Arbitration in writing, which shall, *inter alia*, specify:

   (i)   the names and addresses of the claimant and the respondent, including the zip code, telephone, telex, fax, and cable numbers or any other means of electronic telecommunications, if any;

   (ii)   the arbitration agreement relied upon by the claimant;

   (iii)   the facts of the case and the main points of dispute; and

   (iv)   the claimant's claim and the facts and reasons on which the claim is based.

   The Application for Arbitration must be signed by, and/or affixed with the seal of the claimant and/or the authorized agent of the claimant.

(b)   The relevant documentary evidence which supports the facts on which the claimant's claim is based must be attached to the Application for Arbitration.

---

14   Article 4 of the CIETAC Rules and article 20 of the Arbitration Law.
15   Article 6 of the CIETAC Rules.
16   Article 13 of the CIETAC Rules.
17   Article 14 of the CIETAC Rules.

(c)   Pay an arbitration fee in advance to the CIETAC according to the CIETAC Arbitration Fee Schedule.

8-403 Upon receiving the Application for Arbitration and its attachments, the CIETAC will examine the aforesaid Application and attachments. If, after examination, the CIETAC finds that the claimant has not yet completed the formalities required for arbitration, it will request that the claimant complete such formalities. Only when the CIETAC is satisfied that the claimant has completed such formalities will the following be sent to the respondent:[18]

(a)   Notice of Arbitration;

(b)   a copy of the claimant's Application for Arbitration and its attachments;

(c)   a copy of the CIETAC Arbitration Rules;

(d)   a copy of the Panel of Arbitrators; and

(e)   the Arbitration Fee Schedule of the CIETAC.[19]

8-404 All the above items, with the exception of item (b) will be sent to the claimant as well.

8-405 After sending the Notice of Arbitration to the claimant and respondent, the CIETAC will appoint one of the staff-members of its Secretariat to take charge of procedural administration of the dispute.

8-406 The respondent's written defence and any relevant documentary evidence shall be submitted to the Secretariat of the CIETAC within 45 days from the date of receipt of the Notice of Arbitration.[20]

8-407 The respondent's counterclaim, if any, shall be submitted in writing to the CIETAC within 60 days from the date of receipt of the Notice of Arbitration. The arbitration tribunal may, at its discretion, extend that time limit if it deems that there are 'justified reasons'.[21]

8-408 The respondent must specify in the counterclaim the specific counterclaim brought against the claimant and the facts and reasons upon which the counterclaim is based. The respondent must also attach to the counterclaim any relevant documentary evidence.

8-409 When filing a counterclaim, the respondent must pay in advance an arbitration fee according to the CIETAC Arbitration Fee Schedule.

---

18 Article 15 of the CIETAC Rules.
19 See Appendix 1 to this chapter.
20 Article 17 of the CIETAC Rules.
21 Article 18 of the CIETAC Rules.

8-410   The claimant and the respondent may submit a request to the arbitration tribunal to amend the claim or counterclaim respectively. However, the arbitration tribunal may refuse such an amendment if it considers that the request has been submitted too late and may prejudice the arbitration proceedings.[22]

8-411   Generally, the following documents must be submitted to the CIETAC in quintuplicate:

(a)   Application for Arbitration;

(b)   written defence;

(c)   statement of counterclaim; and

(d)   documentary evidence or any other relevant documents.

8-412   Presumably, each of the three arbitrators in the tribunal will be provided a copy, with the remaining copy given to the other party to the dispute. If the dispute involves more than two parties, additional copies will have to be submitted accordingly. If the arbitration tribunal is composed of only one arbitrator, the number of copies submitted may be reduced to two.[23]

8-413   The arbitration shall proceed notwithstanding the failure of the respondent to submit a written defence or the failure of the claimant to submit a written defence against the respondent's counterclaim.[24]

8-414   Chinese and foreign citizens may be authorized by the parties to act as arbitration agents dealing with matters in relation to the arbitration. However, the authorized arbitration agent must produce a duly executed Power of Attorney to the CIETAC.[25]

8-415   If any party makes an application for the freezing of assets or for 'property preservative measures', the CIETAC shall submit the aforesaid application to the appropriate People's Court for ruling and enforcement. The People's Court will be chosen on the basis of either proximity to the location of the assets or property to be frozen or the domicile of the party against whom the application is made.

8-416   If any party makes an application for interim measures to protect the evidence, the CIETAC shall submit the aforesaid application to the People's Court in the place where the evidence is located for ruling and enforcement.[26]

---

22   Article 19 of the CIETAC Rules.
23   Article 20 of the CIETAC Rules.
24   Article 21 of the CIETAC Rules.
25   Article 22 of the CIETAC Rules.
26   Article 23 of the CIETAC Rules.

Formation of arbitration tribunal

8-417 The arbitration tribunal usually consists of three arbitrators from the CIETAC Panel of Arbitrators, with each party appointing one arbitrator and both parties jointly appointing the third arbitrator, who shall be the presiding arbitrator. The presiding arbitrator and the two appointed arbitrators will jointly form an arbitration tribunal to hear the case jointly.[27]

8-418 The parties are free to entrust the appointment of arbitrators to the Chairman of the CIETAC. The presiding arbitrator may also be appointed by the Chairman of the CIETAC upon the parties' joint authorization.

8-419 The claimant and the respondent shall, within 20 days from the date of receipt of the Notice of Arbitration, each appoint an arbitrator from the CIETAC Panel of Arbitrators or authorize the Chairman of the CIETAC to make such appointment.[28]

8-420 If the claimant or the respondent fails to appoint or authorize the Chairman of the CIETAC to appoint an arbitrator within 20 days from the date of receipt of the Notice of Arbitration, the Chairman of the CIETAC will appoint an arbitrator for the claimant or the respondent.[29]

8-421 The Chairman of the CIETAC may also appoint the presiding arbitrator if the presiding arbitrator is not appointed by the parties within 20 days from the date on which the respondent receives the Notice of Arbitration.

8-422 The claimant and the respondent may jointly appoint or jointly authorize the Chairman of the CIETAC to appoint a sole arbitrator to form an arbitration tribunal to hear the case alone. If both parties agree to having a sole arbitrator to hear their case but are unable to agree on the choice of the sole arbitrator within 20 days from the date on which the respondent receives the Notice of Arbitration, the Chairman of the CIETAC will appoint the sole arbitrator.[30]

8-423 Where there are two or more claimants and/or respondents involved in an arbitration case, the claimants' side and/or the respondents' side shall each, through consultation, appoint one arbitrator from the CIETAC Panel of Arbitrators. The claimants' side and/or the respondents' side may entrust the Chairman of the CIETAC to appoint the arbitrator on their behalf.

---

27 Article 24 of the CIETAC Rules.
28 Article 16 of the CIETAC Rules.
29 Article 26 of the CIETAC Rules.
30 Article 25 of the CIETAC Rules.

8-424   If the claimants' side or the respondents' side fails to make such appointment or entrust the Chairman of the CIETAC to make such appointment within 20 days from the date on which the respondents' side receives the Notice of Arbitration, the appointment will be made by the Chairman of the CIETAC.[31]

8-425   An arbitrator shall withdraw, and the parties to the arbitration shall have the right to request the withdrawal of an arbitrator, in the event of the following:[32]

(a)   where the arbitrator is one of the parties in the arbitration, or is a close relative of any party, or a relative of the attorney involved in the arbitration;

(b)   where the arbitrator has a vital interest in the arbitration;

(c)   where the arbitrator is related to either party, or their attorneys, in a manner beyond the context of the arbitration and the relationship may affect an impartial arbitration; or

(d)   where the arbitrator has had private meetings with the parties or with their attorneys, or when the arbitrator has accepted the invitation of the parties or their attorneys, to dine, or accepted their gifts.

8-426   Under the CIETAC Rules, any appointed arbitrator with a personal interest in the case shall disclose such circumstances to the CIETAC and submit an application to withdraw from his appointment.[33]

8-427   Any party with justified reasons to suspect the impartiality and independence of an appointed arbitrator may submit a request in writing to the CIETAC for the withdrawal of the arbitrator. The aforesaid request must state the facts and reasons on which the request is based and provide supporting evidence. A request for the withdrawal of an arbitrator must be put forward in writing no later than the first oral hearing. If the grounds for the request arise or become known only after the first oral hearing, the request may nevertheless be submitted prior to the conclusion of the last hearing.[34]

8-428   The decision to withdraw an arbitrator from the arbitration tribunal shall be made by the Chairman of the CIETAC. Prior to the final decision of the Chairman of the CIETAC, the arbitrator in question shall continue to serve on the tribunal.[35] If the arbitrator in question is the Chairman of the CIETAC himself, the other members

---

31   Article 27 of the CIETAC Rules.
32   Article 34 of the Arbitration Law.
33   Article 28 of the CIETAC Rules.
34   Article 29 of the CIETAC Rules and article 35 of the Arbitration Law.
35   Article 30 of the CIETAC Rules.

of the CIETAC shall make the decision for the withdrawal of the Chairman of the CIETAC collectively.[36]

8-429 If an arbitrator is unable to perform his/her duties as an arbitrator owing to his/her withdrawal, demise, removal from the Panel of Arbitrators or any other reason, a substitute arbitrator shall be appointed in accordance with the procedure by which the outgoing arbitrator was appointed.

8-430 After the appointment of the substitute arbitrator, the parties to the arbitration may request that the arbitration process begin afresh. The arbitration tribunal may exercise its discretion to grant the request by restarting the arbitration process or by repeating some of the previous procedures.[37]

8-431 An arbitrator may be in breach of his legal responsibilities and may be removed from the Panel of Arbitrators if the arbitrator:

(a)   solicited or accepted bribes;

(b)   practised favouritism or bent the law while arbitrating a case or making a ruling;

or, depending on the severity,

(c)   has had private meetings with the parties and/or their attorneys;

(d)   accepted the invitation of the parties and/or their attorneys to dine; or

(e)   accepted gifts from the parties and/or their attorneys.[38]

Hearing

8-432 Generally, the arbitration tribunal will conduct oral hearings. At the request of the parties or with their consent, the arbitration tribunal may, if it considers oral hearings unnecessary, exercise its discretion to dispense with oral hearings and hear and decide a dispute on the basis of documents only.[39]

8-433 The date of the first oral hearing shall be decided by the arbitration tribunal in consultation with the Secretariat of the CIETAC. The Secretariat shall notify the relevant parties of the decision at least 30 days before the date of the hearing. Any party having justified reasons may request a postponement of the hearing, but a written request must be submitted to the Secretariat of the CIETAC at least 12 days before the date of the hearing. The arbitration tribunal will then decide whether to postpone the

---

36   Article 36 of the Arbitration Law.
37   Article 31 of the CIETAC Rules and article 37 of the Arbitration Law.
38   Article 38 of the Arbitration Law.
39   Article 32 of the CIETAC Rules.

hearing.[40] Any notices in respect of subsequent hearings are not subject to the 30-day time limit.[41]

Location of arbitration

8-434 The arbitration shall take place at a location agreed upon by the parties. Unless the parties agree otherwise, disputes submitted to the CIETAC shall be heard in Beijing, or in any other place subject to the approval of the Secretary-General of the CIETAC. Disputes accepted for arbitration by a Sub-Commission of the CIETAC shall be heard in the place where the Sub-Commission is located, or in other places subject to the approval of the Secretary-General of that Sub-Commission.[42]

8-435 Generally, the arbitration tribunal shall not hear disputes in open session. However, if both parties request that an open session hearing be held, the arbitration tribunal shall have the discretion to do so.[43]

8-436 For disputes heard in closed session, the parties, their arbitration agents, witnesses, arbitrators, experts consulted by the arbitration tribunal and appraisers appointed by the arbitration tribunal and the relevant staff-members of the Secretariat of the CIETAC are not to disclose any substantive or procedural matters in relation to the case to any other parties.[44]

8-437 The parties shall produce evidence in support of the facts on which their claim, defence or counterclaim is based. The arbitration tribunal may, on its own initiative, undertake investigations and collect evidence as it considers necessary. When investigating and collecting evidence, if it considers necessary, the arbitration tribunal may inform the parties so that they may be present when the evidence is collected. Should one or both parties fail to appear, the investigation and collection of evidence shall proceed unimpeded.[45]

Experts

8-438 The arbitration tribunal may consult an expert or appoint an appraiser for clarification of the specific issues in relation to a case. Such an expert or appraiser may be an organization or a citizen and may be a Chinese citizen or a foreigner.

---

40 Article 33 of the CIETAC Rules.
41 Article 34 of the CIETAC Rules.
42 Article 35 of the CIETAC Rules.
43 Article 36 of the CIETAC Rules.
44 Article 37 of the CIETAC Rules.
45 Article 38 of the CIETAC Rules.

8-439   The arbitration tribunal has the power to order the parties to submit or produce to the expert or appraiser any relevant materials, documents, or properties and goods for checking, inspection and/or appraisal, and the parties are obliged to submit or produce the aforesaid materials as ordered.[46]

8-440   The expert's report and the appraiser's report shall be copied to the parties so that the parties may have the opportunity to give their opinions thereon. At the request of any party to the case and subject to the approval of the arbitration tribunal, the expert and appraiser may be present at the hearing, and, if considered necessary and appropriate by the arbitration tribunal, be required to explain their reports.[47]

8-441   The evidence submitted by the parties will be examined and evaluated by the arbitration tribunal. The arbitration tribunal shall decide whether to adopt the expert's report and the appraiser's report.[48]

8-442   Should one of the parties fail to appear at the hearing, the arbitration tribunal may proceed with the hearing and make an award by default.[49]

Records

8-443   During the hearing, the arbitration tribunal may make a record in writing and/or by tape-recording. The arbitration tribunal may, when it considers necessary, draw up minutes stating the main points of the hearing and ask the parties and/or their arbitration agents, witnesses and/or other persons involved to sign and/or affix their seal to it.

8-444   The record in writing or by tape-recording is available only for use and reference by the arbitration tribunal.[50]

8-445   Under the CIETAC Rules, if the parties reach an amicable settlement agreement by themselves, they may either request that the arbitration tribunal conclude the arbitration proceedings by making an award in accordance with the contents of their amicable settlement agreement, or request that the dispute be dismissed.

8-446   The decision to dismiss an arbitration matter will be made by the Secretary-General of the CIETAC if the decision is made before the

---

46   Article 39 of the CIETAC Rules.
47   Article 40 of the CIETAC Rules.
48   Article 41 of the CIETAC Rules.
49   Article 42 of the CIETAC Rules.
50   Article 43 of the CIETAC Rules.

formation of the arbitration tribunal, or by the arbitration tribunal if the decision is made after the formation of the arbitration tribunal.

8-447 If either party or both the parties refer a dismissed matter to the CIETAC again for arbitration, the Chairman of the CIETAC shall decide whether to accept the matter for arbitration or not.

8-448 If the parties reach a settlement agreement by themselves through conciliation without involvement of the CIETAC, any of them may, based on an arbitration agreement concluded between them providing for arbitration by the CIETAC and their settlement agreement, request the CIETAC to appoint a sole arbitrator to render an arbitration award in accordance with the contents of the settlement agreement.[51]

8-449 If both parties desire for conciliation or one party so desires and the other party agrees to it when consulted by the arbitration tribunal, the arbitration tribunal may then conciliate the dispute under its cognizance of the process of arbitration.[52]

8-450 The arbitration tribunal may conciliate cases in the manner it considers appropriate.[53]

8-451 The arbitration tribunal shall terminate conciliation and continue with the arbitration proceedings when one of the parties requests a termination of conciliation or when the arbitration tribunal believes that further efforts to conciliate will be futile.[54]

8-452 If the parties have reached an amicable settlement outside the arbitration tribunal in the course of conciliation conducted by the arbitration tribunal, such settlement shall be taken as having been reached through the arbitration tribunal's conciliation.[55]

8-453 The parties shall sign a settlement agreement in writing when an amicable settlement is reached through conciliation conducted by the arbitration tribunal, and the arbitration tribunal will bring the arbitration to a close by making an arbitration award in accordance with the contents of the settlement agreement unless otherwise agreed by the parties.[56]

8-454 Should conciliation by the arbitration tribunal fail, any statement, opinion, view or proposal which has been made, raised, put forward, acknowledged, accepted or rejected by either party or by the arbitration tribunal in the process of conciliation shall not be invoked

---

51 Article 44 of the CIETAC Rules.
52 Article 45 of the CIETAC Rules.
53 Article 46 of the CIETAC Rules.
54 Article 47 of the CIETAC Rules.
55 Article 48 of the CIETAC Rules.
56 Article 49 of the CIETAC Rules.

as grounds for any claim, defence and/or counterclaim in the subsequent arbitration proceedings, judicial proceedings or any other proceedings.[57]

8-455 The party who knows or should have known of any provision or requirement of the CIETAC Rules that has not been complied with and proceeds with the arbitration proceedings without raising any objections to the non-compliance in writing in a timely manner shall be taken to have waived his right to object.[58]

ARBITRAL AWARDS

Rules for making awards

8-501 The arbitration tribunal shall render an arbitral award within nine months from the date on which the arbitration tribunal was formed. The Secretary-General of the CIETAC may extend this time limit at the request of the arbitration tribunal if the Secretary-General of the CIETAC considers the extension necessary and the reasons for such extension are justified.[59]

8-502 According to the CIETAC Rules, the arbitration tribunal is required to make its arbitral award independently and impartially on the basis of the facts, in accordance with the law and the terms of the contract, with reference to international practices and in compliance with the principle of fairness and reasonableness.[60]

8-503 Where a dispute is heard by an arbitration tribunal composed of three arbitrators, the arbitral award shall be decided by the majority of the arbitrators and the minority opinion may be recorded and placed on file. According to the CIETAC Rules, if 'the arbitration tribunal cannot attain a majority opinion, the arbitral award shall be decided in accordance with the presiding arbitrator's opinion'.[61]

8-504 The arbitration tribunal shall state the following in the arbitral award:

(a) the claims;

(b) the facts of the dispute;

(c) the reasons on which the arbitral award is based;

(d) the result of the arbitral award;

(e) the allocation of the arbitration costs; and

(f) the date and location at which the arbitral award is made.

---

57 Article 50 of the CIETAC Rules.
58 Article 51 of the CIETAC Rules.
59 Article 52 of the CIETAC Rules.
60 Article 53 of the CIETAC Rules.
61 Article 54 of the CIETAC Rules.

8-505   The facts of the dispute and the reasons on which the arbitral award is based need not be stated in the arbitral award if the parties have agreed to that effect or the arbitral award is made in accordance with the contents of a settlement agreement reached between the parties.[62]

8-506   Unless the arbitral award is made in accordance with the opinion of the presiding arbitrator or the sole arbitrator, the arbitral award shall be signed by a majority of arbitrators. An arbitrator with a dissenting opinion may opt not to sign the arbitral award.

8-507   The arbitrators shall submit the draft arbitral award to the CIETAC before signing the award. The CIETAC may remind the arbitrator of any issue relating to the form of the arbitral award provided that the arbitrator's independence is not compromised.

8-508   The CIETAC's stamp must be affixed on the arbitral award. The arbitral award comes into legal effect on the date on which it is made.[63]

8-509   An interlocutory award or partial award may be made on any issue of the dispute at any time in the course of arbitration before the final award is made if considered necessary by the arbitration tribunal, or if the parties make such a proposal and it is approved by the arbitration tribunal. Either party's failure to perform the interlocutory award will not affect the continuation of the arbitration proceedings, nor will it prevent the arbitration tribunal from making the final award.[64]

8-510   The arbitration tribunal has the power to determine in the arbitral award the arbitration fee and other expenses to be paid to the CIETAC by the parties.[65]

8-511   The arbitration tribunal has the power to decide in the arbitral award that the losing party shall pay to the winning party a proportion of the expenses reasonably incurred by the winning party as compensation. The amount of such compensation shall not in any case exceed 10% of the total amount awarded to the winning party.[66]

8-512   The arbitral award is final and binding upon both disputing parties. Subject to article 58 of the CIETAC Rules, neither party may bring a suit before a law court or make a request to any other organization for the arbitral award to be reviewed.[67]

---

62   Article 55 of the CIETAC Rules.
63   Article 56 of the CIETAC Rules.
64   Article 57 of the CIETAC Rules.
65   Article 58 of the CIETAC Rules.
66   Article 59 of the CIETAC Rules.
67   Article 60 of the CIETAC Rules.

8-513 Either party may request in writing that a correction be made to any written, typographical, calculation or other errors of a similar nature contained in the arbitral award within 30 days from the date of receipt of the arbitral award. If there is an error in the arbitral award, the arbitration tribunal shall make a correction in writing within 30 days from the date of receipt of the written request for correction. The arbitration tribunal may likewise correct any errors in writing on its own initiative within 30 days from the date on which the arbitral award is issued. The correction in writing shall form a part of the arbitral award.[68]

8-514 If any claims or counterclaims have been omitted from the arbitral award, either of the parties may make a request in writing to the arbitration tribunal for an additional award within 30 days from the date on which the arbitral award is received. If the omission was due to a mistake, the arbitration tribunal shall make an additional award within 30 days from the date of receipt of the written request. The arbitration tribunal may likewise make an additional award on its own initiative within 30 days from the date on which the arbitral award is issued. The additional award forms a part of the arbitral award previously issued.[69]

8-515 The parties must carry out the arbitral award within the time limit specified in the arbitral award. If no time limit is specified in the arbitral award, the parties shall carry out the arbitral award immediately.

8-516 If one party fails to execute the arbitral award, the other party may apply to the People's Court for enforcement of the arbitral award pursuant to Chinese law or apply to a competent foreign court for enforcement of the arbitral award according to the 1958 Convention on Recognition and Enforcement of Foreign Arbitral Awards or other international treaties that China has acceded to.[70]

Repealing of awards

8-517 An arbitral award by the CIETAC will be vacated by the Intermediate People's Court of the location of the arbitration commission if a party can establish the following:[71]

(a) that there is no arbitration agreement;

(b) the dispute to be arbitrated is not within the scope of the arbitration agreement, or one which the CIETAC has no authority to arbitrate;

---

68 Article 61 of the CIETAC Rules.
69 Article 62 of the CIETAC Rules.
70 Article 63 of the CIETAC Rules.
71 Article 58 of the Arbitration Law.

(c)   the formation of the arbitration tribunal or the arbitration process has violated legal procedure;

(d)   the evidence on which the arbitration is based is counterfeited;

(e)   one party has concealed evidence that could affect an impartial ruling; or

(f)   arbitrators have solicited or accepted bribes, practised favouritism and bent the law while arbitrating a case or making a ruling.

8-518   If a party wishes to make a request for the arbitral award to be repealed, it shall do so within six months after receiving the award.[72] The People's Court shall decide, within two months, whether to approve or reject the request to repeal the arbitral award after receiving such a request.[73]

8-519   After accepting the request to repeal the award, if the People's Court maintains that the arbitration tribunal is still the most appropriate forum to resolve the dispute, it shall notify the arbitration tribunal to rearbitrate the dispute within a specified period and it shall also enter a ruling terminating the repeal procedure. If the arbitration tribunal refuses to rearbitrate the dispute, the People's Court shall rule that the repeal procedure be reinstated.[74]

EXECUTION

8-601   Parties are required to abide by the ruling of the arbitration tribunal. If one party fails to abide by the ruling, the other party may, in accordance with provisions in the Law of Civil Procedure, request that the award be executed by the People's Court.[75]

8-602   A ruling shall not be executed if a party is able to produce evidence proving that the ruling contravenes section 2 of article 217 of the Law of Civil Procedure, and the said evidence has been duly verified by a panel formed by the People's Court.[76]

8-603   If one party requests that the ruling be executed and the other party requests that the ruling be repealed, the People's Court shall rule that the execution be terminated. If the People's Court rules that an award be repealed, the execution of the award shall be terminated. Where a request by one party to repeal the award has been rejected by the People's Court, the People's Court shall rule that the award be executed again.[77]

---

72   Article 59 of the Arbitration Law.
73   Article 60 of the Arbitration Law.
74   Article 61 of the Arbitration Law.
75   Article 62 of the Arbitration Law.
76   Article 63 of the Arbitration Law.
77   Article 64 of the Arbitration Law.

SUMMARY PROCEDURE

8-701 Unless otherwise agreed by the parties, the summary procedure described in the CIETAC Rules (Summary Procedure) shall apply to any dispute in which the quantum of the claim does not exceed Rmb 500,000, and to any case in dispute where the quantum of the claim exceeds Rmb 500,000 provided that one party applies for arbitration under the Summary Procedure and the other party agrees to it in writing.[78]

8-702 When an application for arbitration is submitted to the CIETAC, the Secretariat of the CIETAC shall send a Notice of Arbitration immediately to the parties, if such application is examined and found to be acceptable and suitable for application of the Summary Procedure.[79]

8-703 Unless both parties have jointly appointed a sole arbitrator from the Panel of Arbitrators of the CIETAC, they shall jointly appoint or jointly entrust the Chairman of the CIETAC to appoint a sole arbitrator within 15 days from the date on which the Notice of Arbitration is received by the respondent. Should the parties fail to make such appointment or entrust the Chairman of CIETAC to make such appointment, the Chairman of the CIETAC shall immediately appoint a sole arbitrator to form an arbitration tribunal to hear the case.

8-704 The respondent shall, within 30 days from the date of receipt of the Notice of Arbitration, submit his defence and the relevant documentary evidence to the Secretariat of the CIETAC. A counterclaim, if any, shall be submitted with the relevant documentary evidence within the said time limit.[80]

8-705 The arbitration tribunal may hear the case in any way it deems appropriate. The arbitration tribunal may in its full discretion decide to hear the case solely on the basis of the written materials and evidence submitted by the parties or to hold oral hearings as well.[81]

8-706 Generally, if the arbitration tribunal decides to hold oral hearings, only one oral hearing shall be held. However, the arbitration tribunal has the discretion to hold two oral hearings if necessary.[82]

8-707 The parties must submit all written materials and evidence required for arbitration in accordance with the requirements of the arbitration tribunal within the time limit prescribed.[83]

---

78 Article 64 of the CIETAC Rules.
79 Article 65 of the CIETAC Rules.
80 Article 66 of the CIETAC Rules.
81 Article 67 of the CIETAC Rules.
82 Article 70 of the CIETAC Rules.
83 Article 68 of the CIETAC Rules.

8-708 For disputes where an oral hearing has been fixed by the arbitration tribunal, the Secretariat of the CIETAC shall, after the arbitration tribunal has fixed a date for the hearing, inform the parties of the date of the hearing at least 15 days before the date of such hearing.[84]

8-709 Should one of the parties fail to comply with the Summary Procedure during the summary proceedings, such failure shall not affect the arbitration tribunal's conduct of the proceedings and the arbitration tribunal's power to render an arbitral award.[85]

8-710 The conduct of the summary proceedings shall not be affected by any amendment of the claim or by the filing of a counterclaim, except where the disputed amount of the revised arbitration claim or counterclaim is in conflict with the provisions of article 64.[86]

8-711 Where a case is heard orally, the arbitration tribunal shall make an arbitral award within 30 days from the date of the oral hearing if one hearing has been held, or from the date of the second oral hearing if two oral hearings have been held. Where a case is examined on the basis of documents only, the arbitration tribunal shall render an arbitral award within 90 days from the date on which the arbitration tribunal is formed. The Secretary-General of the CIETAC may extend the said time limit if such extension is necessary and justified.[87]

DOMESTIC ARBITRATION

8-801 This section shall apply to the domestic arbitration cases accepted by the CIETAC in respect of the disputes listed in items (3), (4), (5) and (6) of paragraph 2 of article 2 of the CIETAC Rules.

8-802 The provisions of the previous section in relation to Summary Procedure shall apply if the domestic arbitration cases fall within the scope of article 64 of the CIETAC Rules.[88]

Application for arbitration

8-803 Upon receiving the Application for Arbitration, the CIETAC, if it considers that the application formalities stated in article 14 of the CIETAC Rules have been complied with, shall initiate the arbitration proceedings within five days and notify the parties accordingly.

---

84 Article 69 of the CIETAC Rules.
85 Article 71 of the CIETAC Rules.
86 Article 72 of the CIETAC Rules.
87 Article 73 of the CIETAC Rules.
88 Article 75 of the CIETAC Rules.

8-804 Alternatively, the CIETAC may exercise its discretion to initiate arbitration proceedings immediately and notify the parties accordingly. If the CIETAC considers that the application formalities have not been completed, it shall notify the applicant party in writing of its refusal and explain its reasons therein.[89]

8-805 Upon receipt of the Application for Arbitration, if the CIETAC considers that the Application does not fulfil the requirements set out in article 14 of the CIETAC Rules, it may ask the party to rectify it within a specified time limit. If no required rectification is made within that time limit, such Application for Arbitration will be rejected.[90]

8-806 When the claimant or the respondent is required to appoint or authorize the Chairman of the CIETAC to appoint arbitrator(s) in accordance with articles 16, 24, 25 and 27 of the CIETAC Rules, the time limits provided for by each of the abovementioned articles shall be 15 days.[91]

8-807 The respondent shall, within 30 days from the date of receipt of the Notice of Arbitration, submit his written defence and relevant documentary evidence to the Secretariat of the CIETAC.

8-808 The respondent shall, at the latest within 45 days from the date of receipt of the Notice of Arbitration, file with the CIETAC his counterclaim in writing, if any. The arbitration tribunal may extend this time limit if it considers that there are justified reasons.[92]

8-809 For cases requiring oral hearings, the Secretariat of the CIETAC shall notify the parties involved of the hearing date at least 15 days in advance. The arbitration tribunal may, with consent from both parties, hold the hearing ahead of schedule. Any party may request a postponement of the hearing if it has justified reasons, but a written request must be submitted to the arbitration tribunal at least seven days before the date of the hearing. The tribunal will then decide on whether to postpone the hearing.

8-810 The notice of the date of subsequent hearings is not subject to the 15-day time limit stipulated by the preceding paragraph.[93]

8-811 If a case is heard orally, evidence shall be presented during the hearing(s) and submitted within the time limit set by the arbitration tribunal.[94]

---

89 Article 76 of the CIETAC Rules.
90 Article 77 of the CIETAC Rules.
91 Article 78 of the CIETAC Rules.
92 Article 79 of the CIETAC Rules.
93 Article 80 of the CIETAC Rules.
94 Article 81 of the CIETAC Rules.

8-812　The arbitration tribunal shall make a record of the hearing(s) in writing. Any party or participant in the arbitration may apply for correction if any omission or mistake is found in the record of his own statement. Even if the arbitration tribunal refuses to correct the record, such an application shall nevertheless be recorded.

8-813　The written record shall be signed or sealed by the arbitrator(s), the person making the records, the parties, and other participants to the arbitration, if any.[95]

8-814　The arbitration tribunal shall render an arbitral award within six months from the date on which the arbitration tribunal is formed. At the request of the arbitration tribunal, the Secretary-General of the CIETAC may extend this time limit as he considers necessary and justifiable.[96]

MISCELLANEOUS

8-901　The Chinese language is the official language of the CIETAC. If the parties have agreed otherwise, their agreement shall prevail.

8-902　At the hearing, if the parties or their arbitration agents or witnesses require language interpretation, the Secretariat of the CIETAC may provide an interpreter for them. Or the parties may bring with them their own interpreter.

8-903　The arbitration tribunal and/or the Secretariat of the CIETAC may, as it considers necessary, request the parties to hand in the corresponding translation copies in the Chinese language or other languages of the documents and evidential materials submitted by the parties.[97]

8-904　All the arbitration documents, notices and materials may be sent to the parties and/or their arbitration agents in person, or by registered letter or express airmail, telefax, telex, cable or by any other means considered proper by the Secretariat of the CIETAC.[98]

8-905　Any written correspondence to the parties and/or their arbitration agents shall be taken to have been properly served if it is delivered to the addressee or delivered at his place of business, habitual residence or mailing address, or if, after reasonable inquiries, none of the aforesaid addresses can be found, the written correspondence is sent to the addressee's last known place of business, habitual

---

95　Article 82 of the CIETAC Rules.
96　Article 83 of the CIETAC Rules.
97　Article 85 of the CIETAC Rules.
98　Article 86 of the CIETAC Rules.

residence or mailing address by registered letter or by any other means which provides a record of the attempt to deliver it.[99]

8-906 Apart from charging arbitration fees from the parties in accordance with the CIETAC Arbitration Fee Schedule, the CIETAC may collect from the parties other extra, reasonable and actual expenses including arbitrators' special remuneration and their travel and boarding expenses for dealing with the case, as well as the fees and expenses for experts, appraisers and interpreters appointed by the arbitration tribunal, etc.

8-907 If a case is withdrawn after the parties have reached an amicable settlement between themselves or is concluded with an arbitral award made according to paragraph 4 of article 44 of the CIETAC Rules, the CIETAC may charge the parties a certain amount of fees in consideration of the quantity of work and the amount of the actual expenses incurred by the CIETAC.[100]

CONCLUSION

8-1001 China has since the days of the 'open door' policy developed a body of arbitration law and rules of practice. Arbitral awards rendered by the CIETAC have been successfully enforced in China as well as in Hong Kong. China's accession to the WTO will 'force' Chinese courts to rethink their past practice of protecting local interests at the expense of foreign interests, and will open the door to better enforcement of arbitral awards against Chinese local parties by foreign investors.

REFERENCES AND FURTHER READING

Books

Colin Ng & Partners, *People's Republic of China Corporate Secretarial Manual* (Sweet & Maxwell Asia, 1998).

Statutes and Rules

China International Economic and Trade Arbitration Commission Arbitration Rules (revised and adopted by China Council for the Promotion of International Trade/China Chamber of International Commerce on 5 September 2000; effective as from 1 October 2000).

Arbitration Law of the People's Republic of China (adopted at the Ninth Session of the Standing Committee of the Eighth National People's Congress on 31 August 1994; effective as from 1 September 1995).

---

99   Article 87 of the CIETAC Rules.
100   Article 88 of the CIETAC Rules.

China Maritime Arbitration Commission Arbitration Rules (revised and adopted on 22 November 2000 by China Chamber of International Commerce; effective as from 1 January 2001).

APPENDIX 1

China International Economic and Trade Arbitration Commission
ARBITRATION FEE SCHEDULE
(This fee schedule applies to the arbitration cases accepted under item (1) and (2) of paragraph 2 of article 2 of the CIETAC Arbitration Rules, and is effective from 1 October 2000.)

Quantum of Claim	Fees
Rmb 1,000,000 or less	3.5% of the Claimed Amount, minimum Rmb 10,000
Rmb 1,000,000 to RMB 5,000,000	Rmb 35,000 plus 2.5% of the amount above Rmb 1,000,000
Rmb 5,000,000 to RMB 10,000,000	Rmb 135,000 plus 1.5% of the amount above Rmb 5,000,000
Rmb 10,000,000 to RMB 50,000,000	Rmb 210,000 plus 1% of the amount above Rmb 10,000,000
Rmb 50,000,000 or more	Rmb 610,000 plus 0.5% of the amount above Rmb 50,000,000

Each case, when being accepted, shall be charged an additional amount of Rmb 10,000 as a Registration Fee which includes the expenses for examining the Application for Arbitration, initiating the arbitration proceedings, computerizing management and filing of documents.

Where the amount of the claim is not ascertained at the time when application for arbitration is handed in, or there exists special circumstances, the amount of arbitration fee shall be determined by the Secretariat of the CIETAC or the Secretariats of the Sub-Commissions of the CIETAC.

If the arbitration fee is charged in foreign currency, an amount of foreign currency equivalent to the corresponding Rmb value specified in this schedule shall be paid.

Apart from charging the arbitration fee according to this Arbitration Fee Schedule, the CIETAC may collect other extra, reasonable and actual expenses pursuant to the relevant provisions of the Arbitration Rules.

APPENDIX 2

ARBITRATION PROCEEDINGS

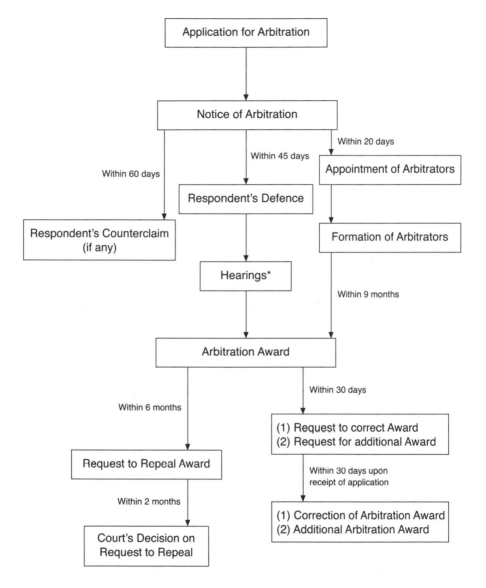

* If oral hearings are to take place, parties will be notified at least 30 days before the hearing date. Any request for postponement of any hearing must be submitted to the Secretariat of the CIETAC at least 12 days before the date of hearing.

Note: The time limits set out above are relevant only for arbitrations heard before the CIETAC. Other arbitration commissions have the power and discretion to impose any time limits or conditions as they see fit.

APPENDIX 3

SUMMARY PROCEEDINGS UNDER THE CIETAC RULES

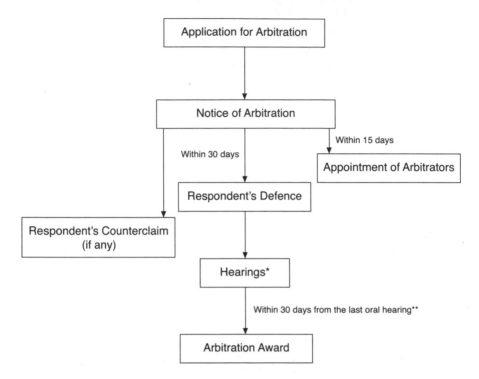

* If an oral hearing is to take place, parties will be notified at least 15 days before hearing date. The arbitration tribunal has the discretion to hold two oral hearings if necessary.

**If the arbitration tribunal decides to hear the case only on the basis of the written materials and evidence submitted by the parties, the arbitral award will be rendered within 90 days from the date the arbitration tribunal was formed.

Note: The time limits set out above are relevant only for arbitrations heard before the CIETAC. Other arbitration commissions have the power and discretion to impose any time limits or conditions as they see fit.

CHAPTER 9

Civil Litigation in the People's Republic of China
Yang Ing Loong

INTRODUCTION

Court system

9-101   According to the Organizational Law of the People's Courts, the People's Courts comprise the Supreme People's Court, specialized People's Courts (the Military, Railroad and Maritime Courts) and all levels of courts in the various localities.

9-102   China's courts are organized in a similar fashion as its geopolitical structure: the highest court in the land is the Supreme People's Court, which sits in Beijing. Next come the Higher People's Courts (which are found at the level of the provincial capital, capital cities of autonomous regions and directly-administered cities). Below that are the Intermediate People's Courts which are located in municipalities or prefectures. The lowest courts are the Basic People's Courts which can be found in the municipal districts (*qu*) or rural counties (*xian*). A simplified diagram of the court hierarchy is set out in Figure 1.

FUNCTION OF THE COURTS

Supreme People's Court

9-201   The Supreme People's Court, as the highest judicial organ of the state, has four primary functions: interpretation of law, adjudication, legislation and administration of the judiciary.

Higher People's Courts

9-202   The Higher People's Courts have five main functions:

(a)   hearing cases (such as commercial matters involving large claims and bankruptcy cases, such as the GITIC case) at first instance;

(b)   confirming the judgments of the Intermediate People's Court in capital cases;

(c)   confirming the judgments of the Intermediate People's Court in which the death penalty is suspended for two years;

(d)   confirming certain capital cases under the authorization of the Supreme People's Court;

(e)   supervising the cases tried by the lower courts. In the event that any error is discovered, it may direct the lower court to retry the case.

Figure 1: Structure of these People's Courts of the PRC

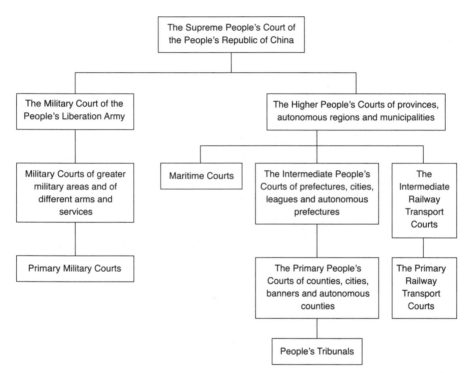

Intermediate People's Courts

9-203   The Intermediate People's Courts have four functions:

(a)   hearing cases at first instance involving substantial commercial disputes, criminal cases involving foreigners and administrative cases involving decisions by municipal level administrative agencies;

(b)   trying a case which is transferred to it from the Basic People's Court;

(c)   hearing appeals from the Basic People's Courts;

(d)   hearing appeals filed by the procuratorate pursuant to the latter's powers of supervision.

9-204 The provisions of the Civil Procedure Law generally direct foreign litigants to the Intermediate People's Courts in the first instance. Hence, of the local courts, foreigners, foreign companies and foreign-invested enterprises (FIEs) are most likely to encounter the Intermediate People's Courts and Basic People's Courts.

Basic People's Courts

9-205 These courts are the first instance trial courts for criminal, civil and administrative cases (unless the law otherwise provides).

Specialized Courts

9-206 The Military Courts hear criminal cases committed by serving military personnel and in practice, may also hear economic cases in which the litigants are military entities. The two-tiered Railroad Transportation Courts hear economic and civil cases involving the railroads, as well as crimes committed on the railroads. This is a special feature of the Chinese court system and is testimony to the importance of the railway as a mode of transport within China. The Maritime Courts, which have a status equivalent to an Intermediate Court, hear tort, shipping, maritime pollution and other maritime cases.

JURISDICTION

9-301 In general, the Basic People's Court of the place in which the defendant is ordinarily resident will have jurisdiction over the case (except for those cases over which the Intermediate, Higher or Supreme People's Courts have jurisdiction). Sometimes, however, more than one court may have jurisdiction over the same matter. For instance, in a contractual dispute, jurisdiction vests in the court located in the place in which the defendant is ordinarily resident, as well as the court located in the place where the contract is to be performed. In such a case, the plaintiff may elect to sue in either of these courts.

9-302 If the subject matter of the dispute is immovable property, the court of the locality in which the property is situated will invariably have jurisdiction.

9-303 The question of which level of court has jurisdiction (ie the Basic People's Court, the Intermediate People's Court or the Higher People's Court) is determined by the size of the claim, the nature of the case, the degree of social impact the case has and the complexity of the case.

JUDICIARY

9-401   Although China is one of the oldest civilizations in the world, its legal history is still in its infancy, as a result of the Cultural Revolution which saw the breakdown of law and order. China's recent history began only in around 1978 and it is quite remarkable that in the short space of just over 20 years, the legal system has made its influence felt.

9-402   In the early years, the judges (who were then only known as *shen pan zhang*, or chief assessors) were drawn from retired military officers or party cadres who knew very little of the law. In recent years, a spirit of professionalism has begun to develop within the judiciary, as legally-educated graduates have made their presence felt.

9-403   The Judges Law has imposed educational requirements on new and serving judges. In particular, it requires new judges to be alternatively: a university law graduate with two years of work experience; a university graduate in a non-law subject with specialized legal knowledge and two years of work experience; an LLB degree holder with one year of work experience; a holder of a masters degree or doctoral degree holders in which case, the work experience requirement is waived.

9-404   In March 2002, a watershed was reached. For the first time, there was a common professional examination for the judiciary, the procuratorate and the legal profession.

LAWYER'S ROLE

Legal representation in civil cases

9-501   Under the Lawyers Law and the Civil Litigation Law, the lawyer acts as the 'agent' (*dai li ren*) of the client. In such capacity, he acts for his principal (the client) in the civil litigation with a view to protecting his client's legal rights and upholding the correctness of the country's laws. The scope of the work which the lawyer can engage in is quite wide-ranging and bears the following characteristics:

(a)   Both the 'agent' and the 'principal' must fulfil the statutory requirements. The principal must be someone who possesses the capacity to sue (ie a citizen), or a corporate person. The agent has to be a legally-qualified person with a practising certificate and practising in a law firm;

(b)   In civil litigation, the lawyer is not an independent contractor. He can only act on the instructions of his client, unlike in criminal cases where he is allowed to act independently. However, this is not to say that the lawyer is merely a mouthpiece of his client. For instance, he has the right to investigate and gather evidence, peruse the files and attend court.

(c) As long as the lawyer acts reasonably within the bounds of his instructions, the client is bound by all his acts and has to bear all consequences flowing from his acts.

Work undertaken by the lawyer

9-502 The work of a lawyer in civil litigation may be divided into three stages: accepting instructions, pre-trial preparation and trial work.

9-503 It is important, when accepting instructions, for the lawyer to require the client to sign an agency contract, as it is the very foundation of the contractual relationship between the attorney and the client. It also serves as a warrant to act.

9-504 Pre-trial work undertaken by the lawyer includes assisting the client to:

(a) draft the statement of case;

(b) apply for an order for preservation of assets or preservation of evidence;

(c) apply for an interim payment order;

(d) draft a statement of defence or counterclaim;

(e) peruse documentary evidence;

(f) draft the opening statement to assist the court;

(g) draft submissions.

9-505 At trial, the lawyer performs the following functions:

(a) at the commencement of the hearing, the lawyer should consider whether to request any member of the tribunal or other court officers to disqualify themselves;

(b) apply for an adjournment if the necessary parties fail to attend court;

(c) apply for an adjournment if the plaintiff raises a new claim and as a result, the defendant requires more time to prepare his defence;

(d) ensure that the tribunal has understood his client's case and the material issues;

(e) make legal submissions and rebut his opponent's submissions;

(f) if the court delays delivering its judgment, the lawyer should, if necessary, write to the court to request for an expeditious judgment;

(g) upon receiving the judgment, the lawyer should analyse the judgment with the client and advise the client whether to file an appeal.

CIVIL PROCEDURE

9-601   In China, the civil litigation system allows only one level of appeal. At first instance, there are two kinds of applicable procedure: the normal procedure and the simplified procedure.

Normal procedure

9-602   Generally, the PRC Civil Procedure Law of 1991 (CPL) is the governing law on both procedure and evidence in civil proceedings. However, on 21 December 2001, the Supreme People's Court issued new regulations entitled Evidence in Civil Proceedings Several Provisions (the Evidence Provisions) which expand and improve on the current CPL provisions regarding evidence. These new regulations became effective on 1 April 2002.

Mode of commencing action

9-603   An action may be commenced orally or in writing, although the former is the exception rather than the rule. An action can be commenced orally:

(a)   when the plaintiff has difficulty in writing; and

(b)   in simplified civil matters.

In such cases, the plaintiff orally narrates his case and this is recorded by the court staff.

9-604   Unless the law otherwise specifies, all actions must be commenced in writing. The written statement of case should set out the following particulars:

(a)   the personal particulars of the plaintiff or, in the case of a corporate plaintiff, the name of its principal representative;

(b)   the facts and reasons for the suit; and

(c)   the source(s) of the evidence, and the names and addresses of the witnesses.

Acceptance of the case by the court

9-605   According to the PRC Civil Litigation Law, the appropriate court shall, within seven days of receiving the statement of case, accept and deal with the suit if all the legal requirements are met. The court shall inform all parties of this.

9-606   Besides ensuring that the relevant provisions of the PRC Civil Litigation Law are satisfied, there are three principal issues which the court will consider:

(a)   whether the subject matter of the suit is actionable under the law;

(b)   whether the parties have the capacity to sue and be sued; and

(c)   whether the matter is repetitious, ie the plaintiff had submitted two or more suits to different courts involving the same subject matter.

9-607   If the statement of case is defective or does not comply with the legal requirements, the court can require the plaintiff to rectify the defect or dismiss the case. If the plaintiff is dissatisfied with the decision of the court, he may appeal to the next higher level of court against the dismissal.

9-608   In most courts in the larger cities, the practice is for the court to rule on the issue of acceptance of the case on the spot, after reviewing the papers and documents submitted.

Pre-trial process

9-609   Once the court accepts the case, it shall deliver a copy of the statement of case to the defendant within five days. The defendant may, within 15 days of receipt of the copy, file a defence. If the defendant is not ordinarily resident in the PRC, he is given 30 days to file his defence. Any extension of time has to be applied for and is entirely in the court's discretion. Filing a defence is not mandatory, however, unless the defendant is raising an objection to the court's jurisdiction. Even if the defendant does not file a written defence, he is entitled to present his defence orally in court. If a written defence is filed, a copy of it shall be delivered to the plaintiff by the court within five days of its filing.

9-610   During the 15-day period for filing a defence, the court may not hold a hearing, unless the defendant confirms his intention not to defend, or the defendant files his defence before the period expires, or gives his consent to the holding of the hearing.

9-611   The fact that the defendant is not required to file a written defence may, in practice, cause substantial delay in the case, because at the commencement of the hearing, if the plaintiff is hearing the defence for the first time, he will usually have to apply for an adjournment to deal with the defence. This is a fairly unsatisfactory state of affairs.

9-612   Before the hearing commences, a tribunal, consisting of three members, will be empanelled and the parties will be notified accordingly. One of the three members of the tribunal will be the presiding judge.

Exchange of evidence

9-613   Once the court accepts the case, it will send out a notice to the parties requiring them to produce their evidence to the court. The notice will stipulate the allocation of the burden of proof, as well as inform the parties of the circumstances under which an application can be made to the courts for an investigation and collection of evidence by the courts. The notice will also stipulate the time period within which the evidence is to be produced (not less than 30 days) and the consequences of non-compliance, ie that the party is deemed to have given up his right to produce evidence. A party is entitled to apply to the court for an extension of time to provide such evidence. Under the Evidence Provisions, the court, upon the application of parties, can arrange for evidence to be exchanged prior to the hearing proper. In the process of the exchange of evidence, the judge shall record in the court's file the facts and evidence to which the parties have no objections, and if there are objections, the grounds for such objections shall also be recorded. The intent behind these rules is that the critical issues of the dispute will surface through the exchange of evidence. Upon the receipt of such evidence, the court will arrange for the parties to exchange their evidence. The objective of the exchange is to avoid any surprises at trial and to give the parties time to prepare, with a concomitant saving of court time. Such an exercise also serves to narrow the issues between the parties.

9-614   Although in principle, the parties ought to produce their evidence before trial, this is not an absolute rule and the court has the discretion to admit evidence even if it is tendered at trial, provided a reasonable explanation is furnished.

9-615   Evidence presented in the courts shall be cross-examined by the parties concerned, and any evidence that has not been subject to cross-examination shall not form the basis for a finding of fact. However, the evidence that has not been objected to in the course of the exchange of evidence can be taken as the basis for a finding of fact.

Burden of proof

9-616   The general rule under the Civil Litigation Law, which is not very different from the common law systems, is that whoever asserts has the burden of proving his assertion.

9-617   The Evidence Provisions provide that the burden of proof is reversed in certain tort claims:

(a)   in patent infringement cases, the defendant has to prove that the infringing product was produced by a different method or means;

(b)   in a personal injury action arising from hazardous operations, the defendant shall produce evidence showing that the plaintiff has voluntarily caused his own injuries;

(c)   in a claim for environmental pollution, the defendant shall provide the evidence showing that he is entitled to statutory exemptions and that there is no direct causation between his acts and the consequences;

(d) in an action for damage caused by the collapse of a building, the defendant owner of the building has to prove that the damage was not caused through his fault;

(e) in an action for damage caused by an animal, the animal's owner has to prove that the victim or some other third party was at fault;

(f) in an action for defects liability, the defendant shall provide evidence showing that he is entitled to statutory exemptions; and

(g) in a medical negligence claim, the medical institution responsible shall provide evidence that there is no direct causation between their acts and the consequences, or that the institution is not at fault.

9-618 The Evidence Provisions also provide for a reversal of burden of proof under certain contractual claims, eg labour disputes, where the burden is on the employer. More importantly, under article 7, the Evidence Provisions recognize that where there are no explicit provisions governing the burden of proof, PRC courts have the ability to determine the burden of proof in accordance with the principles of fairness and honesty, taking into account the ability of a particular party to produce evidence.

9-619 Further, there are five specific types of instances in which proof is dispensed with:

(a) facts which are admitted by the other party;

(b) publicly-known facts;

(c) inferred facts;

(d) *res judicata*, ie facts which have been adjudicated upon by a court or an arbitral tribunal; or

(e) facts which have been verified by a notary. However, if the counterparty adduces evidence which contradicts such facts, then it is still necessary for the first-mentioned party to prove it.

9-620 Other pre-trial matters involve the adding of parties and the bringing in of third parties.

Hearing

9-621 The hearing is an important part of civil litigation and comprises two phases: the first phase involves investigation by the court, while the second phase involves legal submissions.

9-622 China's court system is essentially an inquisitorial, rather than, adversarial system. The judge(s) play a much more active role in the proceedings than a judge in a common law system, by asking questions with a view to investigating the case. The lawyers, correspondingly, play a less active role compared to their counterparts in the common law system.

9-623   During the first phase of the hearing, the parties are allowed to present their cases, adduce evidence and question the other party's evidence. The plaintiff begins the oral presentation by outlining his claim and supporting it with reasons. Next, the defendant orally opens his case by seeking to rebut the plaintiff's case. After that, the plaintiff has the right of reply.

9-624   At the end of the oral presentations, the presiding judge will, according to the nature of the parties' presentations, summarize the issues in the case for the parties to consider.

9-625   If a party is calling oral evidence from a witness, the witness should be summoned by the court to testify. During oral testimony, the court is obliged to inform the witness of his rights and obligations, as well as the consequences of perjury. If the witness has difficulty attending court, the court may allow his written testimony to be read out in court.

9-626   If the evidence sought to be adduced is documentary evidence, the original must be produced in court and inspected by the counterparty. The evidence must also be read out in court. The counterparty may apply to the court to have the evidence examined.

9-627   In the second phase, the focus is on legal arguments. The plaintiff begins, followed by the defendant. Thereafter, the parties can take turns to debate the matter.

Mediation

9-628   In the course of the hearing and before judgment, the court will usually attempt mediation if the parties are agreeable. Sometimes, a mediation session will be arranged before the hearing.

9-629   If the parties reach a settlement after mediation, the court will issue a mediated judgment. Chinese law does not recognize the concept of settlement agreements, and hence the need for a mediated judgment, which is essentially a consent judgment. A mediated judgment, if signed by the parties, has the same legal force as a court judgment and can similarly be enforced by the courts.

Judgment

9-630   Should mediation fail, the court will render a judgment either on the same day or on a later date.

9-631   The court may make partial judgments in respect of issues that have already been decided upon. Further, the court may make supplemental judgments after the main judgment has been issued. Supplemental judgments can only be issued if there is any material omission in the main judgment or the main judgment was ambiguous.

9-632 The contents of the judgment are generally structured as follows:

(a) Heading: this consists of the identity of the court, the title of the case, case number, a brief introduction of the parties, the origin of the case and a brief summary of the trial process. The heading must adhere strictly to the prescribed format.

(b) The plaintiff's contentions and claims.

(c) The facts as found by the court and the applicable legal provisions. This is the core of the judgment.

(d) The verdict.

(e) Conclusion: this should specify who is to bear the litigation expenses. If it is a first instance judgment, it should spell out the right of appeal, the time limited for appeal and the court to which an appeal can be made. Finally, the names of the judges and the court officer and the date of the judgment must be stated, and the court seal affixed.

9-633 Either party may appeal against the judgment within the time allowed by law. Otherwise, the judgment becomes effective and can be enforced by the courts.

9-634 At first instance, a case has to be disposed of by the appropriate court within six months of acceptance by it, unless there are special circumstances justifying an extension.

Simplified procedure

9-635 The simplified procedure is used only in the Basic People's Courts and only in the clearest of cases (in terms of the facts and the law) in which the quantum of claim is very small. An example of such cases is an undisputed loan involving a small sum of money.

APPELLATE PROCEDURE

9-701 Any party who is dissatisfied with the judgment of the court of first instance can appeal within 15 days of the delivery of the judgment. For written judgments, the period is 10 days.

9-702 There may not always be a hearing for the appeal, as the appellate court may decide on the basis of the record of the first instance hearing. However, should there be an actual hearing, the procedure is similar to that at first instance.

9-703 The decision of the appellate court is final and immediately effective and there shall be no further appeal.

9-704   An appeal should be determined within three months. Any extension of time has to be approved by the President of the relevant appellate court and will only be permitted under special circumstances.

PRESERVATION OF ASSETS

9-801   In the course of litigation, the plaintiff can apply to court for preservation of the defendant's assets in order not to render any judgment nugatory.

9-802   In granting such an application, the court may require the plaintiff to furnish an undertaking or guarantee to bear any loss suffered by the defendant resulting from an order being erroneously made against the defendant.

9-803   The court normally decides on an application within 48 hours of it being made. Should the court grant the application, it may freeze, sequester or seize the defendant's assets.

9-804   In certain cases, the plaintiff may also apply for such an order before any action is filed in court, in which case, he has to undertake to file an action within 15 days of the order being made.

RETRIAL

9-901   If any party is of the view that the judgment of the final court of adjudication is wrong, he can apply to that court, or to a court the next level up, for retrial.

9-902   An application for retrial should be made within two years of the judgment. The court has an unfettered discretion whether to grant the application.

9-903   Pending the result of the retrial, the original judgment can be enforced. The court hearing the retrial may decide to affirm the original judgment or reverse it.

ENFORCEMENT

9-1001   In the event that a party fails to satisfy a judgment, the other party can apply to court to enforce the judgment. The courts may freeze or sequester the bank account of the non-complying party, seize and auction his property, or garnish his salary, etc. However, whether enforcement can be successfully carried out ultimately depends on the availability of assets.

COSTS OF LITIGATION

9-1101 The plaintiff has to pay the court fees in advance, in accordance with the relevant rules. Further, the plaintiff has to pre-pay other costs, including but not limited to the preservation fee, enforcement fee, examination fee, accreditation fee, translation fee, application fee and other trial-related fees.

9-1102 Should the defendant lose the case, all the out-of-pocket expenses related to the litigation shall be borne by him.

9-1103 Presently, Chinese jurisprudence does not support the claiming of attorney's fees, that is to say, the victorious party still has to bear his own solicitor-and-client costs.

ADMINISTRATIVE COMPENSATION LITIGATION

9-1201 China has an administrative compensation system: if an administrative organ or a department of the state causes injury to a citizen or a corporate in unlawfully carrying out its duties, the state is liable to that citizen or corporate in damages. These administrative acts could either cause injury to the person (such as wrongful detention or false imprisonment, or assault by police officers), or they could relate to property (such as wrongful fines or wrongful freezing of accounts).

9-1202 Such a compensation system is necessary in China because excesses committed by public officers are not uncommon.

9-1203 An action that is commenced to claim such compensation is termed administrative litigation. However, the limitation period is very short – three months from the date of the act complained of.

CONCLUSION

9-1301 China is a vast country. As such, the courts in China at the various levels are obviously in different stages of development. Users of the higher level courts in the coastal regions and Beijing will find the standard of those courts to be higher than those in the inland or less developed areas.

9-1302 Like its legal system, the courts and the legal profession in China are undergoing tremendous and rapid changes. Also, with China's entry into the World Trade Organization in December 2001, and the consequent rush of foreign investments into the country, there is little doubt that China's legal system and judiciary will have to evolve to cope with the new challenges that these foreign investments and the resulting disputes, present. The judges as well as the lawyers in China are also very much better exposed to the practices in the rest of the world than they were 15 to 20 years ago, and this can only help to uplift the quality of the judiciary and the legal profession generally. It may be that China's litigation procedure may move towards a system that is closer to the adversarial system, with lawyers playing a more important role in the proceedings. However, until the court users see a distinct improvement and gain confidence in the court system, it is likely that the courts will still be regarded as a second choice for dispute resolution compared to arbitration.

REFERENCES AND FURTHER READING

Books

Freshfields Bruckhaus Deringer, *Doing Business In China* (Juris Publishing, Inc, 2001).

APPENDIX

LITIGATION FLOWCHART

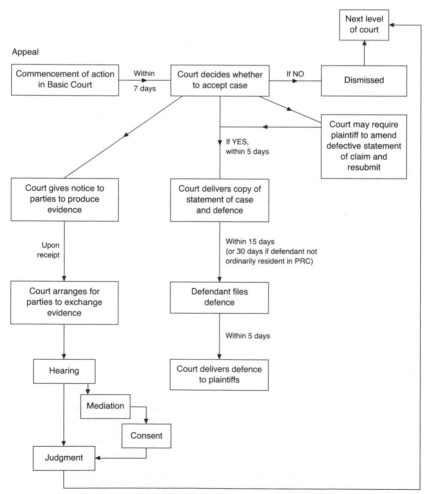

Index